CAN RELIGION BE EXPLAINED AWAY?

CLAREMONT STUDIES IN THE PHILOSOPHY OF RELIGION

General Editor: D. Z. Phillips, Professor of Philosophy, University of Wales, Swansea, and Danforth Professor of the Philosophy of Religion, The Claremont Graduate School

At a time when discussions of religion are becoming increasingly specialised and determined by religious affiliations, it is important to maintain a forum for philosophical discussion which transcends the allegiances of belief and unbelief. This series affords an opportunity for philosophers of widely differing persuasions to explore central issues in the philosophy of religion.

Published title:

RELIGION AND MORALITY (*edited by D. Z. Phillips*)

PHILOSOPHY AND THE GRAMMAR OF RELIGIOUS BELIEF
Timothy Tessin and Mario von der Ruhr (*editors*)

Can Religion be Explained Away?

Edited by

D. Z. Phillips

Professor of Philosophy
University of Wales, Swansea

Danforth Professor of the Philosophy of Religion
The Claremont Graduate School, California

First published in Great Britain 1996 by
MACMILLAN PRESS LTD
Houndmills, Basingstoke, Hampshire RG21 6XS
and London
Companies and representatives
throughout the world

A catalogue record for this book is available
from the British Library.

ISBN 0–333–62065–8

 First published in the United States of America 1996 by
ST. MARTIN'S PRESS, INC.,
Scholarly and Reference Division,
175 Fifth Avenue,
New York, N.Y. 10010

ISBN 0–312–15966–8

Library of Congress Cataloging-in-Publication Data
Can religion be explained away? / edited by D. Z. Phillips.
p.   cm. — (Claremont studies in the philosophy of religion)
Includes bibliographical references and index.
ISBN 0–312–15966–8
1. Religion—Philosophy.   2. Religion—Controversial literature.
I. Phillips, D. Z. (Dewi Zephaniak)   II. Series.
BL51.C3235   1996
200—dc20   95–47035
                                                                CIP

10   9   8   7   6   5   4   3   2   1
05   04   03   02   01   00   99   98   97   96

Printed in Great Britain by
The Ipswich Book Company Ltd
Ipswich, Suffolk

In memory of

EUGENE KAMENKA

who was to have participated in the conference

Contents

Acknowledgements

I am indebted to the contributors to this volume, not only for participating in the 1995 Claremont Conference on the Philosophy of Religion, but for their generous support of the fund which contributes to the holding of future conferences. I am indebted to Jackie Huntzinger and my research assistant, Martha Bailey, at Claremont for their administrative assistance, and to the graduate students who helped, in various ways, to make the conference run smoothly. I am also grateful to Mrs Helen Baldwin at Swansea for administrative assistance in planning the conference. I gratefully acknowledge the financial support for the conference provided by The Claremont Graduate School, Pomona College and Claremont McKenna College.

I am grateful to Martha Bailey for typing the Introduction and Voices in Discussion, and to Timothy Tessin for help with proofreading the collection.

D.Z. Phillips

List of Contributors

John Deigh, Professor of Philosophy, Northwestern University. He is the author of *The Sources of Moral Agency* and Associate Editor and Book Review Editor of *Ethics*.

İlham Dilman, Research Professor, University of Wales, Swansea. He is the author of many books, including *Morality and the Inner Life: A Study in Plato's Gorgias; Quine on Ontology, Necessity and Experience; A trilogy on Freud: Freud and Human Nature; Freud and the Mind; Freud, Insight and Change; Mind, Brain and Behaviour; Philosophy and the Philosophic Life, A Study in Plato's Phaedo; Love and Human Separateness: Existentialist Critiques of Cartesianism*.

Richard Eldridge, Associate Professor of Philosophy, Swarthmore College. He is the author of *On Moral Personhood: Philosophy, Literature, Criticism and Self-Understanding* and the editor of *Beyond Representation: Philosophy and Poiēsis*. He has published papers on aesthetics, philosophy and literature, Wittgenstein and the philosophy of language.

Van A. Harvey, George Edwin Burnell Professor of Religious Studies, Stanford University. He has taught at Princeton, Southern Methodist University, the University of Pennsylvania and Stanford, and has written extensively on nineteenth- and twentieth-century Protestant theology, his best-known work being *The Historian and the Believer*, a study of the ways in which Christian theologians have attempted to deal with the problems raised by biblical criticism. He has twice been awarded a John Simon Guggenheim Fellowship. His most recent book is *Feuerbach and the Interpretation of Religion*.

Lars Hertzberg, Professor of Philosophy, Åbo Academy, Finland. He is the author of *The Limits of Experience* and of papers on the philosophy of mind, philosophy of language, ethics and Wittgenstein.

John Hyman is Fellow and Praelector in Philosophy at The Queen's College, Oxford. He is the editor of *Investigating Psychology* and author of *The Imitation of Nature*.

David McLellan, Professor of Political Theory, University of Kent at Canterbury. Author of several works on Marxism and Marx, his latest publications are *Simone Weil: Utopian Pessimist* and *Unto Caesar: The Political Relevance of Christianity*.

Stephen Mulhall, Reader in Philosophy, University of Essex. He is the author of *On Being in the World: Wittgenstein and Heidegger on Seeing Aspects; Liberals and Communitarians* (with Adam Swift); *Stanley Cavell: Philosophy's Recounting of the Ordinary; Faith and Reason; An Introduction to 'Being and Time'*.

Kai Nielsen, Professor Emeritus of Philosophy at The University of Calgary, now lives in Montreal. He is the author of *After the Demise of the Tradition* and *Why be Moral?*, and is co-editor with Jocelyne Couture, Professor of Philosophy at the Université du Québec à Montréal, of *Méta-philosophie: Reconstructing Philosophy?*. In 1995 Professor Nielsen published three further books: *Transforming Philosophy: A Metaphilosophical Inquiry, Naturalism without Foundations* and *Moral Concerns*.

D.Z. Phillips, Danforth Professor of the Philosophy of Religion, The Claremont Graduate School and Professor of Philosophy, University of Wales, Swansea. He is the author of *The Concept of Prayer; Faith and Philosophical Enquiry; Death and Immortality; Moral Practices* (with H.O. Mounce); *Sense and Delusion* (with Îlham Dilman); *Athronyddu Am Grefydd; Religion Without Explanation; Dramau Gwenlyn Parry; Through A Darkening Glass; R.S. Thomas: Poet of the Hidden God; Belief, Change, and Forms of Life; Faith after Foundationalism; From Fantasy to Faith; Interventions in Ethics; Wittgenstein and Religion; Writers of Wales: J.R. Jones; Introducing Philosophy*. He is the editor of the Macmillan series *Swansea Studies in Philosophy* and *Claremont Studies in the Philosophy of Religion* (co-published by St Martin's Press) and of the journal, *Philosophical Investigations*.

Mario von der Ruhr, Lecturer in Philosophy, University of Wales, Swansea. He is co-editor of *Philosophy and the Grammar of Religious Belief* (in this series) and Associate Editor of *Philosophical Investigations*. He has contributed to a collection on *Particularity and Commonality in Ethics*.

Peter Winch, Professor of Philosophy, University of Illinois at Urbana/Champaign, and Emeritus Professor of Philosophy at the

University of London. He is one of the Trustees of Wittgenstein's *Nachlass*. He is the author of *The Idea of a Social Science and its Relation to Philosophy; Ethics and Action; Trying to Make Sense; Simone Weil: 'The Just Balance'*. He has also edited a number of collections.

Introduction

D.Z. Phillips

How are we to think of religion as the twentieth century draws to its close? The essays in this volume show that a number of different answers are given to this question.

Some argue that religion is an outmoded, primitive way of thinking in our midst. They say it belongs to an infantile morality, and that this has been amply demonstrated by the physical, natural and social sciences. It will be admitted that some demonstrations which seek to reach these conclusions are crude, even vulgar, but crudity and vulgarity can be found in religion, too. It is argued that now we have more sophisticated forms of materialism, which show that religion can be explained away. Again, it may well be that a single reductionist analysis of religious belief cannot do justice to its complexity, but when all the reductionist analyses are combined, the unintelligibility of religious belief is demonstrated clearly.

Given this conclusion, why do so many people still believe in God? If the light of enlightened, secular thought has shone in the darkness, why do so many choose to live in darkness? The reply is that some, who should know better, simply refuse to recognize the confusion involved in the beliefs they entertain. But there are many religious believers of whom this cannot be said. Their social deprivations are such that they cannot be blamed for succumbing to the false promises of religion. This is a tragedy since, in this way, religion reinforces the deprivation. We need to recognize the extent of the social, economic and psychological harm for which religion is responsible.

Philosophers who argue in this way long for a time when religion disappears as a feature of human life. Other philosophers put forward a modified version of this view. They do not go so far as to claim that the unintelligibility of religious belief has been demonstrated. On the other hand, they do not say that religious belief is intelligible either. Typically, they do not claim to see much sense in religion. When they are impressed by something said about religion, they think this is the creation of a minority of philosophers of religion, and not characteristic of mainstream religious beliefs.

These latter beliefs may well be confused, but that would be no obstacle to holding them. People can hold thoroughly confused beliefs. Philosophers do so all the time.

How are such views countered in this volume? The responses take many forms. One response is to question the conceptual presuppositions of the main reductionist analyses of religion. For example, it is argued that Freud's analysis of religion is conceptually confused. This is unsurprising, it is said, since he was blind to religious meanings, and his analysis of morality is a negative one in terms of enlightened self-interest. Similar charges are made against Marx. Religion shows us what we are not. Its point is completely misunderstood if it is seen as promising us 'pie in the sky'. These critiques of Freud and Marx need not deny that religion often takes the compensatory forms these thinkers criticize, but they also emphasize deep forms of religious spirituality, which are untouched by the reductionist analyses.

What of the claim that these so-called deep forms of religious sensibility are the creation of a few philosophers of religion? It is claimed, in response, that this view is the ironic outcome of the dominance of philosophical theism in the philosophy of religion. That dominance is such that philosophers who see little in religion accept, automatically, that philosophical theism is an accurate reflection of religious belief. They do not see that this mode of philosophizing obscures the spiritual roots of religion. The philosophical account dislocates the religious concepts.

A further response may be made to the claim that religion is a primitive mode of thought, a product of our own projections. 'Projection' is meant to be a derogatory term in this context. Yet, if by 'projection' we mean 'methods of projection', all modes of thought are projections, grids through which we understand reality. It is claimed that these grids can be compared. Some will say that the grids that science and technology provide give us powers of control and prediction over our environment which religion cannot compete with. On the other hand, why should all the features of our existence be thought of in these terms? Even when we are interested in explanations, it is often in relation to matters for which we do not seek further explanations. There are also spiritual needs which arise from our reflections on birth, death and the contingencies of life. It is not at all clear how science is supposed to address these.

There may be objections to this notion of 'grids'. It contains a latent scepticism in that there would be no way of establishing

whether any grid brings us nearer to or distances us from the reality on which it is said to be imposed. Grids are not interpretations,
but, if anything, ways of talking and thinking which are constitutive of different conceptions of the world.

At this point, another philosophical perspective in the collection
becomes relevant. It recognizes that there have been reductionist
criticisms of religion. It recognizes that defenders of religious belief
accuse the critics of being blind to its meaning. What this ignores,
however, is the actual cultural context in which we find ourselves;
a context in which we try to understand ourselves. But we lack the
resources, it is said, for such self-understanding. Charles Taylor has
suggested that this lack is due to our loss of theistic concepts. These
concepts, he argues, explain our confusions about the nature of the
self. This is because secular conceptions of the self are, in fact,
parasitic on the deeper theistic conception. If these conclusions were
established, Taylor would have provided an authoritative narrative
for our time, one which demonstrates the superiority of the theistic
conception of the self over its secular alternatives. Unfortunately,
however, this is not what Taylor achieves. He has not given a theoretical, theistic underpinning of the secular perspectives. In elucidating theism, Taylor is, in fact, elucidating a religious perspective
from within it. He is talking in his own voice in doing so.

How are we to react to this conclusion? Some argue that it is
extremely important to note the importance of speaking in one's
own voice in these matters. This importance, however, has a direct
bearing on our understanding of the clash between belief and
unbelief. That clash need not be seen as the mutual effort to demonstrate contradictions or incoherences in religious or non-religious
systems of thought. Rather, the clash will be between the different
demands which divergent ways of looking at the world make on
us. Those demands will not occur in the abstract, but in the actual
lives of individuals. It is there that they either will or will not cause
difficulties and tensions. There will be no general answer to such
issues. Difficulties may occur for some, but not for others. In succeeding or failing to resolve them, each person will speak in his or
her own voice.

Finally, it is argued, in the collection, that it is possible to have a
distinctive interest in the voices involved in the clashes between
belief and unbelief. This is not an interest in entering the dispute,
or attempting to resolve it, but, rather, an interest in giving as just
a characterization of the voices as possible; letting them speak for

themselves, as it were. Some may see this as an abnegation of moral judgement, but this is not the intention. No judgements are prohibited. It is simply that here, the interest is different. One is not arguing from an embattled position, but striving, with great difficulty, to see what is in perspectives which need not be one's own. If a person passes from secularism to religious belief, or vice versa, it will not be claimed that some general method of doing so has been established. What one will have is particular stories of how these changes came about.

In the light of the kind of interest in different voices in our culture I have mentioned, we can return to our opening question: How should we think of religion as the twentieth century draws to its close? We shall see the possibility of having an interest in the question other than a desire to answer it for others.

The papers in the collection reflect the different points of view I have mentioned in the Introduction. What they do not indicate, of course, is the nature of the discussions they provoked. As before in this series, the notes I took of these discussions became the material from which an 'Afterword' was constructed, one which, hopefully, adds to the usefulness of the collection.

It has to be said, however, that the reactions to the discussions which follow are, of course, mine. I am not pretending to summarize different points of view in such a way that all their proponents would be satisfied. That is one reason why I have not attributed the various voices in the Afterword to specific participants in the conference. Also, where the same points were repeated at different times in the conference, even though they may have been made by different participants, I have not hesitated to bring them together in a single 'voice' where I have thought this to be philosophically or stylistically advantageous. Nevertheless, the different voices I allude to are meant to capture the character of the philosophical exchanges which took place. Once again, I was happy to find the exchanges fulfilling the aim of the philosophy of religion conferences at Claremont to make a distinctive contribution to contemporary discussions.

Part One
Animism and Religion

1

Is Animism Alive and Well?

Richard Eldridge

> What am I believing in when I believe that men have souls? What am I believing in, when I believe that this substance contains two carbon rings? In both cases there is a picture in the foreground, but the sense lies far in the background; that is, the application of the picture is not easy to survey.
>
> (Ludwig Wittgenstein, *Philosophical Investigations*, § 422)

Animism is the belief that human beings have souls, or, by extension, the belief that animals, plants or even rocks have souls; that is, that they are subjects of feeling or consciousness, or display intelligence, in ways that ensouled human beings do. This extended view is sometimes called animatism or panpsychism, in order to distinguish it from the more restricted view, though in common usage 'animism' seems typically to embrace the broader view, often preceded by the adjective 'primitive', to suggest that a belief in the souls of plants is something that has been largely outgrown.

What are the experiences and cultural circumstances that nurture animistic beliefs? To what extent are such beliefs reasonable responses to human beings, other animals, plants or mountains? It is not easy to answer such questions, since an answer to them requires an understanding of how such deep metaphysical beliefs are woven out of and into perceptual experiences, cultural settings, unthinking masteries of repertoires of practice, powerful emotional attitudes and moral aspirations and ideals. In order to approach some answers, and in order to appreciate the complex entanglements of beliefs, experiences, cultural settings, emotions, practices and ideals, it will be useful to begin by considering two sharply opposed thoughts about the motivating experiences and circumstances, and the reasonableness, of animistic beliefs.

I

Animism is dead, a relic of outworn cultures which have not yet learned to think scientifically. Consider some of the things that some animists believe. In *Nanna, or Concerning the Soul-Life of Plants*, G.T. Fechner recounts his observation of a water lily's enjoyment of its environment:

> I stood once on a hot summer's day beside a pool and contemplated a water-lily which had spread its leaves evenly over the water and with an open blossom was basking in the sunlight. How exceptionally fortunate, thought I, must this lily be which above basks in the sunlight and below is plunged into the water – if only it might be capable of feeling the sun and the bath. And why not? I asked myself. It seemed to me that nature surely would not have built a creature so beautiful, and so carefully designed for such conditions, merely to be an object of idle observation. . . . I was inclined to think that nature had built it thus in order that all the pleasure which can be derived from bathing at once in sunlight and in water might be enjoyed by one creature in the fullest measure.[1]

Here Fechner does not use the verb *enjoyed* as a metaphor indicating only that the plant grows well in such surroundings. Instead, the water lily is a subject of experience; it actually feels the happiness of its situation. In *The World as Will and Representation*, Schopenhauer similarly attributes a number of mental properties to various inorganic beings. If we observe attentively, Schopenhauer writes, then we may see

> [the] strong and unceasing impulse with which the waters hurry to the ocean, [the] persistency with which the magnet turns ever to the North Pole, [the] readiness with which iron flies to the magnet, [the] eagerness with which the electric poles seek to be reunited, and which, just like human desire, is increased by obstacles [as well as] the choice with which bodies repel and attract each other, combine and separate, when they are set free in a fluid state, amd emancipated from the bonds of rigidity.[2]

Hurrying, persisting, desiring and choosing – these are likewise not metaphors for Schopenhauer, but indicate instead an internal life of sensation and volition, albeit in different forms from the human, in natural phenomena. 'All motion of matter in space', Hermann Lotze claims, 'may be explained as a natural expression of the inner states of beings that seek or avoid one another with a feeling of their need. . . . [Even particles of physical dust] everywhere and without shortcoming perform the actions permitted to them by the universal order.'[3]

Most or many of us are likely to respond to such claims with a mixture of bemusement, embarrassment and condescension. Surely, these are at best analogies. We do not in fact see sodium and chlorine *choosing* to separate, let alone *divorce*, when salt is placed in water. We just see them doing what sodium and chlorine do in such circumstances, without either consciousness or volition. No facts of an intelligent or volitional life present themselves. It is merely fanciful – and it is not even clear what it means – to say that they choose to act as they do, but in the way that chemicals, not human beings, choose to act. What sense can we make of such a view?

And is the situation any better with regard to human souls? It is true, we may say, that human beings feel and think and choose. They evince these doings in words. But do we need to invoke a soul in order to serve as the locus of these operations? Won't the brain serve just as well? The facts of damage to specific areas of the brain resulting in losses of specific abilities indicate that these operations are localized in the brain. Perhaps the language of feeling, thinking and choosing is categorically orthogonal to that of synapses and neural transmitters, so that the prospects for reductionist materialism are not good. But surely there is nothing else there other than neural material in which such operations are instanced. Why, then, talk of a soul?

Besides, such talk is characteristic of primitive culture, which has not yet learned to seek explanations through the investigations of material states and structures, rather than through appeal to personal or spiritual forces. The anthropologist E.B. Tylor forcefully expresses this sense of the growth of our powers to explain through the rise of materialism when he refers to 'the animism of the ruder tribes of India'[4] who continue to appeal to the actions of personal deities to explain phenomena. Writing in 1910, Northcote Whitbridge Thomas dismissed animism and animatism alike as 'feature[s] of the philosophy of peoples of low culture'.[5]

The historian of science David Lindberg offers a common explanation of the primitive appeal to souls, personal deities, spirits, and

the like when he characterizes it as an instance of seeing the unfamiliar – natural phenomena – in light of the familiar – human
events – without much reflection or testing. Hence it is natural to
describe these appeals as *projections* of properties, rather than as
considered discernments of what is there.

> It is natural that in the search for meaning [preliterate people]
> should proceed within the framework of their own experience,
> projecting human or biological traits onto objects and events that
> seem to us devoid not only of humanity but also of life. Thus the
> beginning of the universe is typically described in terms of birth,
> and cosmic events may be interpreted as the outcome of a strug-
> gle between opposing forces, one good and the other evil. There
> is an inclination in preliterate cultures not only to personalize but
> also to individualize causes, to suppose that things happen as
> they do because they have been willed to do so.[6]

Surely with our own wider experience, and our greater capabilities
to sort things into relevant general classes and to measure physical
properties, we do better. No one has seen Zeus unleashing a bolt of
lightning. In contrast, it is possible to predict with reasonable accuracy that electrical charges in cloud formations will discharge themselves when they reach a certain intensity, under specifiable levels
of humidity, air pressure, and so forth.

No doubt lightning and thunder are sometimes awe-inspiring
and impressive. It may be natural enough to conceive of one's awe
as a response to a higher power, to a divinity manifest in nature.
But, as Alasdair MacIntyre observes, the fact that 'pantheist metaphysics provides a vocabulary which appears more adequate than
any other for the expression of these emotions [of awe and wonder]
. . . does not, of course, give any warrant for believing pantheism to
be true.'[7]

And are things any better for even the more restricted versions
of animism? Is belief in a human soul any less of an emotion-
expressing, but cognitively inept, projection? Human beings indeed
do marvellous and awe-inspiring things. No one should want to
diminish or denigrate either Beethoven's *Grosse Fugue* or Nureyev's
grandes jetés. But do we need to posit a soul in order either to value
or to understand these achievements? Surely, Beethoven and
Nureyev were simply human beings, of flesh and blood, who cul-

tivated valuable abilities through enormous practice and discipline. Positing a soul seems less to explain what they have done than to confess our ignorance.

As our powers to shape nature and to explain natural events have grown, there seems to be a progressive diminution in appeals to personal forces of any kind. While emphasizing that the hypothesis of 'the animistic origin of religion is . . . not proven', partly because it is 'very difficult to get precise information on the subject of the religious ideas of people of low culture, perhaps for the simple reason that the ideas themselves are far from precise', Whitbridge Thomas none the less suggests a progression in stages of religious belief from original, primitive animatism, to polytheism, to monotheism, to atheist materialism, with animism in the narrower sense – the belief only in human souls – as a continuing undercurrent that passes away also at the last stage. There is some suggestion, Whitbridge Thomas finds, of a 'path [from animatism and] towards anthropomorphization and polytheism', and perhaps beyond towards monotheism and then atheism.[8] Writing in *Nature* in 1881, T.H. Huxley observed that 'The essence of modern, as contrasted with ancient, physiological science appears to me to lie in its antagonism to animistic hypotheses and animistic phraseology.'[9] This judgement seems an apt response first to the progress in the powers of modern science and technology to free us from immiseration at the hands of nature and to yield explanations of natural phenomena, and second to the shift in the conceptual structures of modern theories away from personal forces and towards materialism.

Bryan Wilson extends this sense of the passing away of animatism and animism to all forms of religious consciousness generally: 'Religions are always dying,' Wilson remarks. 'In the modern world it is not clear that they have any prospect of rebirth.'[10] How much less likely it is, then, that the more primitive forms of religious belief, animatistic or animistic, should revive in the face of behaviourist, cognitivist and neurophysiological psychologies that hold out promises of explanations of human actions and therapies for disturbances of natural, material human capabilities. Materialism is the working ontology of successful science and scientific culture. What better warrant for its truth, or at least its preferability to the rivals that it has supplanted, could there be? If animism isn't dead, what would the death of any metaphysical belief look like?

II

As a matter of sheer fact, animism obviously isn't dead. Various forms of New Age spirituality and ecological consciousness embody a belief in the spiritual intelligence of inorganic objects, animals and people. Some of the practices of New Age spirituality aim explicitly at resonating with or learning from that spiritual intelligence, rather than at the mastery of natural events and objects through the measurement of physical states and structures. One has only to confront the back pages of the *San Francisco Weekly*, or any other urban American weekly or monthly, to find advertisement after advertisement for various forms of therapy and consciousness raising which encourage appreciation of and resonance with a spiritual intelligence in things, animals or people. The Nature Company does good business in selling Brazilian rain sticks to soothe the soul. Various forms of holistic medicine – from transcendental meditation to laughter therapy to exercises for inducing spiritual well-being – contend with dominant, interventionist, drug and surgery medicine. Perhaps persons, even souls, need adjustment to nature's meanings and thoughts, rather than control. There are at least some reasons to think that efforts at achieving resonance, balance, wholeness or adjustment are not simply ill-motivated or silly.

It is not clear that materialist science is distinctively or uniquely successful in yielding explanations of events in nature. It is notoriously difficult to specify a method that the modern materialist sciences use and that other forms of inquiry do not. Empirical induction proceeds only by taking for granted that things have stable class identities, already at least partially grasped, in ways that admit of generalization about tendencies of motion or action that are associated with those identities. But the best partial grasps of class identities that we have achieved in the past – for example, thinking of bodies as displaying natural motion or as occupying absolute space – have turned out not to support the widest ranging generalizations about tendencies of motion. New conceptions of relevant, generalization-supporting kinds have been necessary, and these new conceptions have not been arrived at inductively. Is it clear, then, that we could not usefully arrive at a new conception, supporting wider generalizations, of things in nature as bearing intelligence?

Other, non-inductivist defences of the distinctiveness of the modern material sciences are equally inconclusive. What counts as falsifying a theory depends on the procedures and techniques that have been adopted for assessing class or kind membership. There is no conclusive, a priori reason to believe that these procedures and techniques must be only those of numerical measurement, rather than, say, techniques of empathic observation or resonance with things.

Or consider the view that the cognitive superiority of the modern material sciences is evident in the fact that they undergird and explain our achievements of technological power over nature. As Quine puts it, electrons and the gods of Homer are alike posits, myths, but 'the myth of physical objects . . . has proved more efficacious than other myths as a device for working a manageable structure into the flux of experience.'[11] But what counts as having a manageable structure for our experiences? In what ways are our lives made uniquely better off by the modern material sciences? It misses the point to say that they afford us more power to build bridges, that more power to build bridges is what we want, and that giving us what we want is the mark of cognitive superiority. The point is that it is unclear – at least in the light of the presence in culture, past and present, of practices that manifest animist beliefs – what we either do or should want. Just why is building bridges so central to managing our experience? As Paul Feyerabend notes, other techniques of engaging with nature and thinking about phenomena within it also yield responses, and perhaps responses that are equally fruitful for human life:

> [I]f Aphrodite exists, and if she has the properties and idiosyncrasies ascribed to her, then she certainly will not sit still for something as silly and demeaning as a test of reproducible effects (shy birds, people who are easily bored, and undercover agents behave in similar ways). . . . The 'scientific entities' mentioned above [alpha particles, quarks, neutrinos] are not simply dreams; they are inventions that went through long periods of adaptation, correction, and modification, and then allowed scientists to produce previously unknown effects. Similarly the gods of antiquity and the triune God of Christianity who replaced them were not just poetic visions. They also had effects. They influenced the lives of individuals, groups, and entire nations.[12]

Instead of dogmatically taking it for granted that we have arrived at techniques and practices of measurement that both work to discern what is already there in nature and in doing so enable us to satisfy our genuine needs for bridges and nuclear power plants, we ought instead, Feyerabend suggests, to conceive of techniques, practices and conceptions as all evolving together, in concert with changing articulations of human needs, for this is in fact what happens in the history of science in culture:

> Every individual, group, and culture tries to arrive at an equilibrium between the entities it posits and leading beliefs, needs, expectations, and ways of arguing. . . . Far from merely stating what is already there, [modern science] created conditions of existence, a world corresponding to these conditions, and a life that is adapted to this world; all three now support or 'establish' the conjectures that led to them. Still, a look at history shows that this world is not a static world populated by thinking (and publishing) ants who, crawling all over its crevices, gradually discover its features without affecting them in any way. It is a dynamical and multi-faceted being which influences and reflects the activity of its explorers. It was once full of gods; it then became a drab material world; and it can be changed again, if its inhabitants have the determination, the intelligence, and the heart to take the necessary steps.[13]

So why not a world of intelligent and sensitive natural objects, or a world of, among other things, human souls? To insist that the modern material sciences discern reality 'in itself' is a form of ahistorical dogmatism and idolatry of culture as it is. Wittgenstein made this point in the *Tractatus*:

> The whole modern conception of the world is founded on the illusion that the so-called laws of nature are the explanations of natural phenomena.
>   Thus people today stop at the laws of nature, treating them as something inviolable, just as God and Fate were treated in past ages.
>   And in fact both are right and both are wrong: though the view of the ancients is clearer in so far as they have a clear and acknowledged terminus, while the modern system tries to make it look as if *everything* were explained.[14]

Reality itself does not tell us what to treat as inviolable. We posit entities, create techniques and practices, and articulate and pursue various needs, therein creating culture, all at once. Is it so clear that we might not be better off to treat something other than mathematically formulated laws of material nature as inviolable, particularly in light of the distortions wrought in our understanding of human life by such things as 'intelligence tests' and models of 'rational economic activity' that capitalize on a prior fetishization of measurement?

Nor is the possibility of a fruitful change in basic conceptions of natural phenomena a merely abstract one. It is not only that the philosophy of science has failed clearly to solve the demarcation problem, so that it is hard to distinguish theoretical fact from speculative fiction. Rather, there is a good case to be made that some animistic beliefs already yield distinctively fruitful theory and practice.

First, as Robin Horton has convincingly argued, some traditional African animistic beliefs, particularly those that involve the belief that spirits may be petitioned to cure various illnesses, do articulate a theory and embody efforts at explaining natural phenomena. Appeal to the actions of the gods is often entered as a straightforward explanation of what makes different cases of observable illnesses fall into a common class, with common aetiologies and possibilities of cure. As Horton puts it,

> [R]ecent studies of African cosmology [show] . . . that the gods of a given culture do form a scheme which interprets the vast diversity of everyday experience in terms of the action of a relatively few *kinds* of forces. . . . Like atoms, molecules, and waves, then, the gods serve to introduce unity into diversity, simplicity into complexity, order into disorder, regularity into anomaly. . . . Both [the traditional African thinker and the physicist] are making the same use of theory to transcend the limited vision of natural causes provided by common sense.[15]

Horton argues that many of the explanations and cures that arise out of animistic theory are aimed at illnesses that plausibly flow in part from 'disturbances in a person's social life'. In explaining and curing mental illnesses that are associated with such disturbances, 'the grand theories of Western psychiatry have a notoriously insecure empirical base and are probably culture-bound to a high degree. . . . Hence the need to approach traditional religious theories of the social causation of sickness with respect.'[16] Second, there are more obviously bodily diseases 'such as malaria, typhoid, small-pox, dysentery, etc.'. In traditional Africa, natural resistance to these diseases is comparatively high, and antibiotics are, or were, typically absent:

> In such circumstances, an adult who catches one of these (for Europeans) killer diseases has good chances both of life and of death. In the absence of antimalarials or antibiotics, what happens to him will depend very largely on other facts that add to or subtract from his considerable natural resistance. In these circumstances, the traditional healer's efforts to cope with the situation by ferreting out and attempting to remedy stress-producing disturbances in the patient's social field is probably very relevant.[17]

It requires no great imagination to note that various viruses are now becoming increasingly resistant to treatment by antibiotics, so that our situation in industrial-technological culture is again coming more to resemble the traditional African setting. Hence the possibilities of treatment that animistic therapy discerns may become increasingly relevant for us. In any case, as Horton concludes, there is good reason to think that the practices of appealing to gods and spirits in order to cure illnesses, and the beliefs associated with those practices, 'register certain important features of the objective situation'.[18]

Most importantly, there is another way in which the reasonableness of animistic beliefs, particularly a belief in human souls and in obscure chthonic powers with which human souls might resonate, can be vindicated. It is not just that modern materialist science fails uniquely to pass tests of reasonableness and cannot be clearly demarcated from other systems of belief. It is not just that animistic beliefs figure in some successful explanatory theories and therapeutic practices. There is further a level or region or kind of belief or attitude or comportment – it is difficult to find the right word here – at which animistic beliefs or attitudes are natural and perhaps ineliminable, in some form, in human life; are part, we might say, of a natural poetry of being. This is a considerable part of the point of Wittgenstein's powerful criticism of Frazer's dismissal of primitive practices as inept proto-science.

'I believe', Wittgenstein writes, 'that the characteristic feature of primitive man is that he does not act from *opinions* [*Meinungen*] (contrary to Frazer).'[19] It is, for example, 'surely insane to believe that an *error* is present and that she believes the child has been born' when 'the adoption of a child proceeds in such a way that the mother draws it from under her clothes'.[20] Instead, it is more apt to regard this ceremony as expressing deep attitudes towards family relations, towards relations of intimacy, or of care, or of mutual responsibility, which are now expected naturally to form part of the texture of the developing relationship between mother and child. The ceremony is part of a way of being in which mother and child participate, and it embodies natural attitudes towards that way of being. Elaborating Wittgenstein's views in a similar context – that of our deep attitudes towards human beings – Peter Winch has usefully explicated Wittgenstein's usage of '*Einstellung*' in the phrase '*eine Einstellung zur Seele*', 'an attitude towards a soul'. Here an *Einstellung* is not a belief or opinion, not a *Meinung*. 'It is not a hypothesis, or series of hypotheses, about any particular modes of [another's] consciousness on specific occasions.'[21] It is instead an attitude, or comportment, that is woven through a way of being or living with another human being. It is primitive, and not up for confirmation or infirmation. There is 'an internal relation between the Einstellung and its object'.[22] Only towards a human being can I have this attitude, that she has a soul, and the human being in turn makes this attitude immediate and natural for me. The attitude and the ensouled human being, as it were, reveal each other's nature, without either the need for or the possibility of any experimental testing.

Wittgenstein suggests that a similarly primitive and revelatory attitude or *Einstellung* is what is expressed in some primitive and animistic practices:

> It was not a trivial reason, for really there can have been no *reason*, that prompted certain races of mankind to venerate the oak tree, but only the fact that they and the oak were united in a community of life, and therefore it was not by choice that they arose together, but rather like the flea and the dog. (If fleas developed a rite, it would be based on the dog.)
> ... The form of the awakening spirit is veneration of objects.[23]

Spirit or intelligence or human-mindedness in general, Wittgenstein further suggests, continues to bear marks of its having so awakened. Sometimes such ritual phenomena, embodying animistic attitudes, can be 'brought into connection with an instinct which I myself possess.... [T]hat which brings this picture into connection with our own feelings and thoughts ... gives the account its depth.'[24] It is, and should be, 'from an experience of our own'[25] that we come to appreciate the depth and naturalness of the attitudes expressed in ritual practices. These attitudes, or variations of them, are worked through the fabrics of our own lives as well.

Consider, for example, the practices of making and responding to art, and of leading a moral life. In characterizing beauty in nature and in art, Kant remarks that there is 'an intelligible substrate of external and internal nature',[26] a kind of complete, purposive or design-manifesting ordering of everything that is, and an ordering that obscurely evinces itself in both natural and artistic beauty. It is true that there can be no knowledge of this purposive, rational ordering. We cannot apply a concept to it. Our concepts apply only to objects presented in specific experiences. There is no such thing as a specific experience of the ordering of everything. Such an intelligible ordering can at best be intimated to us in and through certain of our own feelings of pleasure, and a feeling of pleasure or enjoyment in such an ordering – 'is incapable of becoming an element of cognition.'[27] Therefore, this feeling and the intelligible ordering that it dimly reveals have nothing to do with the practices of measurement and theorization in the modern materialist sciences.

But even if it is not an object of theoretical knowledge, such a purposive, rational ordering 'forms the point of reference'[28] for both responding to and making art. This purposive, rational ordering, or supersensible substrate of both humanity and nature, is 'perhaps' the 'determining ground'[29] of the singular, reflective, nonconceptual judgement of taste that something is either artistically or naturally beautiful. That is, this intelligible, supersensible substrate is the something that is internally related to and revealed in the attitude that something is beautiful. Likewise, from the side of the producer of artistic beauty, 'the imagination ... [follows] principles which have a higher seat in reason', and in doing so it achieves 'freedom from the law of association' and acts as 'a powerful agent for creating, as it were, a second nature out of the material supplied to it by actual nature', for creating something that 'surpasses nature'.[30] In artistic creation, as in artistic response, at least as Kant describes it, there is a sense of submission of one's imagination and feeling to a higher, impersonal power, to a non-empirical rational purposiveness that obscurely manifests itself both within and without (the supersensible substrate of humanity *and* nature). Something like this sense of what is going on is what makes talk of art as praise of creation intelligible to us. If any such account of making and responding to art makes sense, then there must in some sense *be* a rational, purposive ordering of things, even though such an ordering is *not* an object of theoretical judgement. Instead, that ordering is dimly manifested to us in the attitudes and senses of our powers that inhabit our making and responding to art. It is not easy to see how that sense of something impersonal and higher inhabiting our making and responding to works of art will readily pass away.

In the moral life, there is a long tradition associating a virtuous character with the achievement of a kind of impersonality that resonates with an obscure rational ordering of things. Evil, in contrast, involves both an assertion of the force and importance of particular desires and inclinations, and a violation of that obscure rational ordering. Kant remarks that 'where the moral law dictates, there is, objectively, no room left for free choice as to what one has to do.'[31] That is to say, when finding oneself in certain circumstances, there is something one must do, a duty that falls to any finitely rational being so situated. The attempt to exempt oneself from one's duty by making an ad hoc exception for oneself in this situation, so as instead to act for the sake of inclination or convenience, is the root of the deformation of one's free choice, or *Willkür*, away from conformity to and information by the demands of impersonal, rational norms of autonomous willing (*Wille*). And not only is there in a certain situation something, a specific act, that one must objectively perform; it is also the case that achieving moral worth involves attaining to a kind of impersonality within, as respect for the moral law and its requirements becomes the motivation for one's actions:

[M]an's moral growth of necessity begins not in the improvement of his practices but rather in the transforming of his cast of mind and in the grounding of a character. . . . [T]he restoration [of the original predisposition to good in us] is but the establishment of the *purity* of this law as the supreme ground of all our maxims, whereby it is not merely associated with other incentives, and certainly is not subordinated to any such (to inclinations) as its conditions, but instead must be adopted, in its entire purity, as an incentive *adequate* in itself for the determination of the will [*Willkür*: choice].[32]

So far as one achieves this restoration, one will objectively do one's duty, will respect persons, both oneself and others. More crucially, however, one will also be living up to the possibilities and demands of one's rational nature. One will be realizing or expressing one's nature fitly, within a system of rational natures, obscure though that system is to us empirically and theoretically. The sense that impersonal motivation by the moral law involves resonating with an obscure rational ordering of things is what leads Kant to say that those who have an interest in beauty, in resonating with that obscure ordering in free perception, have already perhaps begun to achieve that moral motivation. '[T]o take an *immediate interest* in the beauty of *nature* . . . is always a mark of a good soul. . . . [W]e have reason for presuming the presence of at least the germ of a good moral disposition in the case of a man to whom the beauty of nature is a matter of immediate interest.'[33]

It is not easy – certainly not in the terms of the practices of measurement – to say exactly what a realization of one's rational nature involves in all specific situations, let alone who achieves it how, when or where. But to the extent that people continue to feel themselves to be commanded by a rational nature within, as part of an obscure system of nature, to certain modes of action and relation with themselves and with others, then they manifest a commitment to the view that there is a source of such a command within, potentially resonant with an obscure rational ordering without.

In both these regions of human life – in the practices of art and in the moral life – there is a sense, one that seems to force itself on us, that human beings within an ordering of nature have certain empirically unpredictable powers of creation, action and reponse. These powers or potentials, it may seem, show themselves obscurely in virtually everything that human beings do, in their glances, jokes, asides, facial expressions and ordinary actions, as well as in their rituals and lives with art and morality directly. It is perhaps this sense of human beings as possessed of such a power that Winch is voicing when he says about the attitude or *Einstellung* that another has a soul,

> There is no question here of an attitude which I can adopt or abandon at will. My *Einstellung* may no doubt be strengthened, weakened, or modified by circumstances and to some extent by thought too, but usually, in given circumstances, it is a condition I am in vis-à-vis other human beings without choosing to be so.[34]

III

There are, then, these two stances: belief in the soul, whether in human beings or things, is an outgrown relic of a pre-scientific culture, a reaction or projection that is merely subjective when contrasted with the achievements of the modern material sciences and their practices of measurement and theory in discerning what is really there; and belief in the souls of persons as powers, partially manifested in some therapeutic practices, in ritual, in art, morality and in ordinary life, and potentially resonant with an intelligence or purposiveness that obscurely informs things, forces itself on us, and it is as deep, and objective, and fruitful, and inevitable as any fundamental attitude or orientation ever is. What are we to say?

No practice-independent facts – if there are any such things – force either animist or materialist attitudes on us. Instead, which practices, together with their projections of theoretical entities and their ways of being, one inhabits is decisive for the attitudes one will have. What, then, are the outstanding differences between the systems of interrelated practices – the cultures – in which animist attitudes are expressed and nurtured and those in which they are dismissed as merely subjective and suppressed?

Writing on the contrasts between Western material science and African thought, V.Y. Mudimbe and Kwame Anthony Appiah point to 'the totally different social organization of inquiry in traditional and modern cultures'.[35] These different social organizations of inquiry are in turn, they suggest, functions of larger differences in social organization that distinguish modern from traditional culture. Among these larger differences, they point to the social mobility and political individualism of modern societies, both of which are 'rare in the traditional polity'.[36] With social mobility and political individualism, cognitive authority shifts 'from priest and king to commoner'.[37] What one knows is henceforth accredited in competitive discourse, not by a fixed political hierarchy. Horton similarly notes the rise of choice and the separation of aesthetic, emotional and cognitive motives in modern societies.[38] These social developments of mobility, political and cognitive individualism, choice and the emergence of separate spheres of artistic, moral and cognitive activity (in contrast with the unity of these activities enforced under pre-modern rituals) in turn arise out of two related developments. Mudimbe and Appiah, and Lindberg, both appealing to the work of Jack Goody, point first to the development of literacy as underlying and enabling these social developments. As Lindberg puts it:

> The decisive development seems to have been the invention of writing, which occurred in a series of steps. . . . One of the crucial contributions of writing, especially alphabetic writing, was to provide a means for the recording of oral traditions, thereby freezing what had hitherto been fluid, translating fleeting audible signals into enduring visible objects. Writing thus served a storage function, replacing memory as the principal repository of knowledge. This had the revolutionary effect of opening knowledge claims to the possibility of inspection, comparison, and criticism. Such comparison encourages skepticism and, in antiquity, helped to create the distinction between truth, on the one hand, and myth or legend, on the other . . .[39]

While other developments may also be necessary for and enable a modern culture of social mobility and cognitive competitiveness – Mudimbe and Appiah mention agricultural developments, modern warfare, experience with machinery, the Reformation and the development of universities, among other things – the development of writing 'seems certainly necessary. . . . Without widespread literacy it is hard to see how science could have got started.'[40]

Second, there is industrialization. Industrial technology both requires and promotes the existence of specialized bodies of knowledge, freed from direct political control. It builds a world in which the techniques of measurement and theorization used in the modern material sciences have an immediate pertinence and usefulness. And it is the coming into being of this world, Horton suggests, that explains the attenuation of animistic beliefs and practices in modern, scientific cultures:

> In complex, rapidly changing industrial societies the human scene is in flux. Order, regularity, predictability, simplicity, all these seem lamentably absent. It is in the world of inanimate things that such qualities are most readily seen. This is why many people can find themselves less at home with their fellow men than with things. And this too, I suggest, is why the mind in quest of explanatory analogies turns most readily to the inanimate. In the

traditional societies of Africa, we find the situation reversed. The human scene is the locus *par excellence* of order, predictability, regularity. In the world of the inanimate, these qualities are far less evident. Here, being less at home with people than with things is unimaginable. And here, the mind in quest of explanatory analogies turns naturally to people and their relations.[41]

It is, perhaps, something like this thought that lies behind the claim that animistic beliefs and practices are dead. Though it is difficult to demarcate science from non-science, and difficult to see how to demonstrate the cognitive superiority of materialist science to animistic therapy by appeal to a priori knowable epistemic principles, it is also difficult to imagine the reversal or undoing of the development of technological culture.

IV

And yet things are not so clear, for the sociocultural developments through which modern scientific theories and practices, together with their attitudes towards nature, have been brought into being are themselves neither autonomous from developments in attitudes nor complete and absolute.

First, these sociocultural developments are not autonomous from developments in metaphysical attitudes and ways of being. Writing and technology developed in part because people found them to be useful, in light of the attitudes, projects and interests that they already possessed. Writing and the development of the university are interwoven with the development of handicraft technologies; they precede the development of market economies, which in turn precede the development of industrial technologies and economies. At each stage the relation of attitude to practice to technology is complex. The idea that a single, underlying, master imperative that the forces of production shall develop makes itself felt in history is an ahistoricial fiction. As Charles Taylor usefully observes:

[A]ll historiography (and social science as well) relies on a (largely implicit) understanding of human motivation: how people respond, what they generally aspire to, the relative importance of given ends and the like. . . . One reason why vulgar Marxism is so implausible is that its reductive accounts of, say, religious or moral or legal-political ideas seem to give no weight at all to their intrinsic power.... [M]oral ideals, understandings of the human predicament, [and] concepts of the self for the most part exist in our lives through being embedded in practices.... It is clear that change can come about in both directions, as it were: through mutations and developments in the ideas, including new visions and insights, bringing about alterations, ruptures, reforms, revolutions in practices; and also through drift, change, constrictions or flourishings of practices, bringing about the alteration, flourishing, or decline of ideas. But even this is too abstract. It is better to say that in any concrete development in history, change is occurring both ways.[42]

Second, these sociocultural developments do not, again, establish the cognitive superiority of the beliefs and attitudes that they embody. As Feyerabend argues, 'the Greek gods were not "removed by argument." The opponents of popular beliefs about the gods never offered reasons that, using commonly held assumptions, showed the inadequacy of the beliefs. What we do have is a gradual social change leading to new concepts and new stories built from them.'[43] That social change is not a proof of epistemic merit; it is both cause and effect of changes in attitudes, interests, practices and beliefs.

Third, and most important, the development of a modern, materialist culture is incomplete. Practices of art and morality survive, and they seem to resist having their achievements and requirements recast in wholly utilitarian terms. The attitude that a human being has a soul, a locus of agency and responsibility, capable perhaps of resonance with impersonal requirements of reason dimly embodied elsewhere, is itself built into modern familial, pedagogic and legal practices, as well as artistic and moral ones. Morover, premodern cultures, while they no doubt are more thoroughly organized under wider-ranging rituals than modern cultures, also include technological devices for mastering a nature that in some ways is regarded as a fit object of use or domination. Various agricultural implements and tools for hunting, intended for use on nature, arise in the midst of animistic practices and beliefs. As a result, it is difficult to distinguish traditional from modern culture sharply or absolutely. They are not full opposites.

V

It seems, then, that both traditional, more animistic cultures and practices, as well as their contemporary analogues, and modern, scientific, materialist cultures and practices express persistent human interests and responses to reality. In a more traditional culture, more weight or scope is given to the expression of a sense of human ensoulment and resonance with nature, thus leading to what Horton calls 'an intensely poetic quality in everyday life'.[44] In modern, materialist culture, more weight or scope is given to the control of nature, the satisfaction of material needs, the development of power, and the exercise of choice in the fulfilment of desire.

It is, I think, a mistake to wish to absolutize and perfect the expressive achievements of either form of culture at the expense of the other. At any rate, I do not have that wish. Consider, for a moment, what an absolutized materialist culture might look like. Without a sense of the ensoulment of human beings, and without a sense of possible resonance with a meaningful order that we might bring to our actions and relations, we are likely to be left with what are often described as the sins of modernity: alienation, anomie, egoism, acquisitiveness and instrumentalism – everything that Weber saw as falling under the heading of the suppression of *Wertrationalität* by *Zweckrationalität*, or what Hegel memorably describes when he characterizes modern civil society as a culture in which

> Particularity by itself, given free rein in every direction to satisfy its needs, accidental caprices, and subjective desires, destroys itself and its substantive concept in this process of gratification. At the same time, the satisfaction of need, necessary and accidental alike, is accidental because it breeds new desires without end, is in thoroughgoing dependence on caprice and external accident, and is held in check by the power of universality [rather than expressing universal reason]. In these contrasts and their complexity, civil society affords a spectacle of extravagance and want as well as of the physical and ethical degeneration common to them both.[45]

Up to a point, this is a possible, and deplorable, and actual line of development. Modern society has its ills. But fortunately it is not everywhere as bad as all that. Morality and art and religion and the experience of nature do, fitfully, continue to have important roles in our culture.

Or consider an absolutized animist culture. The practices of measurement and the achievements of modern technology would be largely abandoned. Rituals of responsiveness to a meaningfulness discerned principally by authoritative priests and seers would be pervasive. Coerciveness, cultism, quietist anti-ameliorism and collectivism would reign. Up to a point, this is a possible, and deplorable, and actual line of cultural development. But fortunately, it is not everywhere as bad as all that in traditional cultures, which develop their own technologies and practices of measurement, take up new ones, and allow for various forms of individuality within them.

VI

Each culture – modern-scientific-material and traditional-animistic – with its distinctive weightings towards the articulation and expression of persistent human interests and fundamental attitudes – can serve in a way as a measure of the other. Each highlights the other's achievements and failings.

What is it like, then, to live with an articulate interest in both the practices and achievements of modern, materialist science and culture and the practices and achievements of wonder, and dignity, and the poetry of daily life of traditional, animist culture, in so far as one inhabits oneself a complex culture that embodies both kinds of practices and achievements? Thinking of things in this way makes the inheritance of culture a standing problem. How is one to enter into, and react against, a complex culture as it stands? It is difficult to say much with confidence here. Surely there is no one right direction or manner of engagement with a complex culture. But perhaps I can suggest something of the complexity and interest of this problem by pointing briefly to one of the most interesting and complex treatments of it in Western literature, Thomas Mann's *Doctor Faustus*.

In this novel, the composer Adrian Leverkühn is determined to develop a form of artistic, compositional practice that will overcome the failings of materialist modernity and bring a sense of power and meaningfulness into daily life. At university he initially studies theology, accepting the view that 'What we call prayer is really the statement of this confidence [in the angelic direction of one's life], a notice-giving or invocation. But prayer it is correctly called, because it is at bottom God whom we thus address.'[46] In later taking up his career as a composer, he pursues the formulation of a new system of musical conventions that are to be what the old conventions, now outworn, once were: 'They were crystallizations of living experiences and as such long performed an office of vital importance: the task of organization. Organization is everything. Without it there is nothing, least of all art.'[47] To the end of formulating and enacting such conventions, thereby to reintroduce organization, art and meaningfulness into decayed modern life, he forms a pact with the devil, giving himself over to 'that world of the spirit which one approaches only at one's peril', 'to the influence of the powers of the underworld'.[48] He leads a life that is memorable, and magnificent, and horrible in its austerities and casual cruelties.

Against the figure of Leverkühn is set the narrator, his friend, the humanist and teacher, Serenus Zeitblom. Zeitblom is, he tells us, 'by nature wholly moderate, of a temper, I may say, both healthy and humane, addressed to reason and harmony ... the daemonic, little as I presume to deny its influence upon human life, I have at all times found utterly foreign to my nature.'[49] He is scholarly, decent, well-adjusted and more than a bit dull, a figure, in part, of routine in material modernity.

So they are different. One achieves much, in alliance with chthonic creative forces that make ritual and artistic expression possible, but that undo common human decency. The other is decent, measured and dull. And yet, for all his decent dullness, Zeitblom is also interested in and affected by Leverkühn's personality and powers and achievements. He enters into them vicariously. Music, he says, 'seems to me, in all its supposedly logical and moral austerity, to belong to a world of the spirit for whose absolute reliability in the things of reason and human dignity I would not just care to put my hand in the fire. That I am even so heartily affected by it is one of those contradictions which, for better or worse, are inseparable from human nature.'[50] In so far as we find ourselves both drawn to and resistant to Leverkühn's powers and achievements of meaningful expression, however obscure, through these reactions of Zeitblom who guides our perceptions, perhaps our own situation is no less complex and contradictory and interesting than his.

Notes

1.	G.T. Fechner, *Religion of a Scientist*, trans. W. Lowrie (New York: 1946), pp. 176–7; cited in Paul Edwards, 'Panpsychism', *The Encyclopedia of Philosophy* (New York: Macmillan, 1967), vol. 6, p. 22B.

2.	Arthur Schopenhauer, *The World as Will and Idea*, trans. R.B. Haldane and J. Kemp (London: 1883), Book II, section 23; cited in Edwards, 'Panpsychism', p. 25A.

3.	Hermann Lotze, *Mikrokosmus* (Leipzig: 1856–64); *Microcosmus*, trans. E. Hamilton and E.E.C. Jones (New York: 1890), vol. I, p. 363; cited in Edwards, 'Panpsychism', pp. 22B–23A, 23B.

4.	E.B. Tylor, *Primitive Culture*, cited in *The Oxford English Dictionary*, s.v. 'animism', p. 336A.

5.	Northcote Whitbridge Thomas, 'Animism', *Encyclopedia Britannica*, 11th edition (New York: The Encyclopedia Britannica Company, 1910), p. 52A.

6.	David C. Lindberg, *The Beginnings of Western Science* (Chicago: The University of Chicago Press, 1992), p. 7.

7.	Alasdair MacIntyre, 'Pantheism', *The Encyclopedia of Philosophy*, vol. 6, p. 35A.

8.	Whitbridge Thomas, 'Animism', pp. 55A, 54A.

9.	T.H. Huxley, *Nature* (1881), no. 615, p. 344; cited in *The Oxford English Dictionary*, s.v. 'animism', p. 336B.

10.	Bryan Wilson, *Contemporary Transformations of Religion* (Oxford: Oxford University Press, 1976), p. 116.

11.	W.V.O. Quine, 'Two Dogmas of Empiricism', *Philosophical Review* (January 1951); reprinted with minor revisions in Quine, *From a Logical Point of View* (Cambridge, Mass.: Harvard University Press, 1953, 1961); reprinted (New York: Harper & Row, 1963), p. 44.

12.	Paul Feyerabend, 'Realism and the Historicity of Knowledge', *The Journal of Philosophy* LXXXVI, 8 (August 1989), pp. 398, 400.

13.	Ibid., pp. 405, 406.

14.	Ludwig Wittgenstein, *Tractatus Logico-Philosophicus*, trans. D.F. Pears and B.F. McGuinness (London: Routledge & Kegan Paul, 1961), §§ 6.371–2, p. 143.

15.	Robin Horton, 'African Traditional Thought and Western Science', in *Rationality*, ed. Bryan R. Wilson (Oxford: Basil Blackwell, 1970), pp. 133, 134, 136.

16.	Ibid., pp. 137, 138.

17.	Ibid., p. 138.

18.	Ibid., p. 137.

19.	Wittgenstein, 'Remarks on Frazer's *Golden Bough*', trans. John Beversluis, in *Wittgenstein: Sources and Perspectives*, ed. C.G. Luckhardt (Ithaca, NY: Cornell University Press, 1979), p. 71.

20.	Ibid., p. 65.

21.	Peter Winch, 'Eine Einstellung zur Seele', in *Trying to Make Sense* (Oxford: Basil Blackwell, 1987), p. 146.

22.	Ibid., p. 147.

23.	Wittgenstein, 'Remarks on Frazer's *Golden Bough*', pp. 72–3.

24. Ibid., pp. 72, 74.
25. Ibid., p. 77.
26. Immanuel Kant, *The Critique of Judgement*, trans. James Creed Meredith (Oxford: Clarendon Press, 1928), p. 213.
27. Ibid., p. 30.
28. Ibid., p. 212.
29. Ibid., p. 208.
30. Ibid., p. 176.
31. Ibid., p. 50.
32. Kant, *Religion Within the Limits of Reason Alone*, trans. Theodore M. Greene and Hoyt H. Hudson (New York: Harper & Row, 1960), pp. 43, 42.
33. Kant, *The Critique of Judgement*, pp. 157, 160.
34. Winch, 'Eine Einstellung zur Seele', pp. 149–50.
35. V.Y. Mudimbe and Kwame Anthony Appiah, 'The Impact of African Studies on Philosophy', in *Africa and the Disciplines*, ed. Robert H. Bates, V.Y. Mudimbe and Jean O'Barr (Chicago: University of Chicago Press, 1993), p. 126.
36. Ibid., p. 132.
37. Ibid.
38. Horton, 'African Traditional Thought and Western Science', pp. 160, 161.
39. Lindberg, *The Beginnings of Western Science*, pp. 11, 12. Compare Mudimbe and Appiah, 'The Impact of African Studies on Philosophy', p. 132.
40. Mudimbe and Appiah, 'The Impact of African Studies on Philosophy', p. 133.
41. Horton, 'African Traditional Thought and Western Science', p. 147.
42. Charles Taylor, *Sources of the Self: The Making of the Modern Identity* (Cambridge, Mass.: Harvard University Press, 1989), pp. 203, 204, 205.
43. Feyerabend, 'Realism and the Historicity of Knowledge', p. 51.
44. Horton, 'African Traditional Thought and Western Science', p. 170.
45. G.W.F. Hegel, *Philosophy of Right*, trans. T.M. Knox (Oxford: Oxford University Press, 1952), para. 185, p. 123.
46. Thomas Mann, *Doctor Faustus*, trans. H.T. Lowe-Porter (New York: Alfred A. Knopf, 1948), p. 94.
47. Ibid., p. 190.
48. Ibid., p. 8.
49. Ibid., pp. 4, 5.
50. Ibid., p. 9.

2

Is Animism Alive and Well? A Response to Professor Eldridge

Mario von der Ruhr

I INTRODUCTION

Professor Eldridge's paper is an attempt to shed light on the genesis and rationality of animism, which is

> the belief that human beings have souls, or, by extension, the belief that animals, plants or even rocks have souls; that is, that they are subjects of feeling or consciousness, or display intelligence, in ways that ensouled human beings do.[1]

It is not difficult to see why there should be an inclination to wonder about the rationality of animism even at this early stage in the discussion. Does the animist, so one would like to ask, conceive of the human soul as something radically different in kind from, but at the same time inextricably bound up with, consciousness and its behavioural manifestations, as a kind of Cartesian immaterial substance mysteriously interacting with the body, perhaps? And what could be made of the analogous belief that trees or rocks, for example, are subjects of feeling or consciousness? What grammatical work, in Wittgenstein's sense, does the word 'soul' do in phrases like 'Human beings have souls', or 'Trees have souls'? If the animist invokes the notion of a soul as an *explanans* for the observable properties of natural objects in the same sense in which a scientist appeals to the chemical structure of a substance in order to explain the way it interacts with other substances, then it would seem that the animist is no more than a primitive scientist in disguise, one who has yet to learn that the *explanans* he is after is to be given in terms of atoms and molecules, rather than in the misleading terminology of souls and spirits, which would seem to have a more natural home in literature and poetry. If, on the other hand, the animist's description of 'how things really are' appeals to ephemeral, metaphysical substances of some kind, then won't his belief require a close shave with Ockham's razor in order to be granted admission to the realm of intelligible discourse? Surely, one would like to object, there is no need for positing the existence of souls, either in human beings or in the natural world at large, as an *additional explanans* to that which the scientist provides in his account of nature. On this view, animism is, as Eldridge rightly characterizes it in the first part of his paper, 'a relic of outworn cultures which have not yet learned to think scientifically';[2] at best an embryonic form of science, or else a mode of pseudo-scientific irrationality. Like Frazer's account of primitive rituals of nature worship, this dismissive gesture is, however, only one way of reacting to animism, and one that appears too restrictive in its conception of the ways in which human beings can intelligibly relate to the natural world. The motivation behind this negative reaction – the uncompromising insistence on the distinction between the rational and the irrational, the intelligible and the unintelligible – may be commendable, but its rejection of animism as irrational may turn out to be just as hasty as Otto Neurath's impatient and frequent interruptions of the Vienna Circle's discussion of Wittgenstein's *Tractatus* with the exclamation: '*Das ist Metaphysik!*'[3] An alternative way of looking at animism is to see animistic beliefs or attitudes as a natural dimension of human life, as an ineliminable part of what might be called 'a natural poetry of being',[4] which carries its justification within itself and neither rests on, nor clandestinely appeals to, metaphysical presuppositions of the sort that Neurath, Frazer and like-minded critics would justifiably object to. It is to the elaboration of this construal that Professor Eldridge devotes the second half of his paper, as well as offering some suggestions on the socio-psychological, socioeconomic and other factors that may have contributed to the gradual, cultural shift away from an animistic, to what might broadly be called a scientific, perspective on nature. While I am in sympathy with the general tenor of Eldridge's discussion, as well as with his final conclusion on the subject to the effect that 'both traditional, more animistic cultures . . . and modern, scientific, materialist cultures and practices express persistent human interests and responses to reality',[5] I think his account requires a number of correctives, as well as some illustrative detail to bring out what might be meant by saying that an attitude towards nature is animistic. What follows is not a vivisectional analysis of Eldridge's argument, however, but a general discussion of the topic from a slightly different perspective. I hope that my criticisms of Eldridge will stand out from that discussion clearly enough, though I have also formulated them more explicitly in sections IV and V.

II ANIMISM AND THE GREAT SPIRIT

Complaining about the way in which hydraulic mining techniques employed in the wake of the relentless search for gold and other precious metals had devastated the environment, an old and 'holy' Wintu woman once lamented:

> The White people plow up the ground, pull down the trees, kill everything. The tree says, 'Don't. I am sore. Don't hurt me.' But they cut it down and chop it up. The spirit of the land hates them. They blast out trees and stir it up to its depths. They saw up the trees. That hurts them. The Indians never hurt anything, but the White people destroy all. They blast rocks and scatter them on the ground. The rock says, 'Don't. You are hurting me.'[6]

The view expressed here is an intelligible one, especially when it is supplemented with further details of the North American Indians' way of life, in which reverence for nature played an essential role. The belief that trees are animated by the 'spirit of the land' was as much part of their way of thinking as the idea that trees can talk. As the Stoney Indian Walking Buffalo puts it:

> Indians living close to nature and nature's ruler are not living in darkness. Did you know that trees talk? Well they do. They talk to each other, and they'll talk to you if you listen. Trouble is, white people don't listen. They never learned to listen to the Indians so I don't suppose they'll listen to other voices in nature. But I have learned a lot from trees: sometimes about the weather, sometimes about animals, sometimes about the Great Spirit.[7]

There seem, on the face of it, to be only two possible reactions to these remarks. One is to insist that they are doubtlessly intended to be taken *literally*: not only are trees conscious, sentient beings, susceptible to pain and pleasure, but they can also talk, to each other as well as to human beings. Sir James Frazer, in *The Golden Bough*, is inclined towards this reading when he says:

> If trees are animate, they are necessarily sensitive and the cutting of them down becomes a delicate surgical operation, which must be performed with as tender a regard as possible for the feelings of the sufferers.[8]

Indeed, for Frazer, to regard trees and plants as animate *is* to ascribe to them the very same feelings, desires and states of consciousness that are ordinarily attributed to human beings:

> The conception of trees and plants as animated beings naturally results in treating them as male and female, who can be married to each other in a real, and not merely in a figurative or poetical, sense of the word.[9]

Not surprisingly, Frazer can make little of the belief that two trees can, quite literally, be married to each other, feel pain or talk to each other. Given the grammar of terms like 'marriage', 'pain', 'conversation', etc., as revealed in ordinary discourse, Frazer, quite rightly, wants to reject a confused application of such terms to objects that *could not* have the capacities for exhibiting the relevant kind of behaviour that is typically associated with being married, in pain or engaged in a conversation. This is a conceptual point about the grammar of the terms in question, and not a hasty dismissal of something that should, perhaps, be taken seriously. On the contrary, the suggestion that trees could feel pain or talk to each other would, in the absence of an elaborate and intelligible story, be dismissed as sheer nonsense. It may be objected that this construal of the North American Indians' reverence for nature is itself wildly implausible, and that the above remarks are obviously *not* intended to be taken literally but, *pace* Frazer, merely *metaphorically*. When the Wintu woman says that trees don't want to be hurt, she is not ascribing to them certain states of consciousness, but condemning the practice of felling trees. Her remark has the force of a reproach. Similarly, the expression 'spirit of the land' is just a poetic way of saying that the ecosystem should not be upset in that way, etc. And when

Walking Buffalo insists that trees 'talk' to him about the weather, he is simply using the term to express, metaphorically, the idea that trees may be used in a primitive sort of weather forecast, etc. Hence, we can make perfectly good sense of what the North American Indians say, once we recognize that they are speaking metaphorically rather than literally; there is no need to accuse them of conceptual confusion.[10]

While I would certainly agree with the last sentence, it seems to me that this second construal is, in other respects, just as problematic as the first, and for exactly the same reason. Both readings are based on the questionable assumption that what the Indians say must be taken either *literally* or *metaphorically*, since there is no third alternative. Following the language of the *Tractatus*, this is the view that the Indians are either *saying* something, advancing *propositions* about what is objectively the case; or they are merely expressing, in a poetic way, their own, subjective feelings about the world. The contemporary philosophical analogue of this conception of the relation between language and reality is the claim that the Indians must be either realists or non-realists about the properties they ascribe to trees and to 'the spirit of the land', that they must unequivocally put their 'ontological commitments' on the linguistic table if they want us to take their language-games seriously. That this approach is not as helpful as it looks, and indeed distortive of the phenomena under investigation, is easy to see. For if the literal/metaphorical dichotomy is taken as a touchstone of intelligibility, the Indians' beliefs and rituals become either ridiculous or cheap, *saying* either too much to be intelligible, or too little to convey the meaning intended. A possible way out of this dilemma is hinted at by Wittgenstein in his remark on Ludwig Uhland's poem *Count Eberhard's Hawthorn*, when he says that its meaning will be preserved without loss 'if only you do not try to utter what is unutterable'.[11] The poem *shows* us a certain – in this case a religious – attitude towards life, just as the Indians' remarks about trees reveal a distinctive attitude towards nature, and both are expressed in a language that is essential to their being the kinds of attitude they are. The picture of nature suggested by the Indians speaks for itself. To be sure, for an adequate appreciation of the latter, more detail is required than I have provided so far, but the following comments will, perhaps, go some way towards remedying this defect. It is clear that the Indians' remarks are part of a wider framework of thinking, which involves such ideas as that the Great Spirit is our father, but the earth is our mother. She nourishes us; that which we put into the ground she returns to us, and healing plants she gives us likewise.[12]

What Big Thunder, a member of the Wabanakis Nation, says here about the earth allows us to see why the Indians would regard the felling of a tree as a sacrilegious act, as a rejection of the gifts of Mother Earth, as an abhorrent crime. That this attitude towards the earth is not adequately circumscribed in terms of utilitarian concerns for the preservation of the ecosystem, for instance, comes out even more clearly in this remark by Smohalla, a Nez Percé Indian:

You ask me to plow the ground. Shall I take a knife and tear my mother's breasts? Then when I die she will not take me to her bosom to rest. You ask me to dig for stone. Shall I dig under her skin for her bones? Then when I die I cannot enter her body to be born again. You ask me to cut grass and make hay and sell it and be rich like white men. But how dare I cut off my mother's hair?[13]

For the Indian, it was essential to be in close contact with the earth and everything on it. Chief Standing Bear, a Sioux Indian who joined Buffalo Bill's Wild West Show in 1898 as an interpreter and spent his later years lecturing and writing, put it thus:

The Lakota was a true naturist – a lover of nature. He loved the earth and all things of the earth, the attachment growing with age. The old people came literally to love the soil and they sat or reclined on the ground with a feeling of being close to a mothering power. It was good for the skin to touch the earth and the old people liked to remove their moccasins and walk with bare feet on the sacred earth. Their tipis were built upon the earth and their altars were made of earth. The birds that flew in the air came to rest upon the earth and it was the final abiding place of all things that lived and grew. The soil was soothing, strengthening, cleansing and healing. That is why the old Indian still sits upon the earth instead of propping himself up and away from its life-giving forces.[14]

It would be a mistake simply to equate the 'mothering power' of the earth, its 'life-giving forces' with whatever material goods the environment provided for the Indians, or the 'soothing' and 'heal-ing' powers of the soil with the psychological benefits of sitting on the ground, rather than on chairs. For it is important that the earth is considered 'sacred', and that 'altars' are erected on it for the worship of the Great Spirit. Indeed, the 'healing' and 'life-giving' forces of the earth are to be understood in a spiritual sense as well:

> For [the Lakota], to sit or lie upon the ground is to be able to think more deeply and to feel more keenly; he can see more clearly into the mysteries of life and come closer in kinship to other lives about him . . .[15]

The idea echoed in this passage is not dissimilar from that expressed in the penultimate stanza of Uhland's poem on the hawthorn tree, 'neath which the old man oft/would sit in reverie', contemplating not only his own past, but the mystery of creation as a whole, rather than the aesthetic qualities of the tree. This does not mean that there is no conceptual connection between regarding a tree or the soil as sacred, and the economic role it may play in the lives of those who depend on it. As Frazer observes:

> The Wanika of Eastern Africa fancy that every tree, and espe-cially every coco-nut tree, has its spirit; 'the destruction of a coco-nut tree is regarded as equivalent to matricide, because that tree gives them life and nourishment, as a mother does her child.'[16]

What does *not* follow from Frazer's example, however, is that the Wanika merely worship trees *because* of the nourishment these trees provide. That would be a misconstrual of the case, based on the failure to see that, while there may indeed be a necessary relation between the former and the latter, it is not a reductive relation, for the reasons I sketched out in connection with the literal/metaphor-ical dichotomy above. But it may be useful at this point to turn to Frazer's own discussion of tree worship, so as to throw the difficul-ties of his approach into relief.

III FRAZER ON TREE CULTS

Frazer thinks it necessary to 'examine in some detail the notions on which the worship of trees and plants is based', because tree worship

constitutes for him an early stage in man's intellectual development
from animistic, to polytheistic, to monotheistic, systems of belief.
To the savage, Frazer contends, 'the world in general is animate,
and trees and plants are no exception to the rule. He thinks that
they have souls like his own, and he treats them accordingly.'[17]

For Frazer, the inclination to believe that trees are ensouled seems
to be grounded in, among other things: the economic relation between the savage and his environment, certain natural reactions of
fear and awe, and the ensuing desire to influence nature by magical
means. In the spiritual history of Western Europe, we are told, the
worship of trees does not come as a surprise:

> Nothing could be more natural. For at the dawn of history Eu-
> rope was covered with immense primaeval forests, in which the
> scattered clearings must have appeared like islets in an ocean of
> green.[18]

And, 'the solitude, the gloom, the silence of the forest appear to
have made a deep impression' on people.[19] Uhland, it should be
noted, also admits that certain ways of thinking may force themselves on an individual in his dealings with the natural world when
he says that

> the spirit of man ... well aware that it will never comprehend
> within itself and with total clarity the infinite, and weary of its
> indeterminate longing, soon begins to associate the latter with
> worldly pictures, which appear to offer it a glimpse of the super-
> natural. It embraces such pictures with a pious love, and is atten-
> tive to their most secret admonitions.[20]

Unlike Frazer, however, Uhland insists that a poetic perspective
on nature need not be re- or deconstructed in quasi-scientific, socio-
psychological or socioeconomic terms to be rendered intelligible. It
speaks for itself. That is why Romanticism, too, is for him nothing but

> sublime, eternal poetry, which represents in a picture what words
> only express inadequately or not at all; it is the book filled with
> strange magic symbols which keep us in communion with the
> sinister world of spirits; it is the shimmering rainbow, the bridge
> of the gods on which, according to the Edda, they descend to the
> mortals, and on which the elect climb up to them.[21]

Wittgenstein, it seems to me, would have endorsed this point, as well as the question Uhland appends to it: 'Is the ... unbelief of the modern age more rational than the notorious superstitions of the ancients?'[22] Frazer's answer to this question, however, is an unqualified yes. In the preface to the first edition of his work, he argues that tree cults interest him only in so far as they are informed by a fear of the dead – 'the most powerful force in the making of primitive religion' – and leaves no doubt that he regards these cults as deeply confused:

> I hope that after this explicit exclaimer I shall no longer be taxed with embracing a system of mythology which I look upon not merely as false but as preposterous and absurd.[23]

There appear to be primarily two reasons for Frazer's harsh judgement. One has to do with the *character* of some of the practices surrounding the tree cults; the other, with their animistic foundation. In 'holy groves about ... villages or houses, where even to break a twig would have been a sin',[24] Frazer may have seen a relatively harmless superstition, but there are more provocative cases, clearly intended to appeal to the reader's sense of moral propriety:

> Among the Kangra mountains of the Punjaub a girl used to be annually sacrificed to an old cedar-tree, the families of the village taking it in turn to supply the victim. The tree was cut down not very many years ago.[25]

'And not before time!' Frazer might conceivably have added. How *could* a human life be sacrificed to a tree? Does not the very practice, so one is tempted to ask, constitute a *reductio ad absurdum* of the very beliefs that underpin it? Are we not presented here with a case of irrationality resulting in the grossest form of immorality? Frazer does not put it like that, but the question seems to be written all over his description of the cases in question, even where he gets close to seeing something about the depth of tree worship:

> How serious that worship was in former times may be gathered from the ferocious penalty appointed by the old German laws for such as dared to peel the bark of a standing tree. The culprit's navel was to be cut out and nailed to the part of the tree which he had peeled, and he was to be driven round and round the tree

till all his guts were wound about its trunk. The intention of the punishment was clearly to replace the dead bark by a living substitute taken from the culprit; it was a life for a life, the life of a man for the life of a tree.[26]

Frazer finds these practices revolting, and I am sure most readers would agree with him. But the question of whether we find them morally abhorrent needs to be carefully separated from the different question of whether these practices rest on an irrational foundation, on false or confused beliefs about spirits and the natural causal order of things, as Frazer seems to be suggesting. The problem is that the above examples hardly warrant that charge. For one thing – and I think this is a general deficiency in his discussion of the matter – Frazer's descriptions often provide little exposition of the 'grammar' of the vocabulary they employ; it is no wonder, therefore, that little can be made of the practices in question. In addition, Frazer tends to trade on common moral sensibilities in order to boost what is really an epistemological point, viz. that animism rests on shaky epistemic grounds, on false causal hypotheses or, indeed, on 'preposterous' ideas about spirits, and the like. But, as Wittgenstein rightly notes, this latter claim makes the veneration of trees appear absurd, since it posits an *explanation* that is cruder than the practice itself:

> It was not a trivial reason, for really there can have been no *reason*, that prompted certain races of mankind to venerate the oak tree, but only the fact that they and the oak were united in a community of life, and thus that they arose together not by choice, but rather like the flea and the dog. (If fleas developed a rite, it would be based on the dog.)[27]

Rather than searching for an explanation of the practice, one needs to look at the practice itself, at the utterances and thoughts that surround it, and to describe the use to which expressions like 'the spirit of the tree', etc., are put. Given this emphasis on *description*, it is, of course, important that the description of the practice in question not be too scanty. Frazer's point that, according to the animist, animals and plants 'have souls like his own, and he treats them accordingly', is as unhelpful as Big Thunder's remark that 'when we go hunting, it is not our arrow that kills the moose however powerful be the bow; it is nature that kills him.'[28] This statement,

taken on its own, might easily be read as expressing a very peculiar
conception of the course of nature; if a bow is sufficiently powerful,
then surely it *will* be the cause of the moose's death! Fortunately,
Big Thunder is not Frazer and his elaboration on this remark leaves
no doubt that, contrary to Frazer's suspicions, it does not rest on a
confused picture of causal relations in the natural world:

> The arrow sticks in his hide; and, like all living things the moose
> goes to our mother to be healed. He seeks to lay his wound
> against the earth, and thus he drives the arrow farther in. Mean-
> while I follow. He is out of sight, but I put my ear to a tree in the
> forest, and that brings me the sound, and I hear when the moose
> makes his next leap, and I follow. The moose stops again for the
> pain of the arrow, and he rubs his side upon the earth and drives
> the arrow farther in. I follow always, listening now and then with
> my ear against a tree. Every time he stops to rub his side he
> drives the arrow farther in, till at last when he is nearly exhausted
> and I come up with him, the arrow may be driven cleanly through
> his body . . .[29]

The way in which the expression 'mother earth' is applied in the
Indians' life shows, as Wittgenstein notes, that 'if they were to write
it down, their knowledge of nature would not differ *fundamentally*
from ours',[30] even though the description of that knowledge involves
such expressions as 'mother earth', 'the spirit of the land', 'The
Great Spirit', etc. Indeed, the Indians' hostile reaction towards
Christian missionaries could not be understood without ascribing
to them the very knowledge of nature that Frazer denies them:

> The black coats tell us to work and raise corn; they do nothing
> themselves and would starve to death if someone did not feed
> them. All they do is to pray to the Great Spirit; but that will not
> make corn and potatoes grow; if it will why do they beg from us
> and from the white people?[31]

Where does this leave Frazer's discussion of rituals? Its primary
deficiency has been summed up in Wittgenstein's exclamation:

> What a narrow spiritual life on Frazer's part! As a result: how
> impossible it was for him to conceive of a life different from that
> of the England of his time![32]

The charge against Frazer is that there is a sense in which *The Golden Bough* is a *reductio ad absurdum* of the intention that underlies it, viz. to contribute to the reader's understanding of rituals that would otherwise remain unintelligible. Frazer's interpretative comments on these rituals frequently turn *The Golden Bough* into a mirror of his own, rather narrow conception of what is rational and intelligible. This conception is spiritually impoverished, because the significance of the rituals in question, their significance for those who engage in them, is not captured in the scientific language of hypothesis, confirmation or causal efficacy. 'Soul' and 'spirit' are not quasi-scientific names failing of reference to anything confirmable by experience, but part of an irreducibly 'spiritual' vocabulary employed to express dimensions of human life not expressible in any other way. It is not surprising that the failure to see this irreducibility produces a crude picture of tree cults and other primitive rituals. Nor is it surprising to find a striking resemblance between Wittgenstein's response to Frazer's verdict on primitive rituals and Walking Buffalo's riposte to so-called 'enlightened' criticisms of Indian spirituality:

> You whites assumed we were savages. You didn't understand our prayers. You didn't try to understand. When we sang our praises to the sun or moon or wind, you said we were worshipping idols. Without understanding, you condemned us as lost souls just because our form of worship was different from yours. We saw the Great Spirit in almost everything: sun, moon, trees, wind, and mountains. Sometimes we approached him through these things. Was that so bad? I think we have a true belief in the supreme being, a stronger faith than that of most whites who have called us pagans.[33]

IV SCHOPENHAUER'S *WILLE* AND ANIMISM

At this point, it may be objected that, as a criticism of Frazer, this is an *ignoratio elenchi*. Frazer's discussion of tree cults concerns *animistic* beliefs, whereas I have been talking about Indian polytheism, which, according to Frazer, constitutes an intellectual advance over animism and should not be equated with it. The animist regards individual trees as living, conscious beings, whereas the polytheist sees in [them] merely a lifeless, inert mass, tenanted for a longer or shorter time by a supernatural being who, as he can pass freely from tree to tree, thereby enjoys a certain right of possession or lordship over the trees, and, ceasing to be a tree-soul, becomes a forest god.[34]

'Animism', so the objection continues, 'must be carefully distinguished from polytheistic and monotheistic religion, since it involves quite different language-games and beliefs. The former attributes consciousness to plants and rocks, the latter does not. Indeed, that is why the former is irrational in ways the latter is not; it contains pseudo-scientific hypotheses about natural events, whereas religion – at least in its more sophisticated variants – need not do so.' But this won't do. The objection would hold only if Frazer's examples of animism clearly showed, for example, that the 'savages' who engaged in them *did* believe that trees were conscious in exactly the same way in which human beings are conscious. But Frazer's fragmentary descriptions of tree cults show no such thing, not least because he mistakenly thinks the grammar of the claim that nature is ensouled to lie open to view. But to insist that our ancestors *did* literally believe that trees were conscious, felt pain, and talked, etc., is 'shadow-boxing, for it is a superfluous assumption that explains *nothing*'.[35]

This leads me to Professor Eldridge's paper on the topic. Quite appropriately, his discussion of animism begins with Wittgenstein's question in *Philosophical Investigations*:

What am I believing when I believe that men have souls? What am I believing in, when I believe that this substance contains two carbon rings? In both cases there is a picture in the foreground, but the sense lies far in the background: that is, the application of the picture is not easy to survey. (§ 422)

It is greatly to Eldridge's credit that he adopts this remark as the guiding motto for his discussion, but – and this is ironic – the examples of animistic belief presented in the first part of his paper seem to betray forgetfulness of that motto, for *their* sense is taken to lie, not 'far in the background', but plainly in the foreground. It is true that the reading of G.T. Fechner, H. Lotze and Arthur Schopenhauer that follows Eldridge's quotations is set within the context of *one* perspective on animism, contrasted with a different perspective in the second part of the essay. But if the latter is also intended to offer an alternative construal of Fechner, Lotze and Schopenhauer, then this should, in fairness to these thinkers, be made explicit. That Eldridge does not do so is unfortunate for two reasons. First, it would have shown something about the difficulty involved in producing a clear example of the belief that trees and plants are conscious in the *same* way human beings are. Who, one would like to ask, believes this, and what criteria are employed in determining that this *is* what is believed? Second, a closer look at the thinkers presented as 'animists' may well reveal that their positions are, in fact, opposed to animism as Eldridge defines it at the outset. Take Fechner's description of a water lily's enjoyment of its environment, for example. For Fechner, it is argued, the plant 'enjoys' its environment in more than a metaphorical sense. The water lily is for him 'a subject of experience' which 'actually feels the happiness of its situation'.[36] Does Fechner believe that the water lily is conscious then? Or that it might get bored, that it knows how fortunate it is, and wishes night would never come, in the sense in which Fechner might say these things of himself? And what would *that* mean? Taken by itself, the quote from Fechner's *oeuvre* shows too little about its application, and certainly less than Eldridge's reading of it suggests. But a more interesting case is Schopenhauer. His position is even more clearly incompatible with Eldridge's working definition of animism, as well as shedding considerable light on the subject. In *The World as Will and Representation*, Schopenhauer speaks of natural processes and events in terms which suggest that he 'attributes a number of mental properties to various inorganic beings'.[37] This prompts Eldridge to argue that

> Hurrying, persisting, desiring and choosing – these are likewise not metaphors for Schopenhauer, but indicate instead an internal life of sensation and volition, albeit in different forms from the human, in natural phenomena.[38]

When Schopenhauer sees in natural processes manifestations of 'volition', or *Wille*, this is, indeed, not just a metaphor for mechanical processes describable in the language of scientific enquiry. But neither is Schopenhauer's idealism a brand of Cartesian dualism, postulating the existence of spirits animating the material world. On the contrary, he laments the fact that 'there still exists the old fundamentally false contrast between *spirit and matter*',[39] and the primary concern of his philosophy is to overcome this contrast; to show that a crude, mechanistic account of the natural world is just as inadequate as its idealistic counterpart. The former is reductive, whereas the latter explains nothing. As Schopenhauer insists:

> Physical and chemical effects are admittedly incomprehensible to you so long as you are unable to reduce them to *mechanical*. In precisely the same way, these *mechanical* effects themselves and thus the manifestations that result from gravity, impenetrability, cohesion, hardness, rigidity, elasticity, fluidity, and so on, are just as mysterious as are those others, in fact as is thinking in the human head. If matter can fall to earth without your knowing why, so can it also think without your knowing why.[40]

Encapsulated in this passage is the thought, familiar from Wittgenstein's *Tractatus*, that what the scientist *says* about the world still leaves out a dimension of reality that can only be *shown*. This is the mysterious and inexplicable, viz. such familiar phenomena as human consciousness and other aspects of reality:

> The tendency to gravity in the stone is precisely as inexplicable as is thinking in the human brain, and so on this score, we could also infer a spirit in the stone.[41]

Cartesian 'explanations' of thought and consciousness in terms of immaterial substances or spirits are mere pseudo-explanations, for

> if you assume in the human head a *spirit*, like a *deus ex machina*, then . . . you must also concede to every stone a spirit. On the other hand, if your dead and purely passive *matter* can as heaviness gravitate, or as electricity attract, repel, and emit sparks, so too as brain-pulp can it think. In short, we can attribute matter to every so-called spirit, but also spirit to all *matter*, whence it follows that contrast is false.[42]

Strongly influenced by the Kantian idea that 'everything empirically real retains transcendental ideality',[43] Schopenhauer wants to present a perspective on the natural world that is neither reductivist nor idealist in the traditional sense of these terms, a perspective that firmly integrates man into nature while at the same time according him attributes that distinguish him from it. Man remains an enigma, on this account, precisely because, and in so far as, nature itself is essentially mysterious. In this context, Schopenhauer is careful to note that, in seeing in natural objects and processes manifestations of *Wille*, he is not ascribing to them anything like human consciousness or volition:

> Vital force [*Lebenskraft*] is absolutely identical with the will, so that what appears in self-consciousness as will, is in unconscious organic life the *primum mobile* thereof which has been very appropriately described as vital force. Merely from the analogy with this, we infer that the other forces of nature are also fundamentally identical with the will, only that in them the will is at a lower stage of its objectification.[44]

Schopenhauer's attitude towards nature is not pantheistic; indeed, he rejects pantheism along with Cartesian dualism because it 'states nothing',[45] and only leads to confusion. But if Schopenhauer is neither an animist in Eldridge's sense, nor a pantheist, nor indeed an apostle of Christianity, what are we to make of his view? The attempt to categorize his position in terms of realism or anti-realism seems to me to be a fruitless endeavour. More helpful would be a discussion of the similarity between his notion of *Wille* and Spinoza's idea of *conatus*[46] on the one hand, and of the relation between *Wille* and Kant's conception of the noumenal, on the other. But this would require a separate paper. However, the relevance of Schopenhauer's work for an examination of animism is apparent if one takes it as a philosophical articulation of the attitude towards nature revealed in the ritual practices and thoughts described above. This does not mean that the veneration of trees presupposes as an intellectual foundation something like Schopenhauer's philosophy, which is what Frazer is suggesting when he speaks of the 'savage' as a 'primitive philosopher'.[47] Nevertheless, certain aspects of Schopenhauer's thought, such as the rejection of any sharp distinction between spirit and matter, can be said to reveal themselves *in* the rituals and thoughts described above. It is interesting that, in his notes on Frazer's *Golden Bough*, Wittgenstein himself draws attention to Schopenhauer's work. Wondering whether the ancient Greek view 'which ascribes the same multiplicity to the soul as to the body' may not be closer to the truth than a 'modern watered-down theory', he notes: 'Frazer doesn't notice that we have before us the teaching of Plato and Schopenhauer.'[48]

Wittgenstein does not elaborate on this point, but I read it as a positive comment on Plato and Schopenhauer, and it is noteworthy that the remark stems from a late, second encounter[49] with Frazer, which took place 'not earlier than 1936 and probably after 1948',[50] which suggests that even the later Wittgenstein considered a closer look at Schopenhauer's discussion of the relation between mind and body, spirit and matter, a rewarding enterprise.[51]

V ANIMISM – A BETTER EXPLANATION?

I said at the beginning of this paper that, while I agreed with the general tenor of Eldridge's discussion, I thought it required certain correctives. In addition to the points already made, there are the following considerations:

Eldridge is, of course, quite right in noting that 'both traditional, more animistic cultures ... and modern, scientific, materialist cultures and practices express persistent human interests and responses to reality',[52] as well as in rejecting the claim that the former *must* be irrational, in the sense suggested by Frazer and his intellectual successors. Frazer's 'savages' did not engage in false science, nor is there any reason for making the language of science the touchstone of rationality and intelligibility. However, rather than consistently following Wittgenstein's exhortation that 'here one can only *describe* and say: this is what human life is like',[53] Eldridge also argues for the rationality of *some* animistic beliefs by suggesting that they play a role akin to scientific beliefs, in that they are explanatory and efficacious components of a successful theory: 'It is not just that animistic beliefs figure in some successful explanatory theories and therapeutic practices',[54] they also have a decent record in achieving successful explanations and cures.

One of Eldridge's examples in this connection is an appeal by some traditional African animists to gods and spirits in the explanation and cure of mental illness; their rituals, Eldridge thinks, 'may become increasingly relevant for us', too.[55] But this attempt at bolstering the rationality of animistic beliefs by likening them to scientific hypotheses confirmed through experience, is problematic; not so much because African animists are not successful at curing mental illness, but because this construal distorts the very nature of the animist's attitude towards the world. This becomes clear if one asks in what way, according to Eldridge, animistic beliefs 'may become increasingly relevant for us'. An African animist might well persuade me – but without a look at the statistics? – that his rituals have a beneficial effect on my psyche, but so might a visit to a National Park, transcendental meditation, mantra chanting, laughter therapy or a Brazilian rain stick. All these things might, as psychological comforters, become relevant to my life and play an important role in it. But would their relevance to it not also differ, quite radically, from the kind of significance that trees and other natural objects have in the lives of the North American Indians? That significance is, as has been suggested, not reducible to utilitarian considerations, whether physical or psychological, and it would be wrong to focus on such considerations in describing the Indians' rituals. Otherwise, one might think that a belief in 'the spirit of the land', say, simply *was* a belief in something causally operative on the land, something that explained the physical changes on it, etc. Yet sentences like 'The white man is ill because the spirit of the land hates him for what he has done' are no more explanations in the scientific sense than 'Because it was God's will' would be an explanation of why Count Eberhard (in Uhland's poem) survived the war. Both phrases are more like professions of faith; their 'grammar' is not that of the language of science. Finally, there is the question of whether Count Eberhard or Walking Buffalo are not, in some sense, better off than postmodern and 'enlightened' man. Eldridge is inclined to answer in the affirmative when he asks, somewhat rhetorically, 'Is it so clear that we might not be better off to treat something other than mathematically formulated laws of material nature as inviolable?'[56]

But what does 'better off' mean here? Materially better off, or spiritually? The only sense in which animism might make us better off, it seems to me, also makes the question an uninteresting one. Seeing what modernity does to the environment, one might well propagate Walking Buffalo's conduct *vis-à-vis* nature as an example to be imitated, but why should one want to regard the spiritual dimensions of this relation to be *better* than the *Weltanschauung* of a humanist, say, who has made ecological concerns the primary focus of his public and private activities? Both are intelligible attitudes towards nature, but there is no external vantage point from which one could be seen to be superior to the other. To let Wittgenstein conclude this discussion:

One could say 'every view has its charm', but that would be false. The correct thing to say is that every view is significant for the one who sees it as significant (but that does not mean, sees it other than it is.) Indeed, in this sense, every view is equally significant.[57]

Notes

1. Richard Eldridge, 'Is Animism Alive and Well?', this volume, Chapter 1, p. 3.
2. Ibid., p. 4.
3. Manfred Geier, *Der Wiener Kreis* (Reinbek: Rowohlt, 1992), p. 26.
4. Eldridge, 'Is Animism Alive and Well?', p. 12.
5. Ibid., p. 21.
6. T.C. McLuhan, *Touch the Earth. A Self-Portrait of Indian Existence* (London: Abacus, 1980), p. 15.
7. Ibid., p. 23.
8. James George Frazer, *The Golden Bough*, abridged edition in one volume (London: Macmillan, 1983), p. 148.
9. Ibid., p. 150.
10. The notion of the metaphorical here involves the idea that a metaphorical expression is translatable without loss of meaning into a non-metaphorical one. Such a conception of metaphor seems to me narrow and misguided, but since it informs Frazer's discussion of primitive rituals, it also enters into the literal/metaphorical distinction presently under investigation.
11. *Letters from Ludwig Wittgenstein with a Memoir by Paul Engelmann*, ed. Brian McGuinness (Oxford: Blackwell, 1967); letter of 9 April 1917, reprinted in Brian McGuinness, *Wittgenstein: A Life. Young Ludwig 1889–1921* (London: Duckworth, 1988), p. 251.
12. McLuhan, *Touch the Earth*, p. 22.
13. Ibid., p. 56.
14. Ibid., p. 6.
15. Ibid.
16. Frazer, *The Golden Bough*, p. 148.
17. Ibid., p. 146; see also p. 155.
18. Ibid., p. 144.
19. Ibid.
20. Ludwig Uhland, *Werke*, vol. 2, ed. Hans-Rüdiger Schwab (Frankfurt: Insel, 1983), p. 8.
21. Ibid., p. 11.
22. Ibid.
23. Frazer, *The Golden Bough*, p. vii (both quotations).
24. Ibid., p. 146.
25. Ibid., p. 148.
26. Ibid., p. 145.

27.   Ludwig Wittgenstein, 'Remarks on Frazer's Golden Bough', in *Philosophical Occasions*, ed. James C. Klagge and Alfred Nordmann (Indianapolis: Hackett, 1993), p. 139; see also p. 131.

28.   McLuhan, *Touch the Earth*, p. 22.

29.   Ibid., p. 22.

30.   Wittgenstein, 'Remarks on Frazer's Golden Bough', p. 141.

31.   McLuhan, *Touch the Earth*, p. 63; a remark by the Indian Red Jacket, made in 1824.

32.   Wittgenstein, 'Remarks', p. 125.

33.   McLuhan, *Touch the Earth*, p. 23.

34.   Frazer, *Golden Bough*, p. 155.

35.   Wittgenstein, 'Remarks', p. 139.

36.   Eldridge, p. 4.

37.   Ibid.

38.   Ibid., pp. 4–5.

39.   Arthur Schopenhauer, 'On Philosophy and Natural Science', in *Parerga and Paralipomena*, trans. E.F.J. Payne (Oxford: Clarendon, 1974), vol. II, § 74/104.

40.   Ibid., p. 105.

41.   Ibid.

42.   Ibid., p. 106.

43.   Ibid., p. 107.

44.   Schopenhauer, 'On Philosophy and Natural Science', § 94/162.

45.   Arthur Schopenhauer, 'A Few Words on Pantheism', in *Parerga and Paralipomena*, vol. II, § 69/99.

46.   Cf. Spinoza's *Ethics* II, Prop. VI and Proof; III, Prop. VII; IV, Prop. XXI, XXII, Proof.

47.   Frazer, Golden Bough, p. 75.

48.   Wittgenstein, 'Remarks', p. 141.

49.   Wittgenstein first approached Maurice Drury about *The Golden Bough* in 1931, asking him to get hold of a copy and read it out loud to him; cf. Maurice Drury's 'Conversations with Wittgenstein', in Rush Rhees, ed., *Recollections of Wittgenstein* (Oxford: Oxford University Press, 1984), p. 119.

50.   Rush Rhees, in 'Introductory Note', *Synthese*, vol. 17 (1967), p. 234.

51.   For a more detailed discussion of Schopenhauer's influence on Wittgenstein, see Bryan Magee, *The Philosophy of Schopenhauer* (Oxford: Clarendon, 1983), Appendix 8.

52.   Eldridge, p. 21.

53.   Wittgenstein, 'Remarks', p. 121.

54.   Eldridge, p. 12.

55.   Ibid., p. 12.

56.   Ibid., p. 11.

57.   Wittgenstein, 'Remarks', p. 135.

Part Two
Is Religion the Product of Projection?

3

Is Religion a Product of Wishful Thinking?

Lars Hertzberg

> Religion is a dream, a fantasy-picture which expresses man's situation and at the same time provides a fantasy-gratification of man's wish to overcome that situation. . . . In religion man recognizes his helplessness, his dependence, and he seeks to overcome it by calling in the aid of the imagination. Sacrifice and prayer thus stand at the very centre of religion and reveal to us its essential character and aim . . . 'the prayer pregnant with sorrow, the prayer of disconsolate love, the prayer which expresses the power of the heart that crushes man to the ground, the prayer which begins in despair and ends in rapture'.[1]

This, according to the late Eugene Kamenka, was Ludwig Feuerbach's view of religion. In Bertrand Russell, we find another, somewhat cruder version of the view of religion as a projection of human fears or wishes. Thus, Russell wrote:

> Religion is based, I think, primarily and mainly upon fear. It is partly the terror of the unknown, and partly . . . the wish to feel that you have a kind of elder brother who will stand by you in all your troubles and disputes. Fear is the basis of the whole thing – fear of the mysterious, fear of defeat, fear of death.[2]

In fact, notions like those expressed by Feuerbach (on Kamenka's reading) and by Russell could be said to have become part of conventional 'wisdom', to have passed into what might be termed the folk psychology of religion. Thus, they are often used in an attempt to 'explain away' religious belief.

To explain away religion is to attempt to undermine the challenge that the life of faith apparently poses to the non-believer by invoking some explanatory mechanism which radically undercuts the believer's claim to bear witness to the truth. In this essay, I want to take a closer look at the attempt to explain away religion as a form of wishful thinking. I begin by trying to get clear about what is involved in accusing someone of wishful thinking in an everyday context. After that, I address the question whether this accusation can be directed at the believer.

I

1.   In *The Periodic Table*, Primo Levi recounts the following incident: a chemist by profession, he had, as a prisoner at Auschwitz, been put to work in a chemistry laboratory. Years later, by pure chance, he comes to have professional dealings with the civilian who had been overseeing the work. The German confesses his guilt about the Nazi crimes, but it is obvious that his picture of the concentration camps is much too rosy. Among other things, he claims to remember having talked to Levi about scientific problems and the evil of the times. Levi comments: 'Not only did I not remember any such conversations (and my memory of that period . . . is excellent), but against the background of disintegration, mutual distrust, and mortal weariness, the mere supposition of them was totally outside reality, and could only be explained by a very naive ex post facto wishful thinking.'[3]

How are we to understand this explanation? First of all, it is essential that the German's memories of the situation tended to make it less painful and guilt-ridden. Second, what is being claimed is that this fact is precisely what *made* him remember things the way he did; his wish that that was the way they were is offered in explanation of the belief.

But how do wishes bring about false convictions? Is there a peculiar mechanism at work here, rather like that by which a person dying from thirst may come to hallucinate a drink? In other words, are we here up against a psychological phenomenon that can only be measured and recorded but cannot be made intelligible? If that is so, it appears we are at the mercy of our wishes and of what they will do to our ability to understand the world.

We obviously would not *accuse* someone of hallucinating in the way we may accuse a person of wishful thinking. Wishful thinking seems to be a measure of character, a weakness. Even so, wishful thoughts are not something we *decide* to have. They may be an object of guilt, but not of remorse. Thus, apparently, they occupy a somewhat puzzling middle ground between the things we do and things that happen to us.

In this respect, wishful thinking is closely reminiscent of self-deception. Both are ways in which character clouds our perception, in the case of both the resulting judgement is one more to our liking than the truth. However, it is important to be clear about the differences between them. The main difference seems to be this: wishful thinking usually involves something like a hypothesis; that is, it is connected with the possibility of an independent test (the truth may catch up with the wishful thinker), whereas in self-deception what is needed to overcome the error is already available to the self-deceiver; he simply fails to make use of it.

What the self-deceiver falsely represents to himself are mostly matters like his own beliefs, feelings or motives. Now, when someone tells you truthfully what he believes or how he feels, his ability to do so is not dependent on his having managed to learn some fact about himself; on the contrary, the very notion of believing or feeling this or that is partly constituted by the fact that, in the normal case, people are simply able to express what they believe or feel. The self-deceiver, then, is someone who refuses to acknowledge something that, but for his reluctance to acknowledge it, he is at any moment in a position to acknowledge. Indeed, I would venture to suggest that it is *only* by self-deception that we may be wrong about the sorts of thing that may be an object of self-deception.

Wishful beliefs, on the other hand, concern some state of affairs which is independent of the believer. The fault of the wishful believer lies in his failing to make the best possible use of his judgement concerning its likelihood. Wishful thinking involves self-deception: the wishful thinker, we might say, is someone who deceives himself into thinking he has done his best to discover the truth.

2. Part of what makes wishful thinking seem such a paradoxical phenomenon is a way of thinking about belief that is prevalent within the analytic tradition in philosophy. The 'belief that p' is regarded as an unambiguous way of being related to the proposition p, the prime mark of which is a willingness to assent to the assertion 'p'. Thus, according to H.H. Price, two elements can be distinguished in belief: '(1) the *entertaining* of a proposition, (2) the *assenting to* or *adopting of* that proposition.'[4]

A belief, on this view, comes to appear almost like a solid item that may be acquired, possessed and lost (as seen, for instance, in the facile way in which in doing philosophy we tend to speak about a person's 'beliefs' in the plural). A consequence of this is a lack of attention to the variety of things attributing a belief may amount to.

Thus, the context in which I speak of someone's beliefs may be that of reporting what she told me, or trying to make sense of her actions, or trying to explain why she feels the way she does about some imminent event, etc. Some beliefs only exist, say, in the context of a dinner conversation or a Gallup poll, while other beliefs are put to the test in the hurly-burly of life. In such cases there may well be divergences between our various relations to the matter at hand: thus, our actions may belie our words, or both may belie our feelings, etc. As for the question what someone 'really believes', it seems to have no clear sense apart from the purpose for which it is asked. What may have led philosophers to ignore this point is the idea that there must be some specific inner state to which the word 'belief' primarily refers, and which is expressed in various outward manifestations of belief.

A veteran of the Normandy invasion, in a recent memoir, said that regardless of the odds, he and all the combat-bound GIs he knew believed that each of them individually would be the one to survive.[5] The soldiers' confidence in their survival, I take it, consisted primarily in what they were inclined to say about their chances, perhaps in the fact that they did not feel a fear proportionate to the danger, or in a refusal to dwell on the prospect of getting killed.

In the case of some, this might be considered an aspect of their courage, in that of others, it may have been due to a naive confidence in their own invulnerability, to an inability to imagine what was about to happen, to indifference bred of exhaustion and disillusionment, etc. Someone who faces battle with confidence may yet write a letter to his wife to be delivered in the event of his death, draw up a will, etc. Someone else may just go into battle recklessly, perhaps neglecting basic precautions. In the latter case, but not, I think, in the former, we might be prepared to speak about wishful thinking.

3.   Emphasis on the propositional character of believing also leads us to ignore the importance of what surrounds the manifestations of belief. In the case of the German chemist what is crucial is not his having imagined the conversations in question. As far as those were

concerned, he might have simply got Levi mixed up with someone else. As Levi emphasizes, what was important was rather the kind of relation the German had to have to those past events in order to imagine that such an encounter would even have been possible. This must have meant that he had at the time completely failed to take in the reality of the concentration camp which he occasionally visited in order to inspect work at the lab. It also meant that he must have carefully avoided learning more about the camps after the war. What made him a wishful thinker, then, was not the single lapse of memory by itself, but its connection with his failure to come to terms with his country's past and his own role in it.

Compare the situation of the German chemist to the response of someone who first began hearing rumours about the extermination of Jews, say, some time in 1944. We could very well imagine her refusing to believe them, classifying them with the stories about 'Hun soldiers' killing infants or resorting to cannibalism during World War I. And she might back up her disbelief by saying things like, 'Human beings can't be that evil' or even 'God wouldn't permit it'. Are we to consider her a wishful thinker, as compared, say, with someone in a similar position who was ready to lend credence to the rumours right away? Suppose the one who believes the story is a German-hater or a cynic, someone who is always prepared to believe the worst of his fellow man, or the like. Is the latter reaction necessarily more admirable?

Whether something is to be considered a case of wishful thinking is certainly not to be resolved by some kind of inquiry into the mechanisms by which a belief was caused. What seems to be central, on the other hand, is a person's relation to the matter at issue. In the case just outlined, it would make all the difference if the disbeliever were someone in Britain or the United States who was upset by the nationalist fervour and Germanophobia caused by the war, or if, on the other hand, she were a German citizen, especially if she was a supporter of Hitler.

4.   Imagine a group of people trying to make up their mind about some past occurrence, or about the likely outcome of some project, or about the real motives of someone they all know well, etc. If the issue matters to them, each one of those who take part in the discussion will have a stake in the matter, of one sort or another. It may be a question of defending one's own honour or someone else's. Loyalties or commitments, whether personal, collective or

intellectual, may be at stake. Issues of shame or guilt on the speaker's behalf or that of others may arise. Again, the speaker may find his reputation for good judgement subject to challenge. We all have our *idées fixes*, our axes to grind, our sore points and blind spots, etc.

These are the rocks and currents among which real argument takes place. And it is by having taken part in such discussions that we gradually form an idea of what will count as good sense or responsible thought in matters of this or that sort. (By contrast, the 'ideal conversations' imagined by Apel and Habermas, if I have understood them correctly, seem to have something unreal about them, since they presuppose no commitments stronger than a commitment to the truth as such.[6] Where, one would like to ask, could truth get its importance except from the matters at issue? Someone who cares for nothing more than he cares for the truth, I would argue, cannot care much for anything, *including* the truth.)

The notion of 'how it really is' (or was) has a crucial role in such argument: it is the contested borderline we are trying to settle. What each of us carries away from an argument may not be the same; however, it will mainly be determined by the way she perceives the moral economy of the confrontation: by what she takes to be the stakes involved for each participant and what she makes of their character: Might *A* be ready to lie to gain his point? Can *B* really be so blind where these matters are concerned? Is *C* too timid to speak his mind? Is *D* incapable of admitting any error? Is *E* unable to stand unpleasant truths? etc. In the context of issues like these, testing the likelihood of what is claimed against judgements of character and vice versa, one's view of what will constitute responsible thought in the matter will gradually take shape. And it is in this type of context that the notion of wishful thinking has a role.

The object of wishful thinking may be the things we reckon with or remember, the way we read other people's behaviour and expect them to read ours: it consists in a refusal to acknowledge things that reflect unfavourably on ourselves or on those we identify with, or prospects that seem menacing, frightening to contemplate or even just inconvenient.

'Wishful thinking' does not refer to a specific weakness that an individual may display to varying degrees, but rather is a way in which various flaws of character will manifest themselves in the judgements he makes: say, lack of courage, failure to face up to one's guilt or shame, immaturity, love of comfort.

II

5. Let us now consider the idea that religion is to be understood as a product of wishful thinking. For those who view religion in this light, the view is closely linked to faith in science and in the progress it will bring. According to Feuerbach, as presented by Kamenka,

> Religion ... is an attempt to work over reality into something satisfactory to man. But it does so in fantasy, because man is not yet ready, not yet powerful enough or knowledgeable enough, to do it in reality. When man does become knowledgeable or powerful enough, religion withers away and dies; its place is taken by politics and technology as the expression of firmly-centred human wishes ...[7]

And Russell writes:

> Science can help us get over this craven fear in which mankind has lived for so many generations. Science can teach us, and I think our own hearts can teach us, no longer to look round for imaginary supports, no longer to invent allies in the sky, but rather to look to our own efforts here below to make this world a fit place to live in, instead of the sort of place that the churches have made it.[8]

This response to religion is undoubtedly itself supposed to be an expression of the scientific attitude. What is being put forward here at last, so it is argued, is a scientific understanding of religious faith. Viewed in that light, however, it has a rather curious aspect. For one thing, the hopes expressed in these scenarios have a very distinct flavour of wishful thinking themselves. Indeed, the term seems much better suited to them than to many forms of religious faith, as I shall argue.

Also, the claim that wishful thinking could account for the origin and persistence of religious life-forms, if regarded as a scientific hypothesis, leaves a great deal to be wished. For one thing, its sweep is breath-taking, since it apparently claims to span all the different forms of religious life in all human cultures over the entire history of humankind. It also seems to presuppose that the conditions contributing to the formation of religious life-forms are identical to those accounting for its continued existence. And it neglects the impossibility of advancing beyond the merest speculation where such an issue as the origins of religion is concerned.

Quite apart from this, as I have suggested, when we claim that someone is guilty of (or a victim of) wishful thinking, the claim is not based on the prior identification of some peculiar mechanism by which the belief came into existence. Rather, it expresses our attitude towards her belief in the context of her life. But this means that the very idea of trying to decide by means of scientific observation whether religion is a form of wishful thinking is misconceived. For someone to conclude that it is can only be understood as expressing an attitude towards religion, as a claim that gets its sense from its connection with the place of religion in the speaker's own life.

If Feuerbach's and Russell's claims are regarded as the expression of a 'scientific attitude', then, we should be clear that this phrase is being used in a rather peculiar sense here: the attitude in question is not that of the spirit of inquiry, but rather that of being in harness against religion. 'Science' is used here as the name of a world-view locked in deadly combat with its competitor, 'the religious world-view'.[9] The idea seems to be that we have to get things like religion out of the way before we can start being scientific about things (somewhat in the spirit of killing people for the sake of peace).

6. Calling religion a projection of our wishes, then, is a way of distancing oneself from a religious form of life. Religion is seen as grounded in a weakness from which one considers oneself to be free. What gives this idea its appeal? I want to suggest that it comes from a confused way of thinking about the ways in which religious belief may be bound up with human hopes, fears and wishes.

Thus, consider the wish for 'a kind of elder brother who will stand by you in all your troubles and disputes' that Russell speaks about. Suppose we try to take this idea seriously: what might be involved in such a wish? In an actual case, there is, of course, a variety of ways in which an elder brother may make a difference. First of all, he may, as it were, be of practical assistance, for example, by giving you advice on how to make up with your girlfriend, or by lending you money to tide you over until next week's allowance, and, if he's strong enough, by giving the boy next door a sound thrashing so he'll stop pestering you.

Obviously, though, there may be some troubles and disputes he will not be able to sort out for you in one of these ways. (Some of these will belong to the contingencies of life while others are part of the human predicament: for example, the fact that we shall all die, that we are at the mercy of blind fate, etc.[10]) However, in that case too he may make a difference, for he may console you, say, by getting you to look at matters in a different light, by assuring you that you'll get over the shame of defeat or simply by being around so you may feel that you're not alone: there's somebody there who knows how you feel and whom you can talk to. Here the difference he made would not concern the *object* of your grief or worry so much as *your relation* to it.

In which of these ways are we supposed to think about the believer's wish for a God, according to Russell? One gets the impression that Russell neglected to ask himself this question. Anyway, it might be argued that only the latter kind of wish has anything to do with genuine faith. We turn to God to find spiritual guidance, to learn to bear the burdens of life, not to avert them. To think about God as making a practical difference is a vulgarization of faith; it is to commit what D.Z. Phillips has called the naturalistic fallacy in religion. 'The believer cannot expect one thing rather than another – in the world of events. The events do not constitute *evidence* for the goodness of God, since the essence of the believer's belief in divine goodness consists precisely in the fact that the meaning of life does not depend on how it goes.'[11]

However, it is not necessarily clear how we are to draw the line between the kind of belief that commits this fallacy and other kinds of religious belief. Obviously, it would be a misunderstanding to think about reliance on divine intervention as an *alternative* to other methods of making inferences or bringing about results. Thus, if one of the staff officers involved in planning the landings in Normandy had said that there was no need to make contingency plans to be implemented in the case of bad weather since he had taken the precaution of praying for the weather to be good, his fellow officers (whether religious or not) would probably take this as a joke, or alternatively conclude that he had taken leave of his senses. This is not a way in which we are sometimes tempted to misuse religious language; rather, this remark would simply not be intelligible in the context. A child learning to use religious language would be told that such things cannot be said.[12]

However, there are other ways in which religious faith may be bound up with secular beliefs. Thus, someone may tell us he was

confident that God would let his business venture succeed, or someone rescued from a ship wrecked in a storm in which many others
perished may tell us he had been confident all along that God did
not want him to die. Divine intervention is not here regarded as an
alternative to other methods. Thus, the businessman's faith may
not keep him from working hard to ensure the success of his firm,
and the shipwrecked man may have struggled with all his might to
stay afloat until help arrived.

Are we to say that such responses lie outside religion? I am not
at all clear what one is to say in such a case. The obvious objection
to these expressions of faith is to say that they are self-centred in a
way that is in conflict with the very essence of, say, the Christian
faith. Still, one can easily imagine that the lives from which they
grow are devoutly religious in other respects. In fact, the businessman's confidence might make him reject various shady deals that
belonged to the regular practice of his trade, telling his associates
'God will provide'.[13] And the man rescued in the storm might refuse
to get into the lifeboat until all the others were safely aboard.

Considerations like these could make someone say that these
men's confidence was really spiritual acceptance in disguise, and
that they were simply inept at expressing their faith. One can easily
imagine cases in which this would be so, cases in which they would
respond affirmatively to questions like, 'Aren't you really trying to
say that you were ready to accept whatever happened, that you
were placing your fate in the hands of the Almighty?'

It might also be thought that the real test of faith in such a case
would be a person's reaction to things going badly. If after going
bankrupt the businessman were to say, 'So there isn't a God after
all' and to turn his back on the religious life for good, this would
certainly seem to show that his faith had been shallow. On the
other hand, misfortune might bring on a religious crisis, one that
resulted in his coming to think that his earlier faith had been imma-
ture and self-centred. This would not necessarily lead us to conclude that his faith had not been genuine before.

Concerning the loss of faith in the face of adversity, Gareth Moore
writes:

> the same kind of suffering that can make people lose their faith
> in God can also give birth to it in others. This happens particularly,
> not just when people have a difficult time, but when everything
> around them, their whole life, collapses: they lose everything in

a business failure, they suffer a heart-breaking bereavement, they
are thrown into a concentration camp. . . . And yet, in spite of it
all . . . they manage to carry on, even though everything they had
previously relied on for support had gone. It is here that language about God, which has before been available but unused
. . . may suddenly gain a hold.[14]

Here we may want to ask whether the experiences leading to the
rejection or discovery of God are to be regarded as internally related to faith itself. Are we to say that the faith of the fortunate is
a different matter from that of the unfortunate?[15]

Furthermore, suppose the confidence and the disappointment are
not self-centred in the way they are in this example. Imagine, for
instance, a devout believer who rejects the reports about the Holo-
caust because he is confident that God would not let it happen, and
when forced to accept the facts reacts by crying out in despair, 'So
there isn't a God after all.' Are we to say that responses like these
do not belong to a religious life? Could one not call his loss of faith
an expression of religious feeling, as against that of someone who
stops worshipping because he discovers he no longer has a need for
God?

I believe the bewilderment we may feel in the face of such issues
comes from the mistaken idea that it is somehow the task of philosophy to resolve them: that it is the job of the philosopher of
religion to identify the criteria by which it is to be decided whether
a person's faith is genuine or not. Of course, the philosopher has
no such authority. Taking a stand on the genuineness of someone's
faith is part of the religious life, not a philosophical preliminary to
it.[16] Nor do we have to decide which responses are to be considered
genuinely religious before we can do philosophy of religion. The
task of the philosophy of religion is simply to take note of religious
uses of language and to clear up misunderstandings that may appear
in connection with them by pointing to the ways in which they are
similar to, or differ from, other uses of language.

What is important for our present purposes is simply the realization that questioning the depth or genuineness of one's own faith
or that of one's fellow believers may be a part of certain forms of
religious life. Thus, it may be an important part of the way believers
think about their faith that they will occasionally search their hearts
in order to decide, for instance, whether what they harbour is true
love and genuine acceptance or simply a self-centred confidence

that things will turn out their way. It belongs to the philosophical
task of giving an overview of religious phenomena to take note of
the existence of such questions, though not to give guidelines on
the way they are to be answered.

Now, to the extent that there is, in religious life, an element which
consists in the questioning of one's wishes, this part of it cannot at
the same time be regarded as an expression of those wishes. Hence
wishes of this sort cannot account for the existence of religious
belief, since that means that they would be taken to have given rise
to a system of thought in which those very wishes are disallowed.
To this extent at least, the idea that religion might be a form of
wishful thinking is confused.

7.   Let us now consider the other kind of wish: not the wish for a
God who may arrange things to one's own liking, but the wish for
a God who will help one find the right attitude to events. The
attitude sought for may be expressed in various ways: one may
wish for the strength to accept what happens, for the courage to go
on living, or for the ability to retain one's faith in the meaning of
life in the face of failure, humiliation, emptiness, suffering or loss.

Now it should be clear that such wishes may have a secular
motive: they may simply be a wish to be rid of the pain or the
anguish. Thus, someone might envy her friend's peace of mind and
wish that she could share his faith in God so that she too could find
peace. The 'right attitude' here is simply the attitude that will put
an end to the anguish.[17]

However, it should be clear that the idea that 'the right attitude'
to events is the one that lets me get rid of the anguish is not a
religious idea. To think along these lines would mean that what is
central is one's faith in God, whereas to the true believer it is God
who is central. Someone who takes up this attitude has no need for
God, she is simply deceiving herself about her faith. What she hopes
her faith in God will give her (she does not really hope that *God* will
give her anything) might alternatively be got by taking up yoga or
eating a pill.

Someone may, of course, find true faith after seeking it merely
as a means to release. One mark of this might be that she felt gratitude for her former anguish, thinking of it as God's way of helping
her find Him. In other words, the anguish itself would take on a
religious significance for her. In the other case, however, if the
woman's anguish were to subside for some other reason, she might

turn her back on the religious life, even feel relieved. The anguish would be external to her faith. She would not, for instance, think about it as a message the meaning of which it was incumbent on her to understand (except perhaps in a psychiatric sense, which means that it would be a message only metaphorically).

At this point, a clarification may be needed. It will perhaps be thought that I have just violated my own strictures against taking a stand on the genuineness of faith in saying that someone who longs for faith as a means to release is deceiving herself, and in contrasting this with actual faith. However, the situation here is different. What I am trying to argue now is that certain ways of thinking about faith are confused. The claim I wish to make is that there are cases in which, if someone were made aware of certain aspects of their own religious attitude, if she were made to ask certain questions about it and were to answer them honestly, she would no longer wish to call her attitude belief in God. The point, accordingly, is inextricably *ad hominem*. But in this respect it is no different from philosophical argument in general.

8.   In the context of wishes of this kind, then, the idea that religion is a form of wishful thinking would amount to the claim that it always involves a form of self-deception. On this line of thought, there can be no such thing as a 'genuine' instance of religious belief, we simply find a number of anguished people clutching at straws, mesmerizing themselves into a frame of mind which helps them keep their anguish at bay. The continued existence of religious life-forms is solely made possible by the fact that religious believers keep from asking themselves certain questions.

Now, what plausibility this notion may have depends entirely on accepting a radically narrowed down conception of religious life. Peace of mind, release from anguish, though they may be important forms of religious response are not the only or the most essential expressions of belief in God. What will constitute 'the right attitude to events' cannot be laid down once and for all. It is something that the individual believer may have to work out for herself, or in consultation with her priest or rabbi, etc. Though in some forms of religion peace of mind is considered a sign that one has found the answer sought for, this is not necessarily so.

Indeed, some of the things a believer may find to be demanded of her are things that fill her with grief or horror. She may feel it her duty to sacrifice what sh loves the most, to withdraw into a convent, to face hardship and humiliation, even martyrdom as a missionary worker, etc. The priest Brand, in Ibsen's play with that title, finds that what God demands is that he should not forsake his congregation even though his only chance of saving the life of his consumptive son would be to move with him to a warmer region. We may feel horror at the determination with which he accepts, and forces his wife to accept, the death of their beloved child. (Though we should note that even he, earlier on, expresses a faith that God in His goodness will not let it come to that.)

It is hard to imagine anyone *wishing* to be in Brand's position, especially as a way of avoiding anguish and despair. It would be pure sophistry to suggest that his son's life was the price he was willing to pay for religious solace. Perhaps one could even express his predicament by saying that in some sense he wished that the God who made these demands on him did not exist. Yet I would contend that we find no difficulty in recognizing his attitude as one of the forms that religious life may take.

The discussion in this section could perhaps be summed up by saying that 'the right attitude' (in the sense relevant to religion) is not to be seen as something to be achieved *by means of* faith; rather the wish for the right attitude is *itself* an expression of faith.

CONCLUSION

To regard religious belief as a product of wishful thinking is to regard it as a form of thought about matters of human life which is irresponsible, since it expresses a refusal to face up to the reality of those matters. On this view, it either takes the form of imagining that there is a Supreme Being able and willing to stave off ill fortune, or of conjuring up a faith that will help us sustain the strains of human existence. (It is assumed that what constitutes a 'strain' is a matter that people will be able to agree on independently of their religious outlook.) But whether or not such descriptions would fit some of those who would describe themselves as religious believers, there are important elements of religious belief that could not be regarded as products of wishful thinking: first, there is, within religion, a criticism of self-centred faith in God as a protector against misfortune; and second, genuine religious faith is not reducible to a preoccupation with one's own peace of mind.

The relation of religion to wishful thinking is not to be resolved by saying that in religion we are concerned with other-worldly things. Religious faith, for many believers, *is* a way of being concerned with the problems of living in *this* world. However, it is not an irresponsible way of being concerned with such problems, but rather a way of thinking about them in which the limit between responsible and irresponsible thought is drawn differently than in secular thought. The specific way in which it is drawn, however, depends on the particular religious tradition from within which one is speaking.[18]

Notes

1. Eugene Kamenka, *The Philosophy of Ludwig Feuerbach* (London: Routledge & Kegan Paul, 1970), pp. 39f. The concluding quotation is from Feuerbach.
2. Bertrand Russell, *Why I am not a Christian* (London: George Allen & Unwin, 1957), p. 16.
3. Primo Levi, *The Periodic Table* (New York: Schocken Books, 1984), p. 220.
4. H.H. Price, 'Some Considerations about Belief', in A. Phillips Griffiths, ed., *Knowledge and Belief* (London: Oxford University Press, 1967), p. 43. For a more recent case in point, consider the following definition by Dan Sperber: 'a subject's factual beliefs are all the independently stored representations that the subject is capable of retrieving from his encyclopaedic memory and all the representations that, by means of his inferential device, he is capable of deriving from his stored factual beliefs' ('Apparently Irrational Beliefs', in M. Hollis and S. Lukes, eds., *Rationality and Relativism* [Oxford: Basil Blackwell, 1982], p. 172.)
5. William Preston Jr, 'On Omaha Beach', *New York Review of Books*, 14 July 1994.
6. On this, cf. e.g., Karl-Otto Apel, 'Universal Principles and Particular Decisions and Forms of Life', in R. Gaita, ed., *Value and Understanding* (London: Routledge, 1990), pp. 83ff.
7. Kamenka, *The Philosophy of Ludwig Feuerbach*, p. 41.
8. Russell, *Why I am not a Christian*, p. 16. Here one encounters the idea, not uncommon among critics of religion, according to which not only God and the order of things as seen by the believer, but also faith itself, the actual religious traditions and institutions, are somehow alien to the genuine life of human beings, as though they were produced by divine interference. Paradoxically, this comes close to the Christian idea that faith is a gift of God.
9. The fact that the word 'science' has in this way come to be linked to a certain world-view seems to be the result of historical contingencies. Evidently, episodes such as the Church's stubborn defence of

the Aristotelian cosmology had an important part to play in the matter. This, in turn, is probably a reflection of the conservatism natural to any institution in power, in matters of faith no less than natural philosophy. However, the result was that the Church found itself saddled with the role it had arrogated to itself, as arch-rival of science.

10.　It is not quite clear, when Kamenka talks about recognizing our dependence or helplessness, whether he means something that may or may not be so, or a feature of the human predicament. Thus he says, 'The concept of dependence in Feuerbach . . . is not Schleiermacher's vague metaphysical "dependence" . . . It is the concrete empirical dependence of man on nature and other men' (*The Philosophy of Ludwig Feuerbach*, p. 41). Here the suggestion seems to be that the dependence is of a sort that we may overcome by our own efforts.

11.　D.Z. Phillips, *The Concept of Prayer* (Oxford: Basil Blackwell, 1981), pp. 101ff. The quotation is from p. 102.

12.　In the Bible we read about God helping His chosen people to smite their enemies, about Christ performing miracles for those who had faith in him, etc. Hence, it may appear that God's making a practical difference is part of the Judaeo-Christian tradition. However, I believe that matters are not so straightforward. The Bible, for the believer, is not simply a book of stories about the life of the faithful in earlier times. The present life of the believer is not just a continuation of what she reads in the Bible, for in the Bible God and the difference He makes in people's lives is *given*, whereas in her own life the believer must seek for them.

13.　Then again, the significance of this would change if he were to point to his own honesty as the *ground* for his conviction that God would take care of him. Perhaps in this case he might be accused of thinking wishfully *within* religion.

14.　Gareth Moore, *Believing in God: A Philosophical Essay* (Edinburgh: T. & T. Clark, 1988), pp. 131f.

15.　Consider, in this connection, Wittgenstein's remark:

> Life can educate one to a belief in God. And *experiences* too are what bring this about; but I don't mean visions and other forms of sense experience which show us the 'existence of this being', but, e.g., sufferings of various sorts. These neither show us God in the way a sense impression shows us an object, nor do they give rise to *conjectures* about him. Experiences, thoughts, – life can force this concept on us.
>
> So perhaps it is similar to the concept of 'object'.
>
> (*Culture and Value*, Oxford: Basil Blackwell, 1980, p. 86)

In both cases, the suggestion seems to be, we come to use a concept because our life creates a need for it.

16.　This point is forcefully made by O.K. Bouwsma in 'Miss Anscombe on Faith', in the collection of his essays, *Without Proof or Evidence*, ed. J.L. Craft and Ronald E. Hustwit (Lincoln, Neb. and London: University of Nebraska Press, 1984).

17. This type of attitude seems to lie at the basis of the religious reductionism attributed by D.Z. Phillips to Ingmar Bergman. See his essay, 'Ingmar Bergman's Reductionism: "A Modern Cosmology of the Spirit"', in *Through a Darkening Glass* (Oxford: Basil Blackwell, 1982).

18. I wish to thank Olli Lagerspetz for his comments on an earlier version of this essay.

4

Projection: A Metaphor in Search of a Theory?

Van A. Harvey

My purpose in this essay is three-fold. I wish to show, first, that the variety and complexity of projection theories of religion is so great that it is difficult, if not impossible, to generalize about them; second, that any philosophically important criticism of any one of these theories must deal with the term 'projection' in the larger theoretical context within which it functions and acquires its meaning. Finally, I shall argue that to focus on wishful thinking in the ordinary sense of that word as though it were a fundamental element in projection theories is a strategic mistake because it rarely plays a part in the most interesting of these theories, and, to the extent that it does play a role, as in Feuerbach's early theory, its meaning and role can only be understood in the context of the larger theory of consciousness of which it is a part.

I

The claim that the gods are projections is an ancient one, going back to the sixth century BC when Xenophanes sardonically observed that the gods of the Ethiopians are black with snub noses while those of the Thracians are blond with blue eyes. But it has only been in the past century that a contemporary writer, David Bakan, could argue that this idea, which was once 'only on the periphery of science', has become

> what might be termed a credo. It is the belief that the evidence set forth by anthropologists and psychoanalysts, particularly by Frazer and Freud, in favor of the proposition that religions are the products of human imagination revised by rationality, is so

massive and persuasive that it adds up to a veritable discovery, potentially the most consequential since Darwin's discovery of evolution.[1]

It is relatively easy to make fun of the extravagant rhetoric in Bakan's statement, not to mention the way in which a 'belief' in 'evidence' that 'favors a proposition' gradually becomes transformed into a 'veritable discovery'. But it is less easy to ignore the cultural fact to which Bakan attests; namely, that the concept of projection is central to an extraordinary number of widely held theories of religion advanced in the disciplines of sociology, anthropology, psychology, social psychology and even philosophy. Indeed, it is not an exaggeration to say that the concept of projection is close to the centre of some of the most influential currents of modern thought: not only Freudian, Jungian and Object-Relations theory, but neo-Kantian, Heideggerian, neo-Marxist, Durkheimian, as well as those less easy to characterize with such labels, such as Peter Berger's or Fokke Sierksma's.[2] Moreover, the term 'projection' seems to be as much at home in positivistic modes of thought as in those that assume that reality is 'socially constructed'. And although the layperson tends to associate projection theories of religion with the name of Freud and, hence, with hostile interpretations of religion, one also finds projection theories among sociologists, anthropologists and sociologists who are neither hostile to religion nor think of it as a delusion.

It is just this variety of projection theories of religion that should caution us about making any generalizations about them, even about the meaning of the term 'projection'. For even a superficial inspection of a range of such theories immediately reveals that this term is often employed and interpreted in quite different ways. Peter Berger's conception of projection is, as we shall see, fundamentally different from Carl Jung's, just as Durkheim's differs from Sierksma's or from that of Object-Relations psychology. Moreover, not only do the conceptions of projection differ from theory to theory, but they are the basis for radically different interpretations of religion. None of the above, for example, makes any appeal to wishful thinking.

What, then, are we to make of this common use of the term projection which is then embedded in radically different theories? We can charitably say that this diversity of meaning should not surprise us because a technical term acquires its specific meanings from the theoretical context in which it functions or, perhaps, uncharitably that what we have here is a metaphor in search of a theory. What we should not do is assume that the term has a single meaning, isolate what appears to be its association with wishful thinking in one thinker, criticize that notion and conclude that we have dealt with the theory of religious projection.

II

If we attempt to bring some order into this plethora of projection theories, we observe that they tend to fall roughly into two ideal types which, for reasons that follow, I shall label 'beam' and 'grid'. The first type contains those theories in which the term projection refers more narrowly to the externalization of some aspect of the self – its feelings, character traits or personal subjectivity itself. In this type of theory, of which Freudian theory is the best known exemplar, projection is said to be generated by some internal psychic mechanism – although the theorists often disagree about its nature – and, hence, is not a cognitive response to publicly observable aspects of reality. Projection is, therefore, often but not always regarded as an error or an illusion.[3]

Because beam theories of projection appeal to some internal psychic mechanism, they quite often employ metaphors taken from the cinema or, as in the nineteenth century, from the magic lantern. Projections are likened to pictures or images that are thrown or projected by a beam of light onto a blank screen and then, as in Plato's Allegory of the Cave, taken by the denizens of the cave to be real. This type of projection theory is most clearly exemplified in Sigmund Freud's *Totem and Taboo*, where he explains 'primitive religion' as the projection of human subjectivity onto animals and nature. The result is the anthropomorphization of reality, which is then taken to be the original form and even the 'essence' of religion.[4]

Within this general type of beam theory, one may distinguish between those in which projection is associated with a highly technical theory of the psyche and those which do not seem to require any serious conceptual theory at all. Carl Jung's projection theory of religion, for example, presupposes such a theory of the self in which the ego is said to rest on a larger collective unconscious, which contains instinctual patterns called archetypes which seek to compensate for the ego. In the process of this compensation, which Jung calls the 'transcendent function', these archetypes generate religious symbols, the most important of which is the idea of God, the archetype for the self taken as a whole.

It naturally follows that the persuasiveness and viability of the claim that religion is projection is largely dependent upon the persuasiveness of the underlying psychological theory. If one finds Jung's theory of the collective unconscious and the archetypes unconvincing, one will also find his concept of projection and the interpretation of religion to which it leads unconvincing.

But there are those beam theories that presuppose no technical psychological theory at all. They simply attribute religious belief to fear or wishful thinking in the ordinary sense of those words Bertrand Russell's argument, with which Prof. Hertzberg is concerned, seems to be of this type, although, as I shall point out below, Feuerbach's is not. One might even question whether we should dignify Russell's opinions about religion with the term 'projection theory' at all; but were we to do so perhaps we should call it a 'middle range' theory.

This distinction between middle range and complex technical theories is more important than may appear on the surface because there are complex beam theories that make little or no use of either fear or wishful thinking. Jung's theory of religious projection, for example, does not appeal to fear or wish but rather views projection, as I have pointed out, as a manifestation of the archetypes attempting to compensate for some conscious functioning. And it is an ironic and interesting but often unnoticed feature of Freud's thought about religion that (a) he never systematically developed a technical theory of religious projection; (b) to the extent that he did attempt to account for religious projection on technical grounds, as in the Schreber case, he did not appeal to wishful thinking at all but to a convoluted process involving the repression of an unacceptable desire; and (c) the book which is taken as most representative of his thinking, *The Future of an Illusion*, proposes a middle-range theory which even he conceded is quite independent of the technicalities of his psychoanalytic theory.[5]

There is a second type of projection theory which is much more philosophically complex than most beam theories. In these theories, projection is not used to refer to the externalization of some aspect of the self but to the symbolic or categorical schemes that human beings superimpose on their experience in order to make it intelligible.[6] These theories are based on the assumption that human minds have no direct and immediate access to the structures of reality and, hence, that what is called reality is mediated through language, sign and symbol. Just as beam theories appropriate metaphors appropriated from the technology of the cinema, grid theories use metaphors taken from cartography and drafting. Projects are like 'frameworks', 'templates' and grids by means of which human beings organize or construct their experience.

The extension of the term 'projection' to include religion has seemed both legitimate and appropriate to some philosophers and theologians because they believe that any view of the world is scheme-bound and that religions are ways of organizing experience. They are like world-views, writes Gordon Kaufman, because they are able 'to interpret every feature of experience'.[7] This opinion jibes with that of the anthropologist Clifford Geertz who has, in a well-known article, proposed that a religion is:

(1) a system of symbols which acts to (2) establish powerful, pervasive, and long lasting moods and motivations in men by (3) formulating conceptions of a general order of existence and (4) clothing these conceptions with such an aura of factuality that (5) the moods and motivations seem uniquely realistic.[8]

There are, of course, basic structural differences between beam and grid theories of projection that are important to consider because they bear not only on how projection is conceived but the extent to which categories of truth and illusion are appropriate. In beam theories, the religious projection is subjectively generated and bears no relation to the objective nature of the object upon which the image is projected. The metaphor 'beam' suggests an image thrown onto an otherwise blank screen and, hence, is an illusion. In grid theories, by contrast, the categories and basic assumptions of the grid constitute the framework within which judgements of truth or falsity are possible.

Consequently, grid theories make possible a different conception of the relation of religion to science. Both Freud and Russell assume that the religious projection can be contrasted with knowledge and hence must be supplanted by science. This conclusion is naturally reinforced by the view that since projections are externalizations of the self, religions necessarily are anthropomorphic. In grid theories, by contrast, all experience, including scientific experience, is 'constructed' and in that sense a projection. The difference between religion and science is not that the former is a projection while the latter is not. Rather, the difference must be that the scientific projection is in the interest of prediction and control while religion is in the interest of . . . and here the theories diverge. Ernst Cassirer, for example, argued that religion is an attempt to express the feeling that all forms of life are parts of a larger community of life; hence religion is concerned with those aspects of life that bear on this basic feeling.[9]

Once the term projection is used in this extended sense to refer to an experiential grid, this grid may itself be conceived in different ways and with different results. One possibility that is friendly to religion is to argue as Kant and some neo-Kantians have that the grid of reason itself contains certain categories like causality, substance and the like, and that these categories presuppose certain regulative ideals or postulates such as God, the notion of the world and a synthesizing ego. These postulates are not objects of knowledge and experience but are presupposed by all knowledge and experience. Belief in God, then, does not spring out of fear or wish, but is an implicate of the grid of reason.

There is a variant on this Kantian theory that is less friendly to religion. While trading on the metaphor of grid it also contains elements of a beam theory, albeit with a difference. Friedrich Nietzsche agreed with Kant that there are certain fundamental categories like 'cause', 'thing' and 'self' that human reason necessarily uses to organize experience. But unlike Kant he did not regard these as inherent in reason itself but as 'fictions' and 'projections'.[10] He regarded the human intellectual in biological and pragmatic terms, and he concluded that the fundamental categories that we employ are not inherent in reason itself, whatever that might be, but the result of a long evolutionary process of human adaption and survival. Our categories emerge out of our need to simplify and quantify our experience. Our intellects, he argued, are not designed for 'knowledge' but for survival. They impose only as much regularity and form upon the flux of life as our practical needs require. Indeed, Nietzsche suggested, the human intellect may have cast up innumerable categorical schemes before it hit upon those we now employ. The categories are mere 'fictions', 'conditions of life' for us. Moreover, the idea of God, he suggested, reflects our inveterate tendency to postulate an ego behind every action and being. We are drawn to the idea of the whole, to the idea of 'Being', but we then slip an ego or a cause behind this Being. 'I am afraid we are not rid of God because we still have faith in grammar.'[11] But even if it could be shown that the ideas of 'God' and 'ego' are among these necessary conditions of life, Nietzsche argued, they could for all that be 'false' albeit necessary ideas.

There is still another variant on the grid model that is in closer touch with disciplines of psychology and anthropology. In his book, *De religiuze projecti*, the Dutch anthropologist Fokke Sierksma argues that we cannot deal adequately with the phenomenon of religion until we reject metaphors taken from the cinema and deal with the basic perceptual apparatus of the human. He believes that we must begin by observing that every species of biological organism has its own world of signs, which is to say that its sensory organs are 'tuned' to receive only certain aspects of the external world. The dog, for example, has a different world from the amoeba or the spider. Every organism has a world that reflects, to use Wittgenstein's phrase, a 'form of life'.

The human world differs from that of the animals because the human being possesses self-consciousness and can make itself both subject and object. It can distinguish the I from the me. By virtue of this ec-centric position, the self finds itself precariously situated and balanced between the external and the internal world. It can know that it is threatened from without as well as within. If this precarious balance is upset, the I seeks to restore it. It can do this by replacing its lost objectivity by interpreting the world as a subjective reality, or it can, perhaps, take a 'holiday from the ego' and lose consciousness.

Moreover, the human self can know that it has a species-specific perception, that its organs of perception and conceptualization are limited. It suspects that there is a larger environment that escapes it, 'something more', as William James once put it, that plays 'hide and seek' with us, something within and behind the phenomena which escapes the conceptual net we have at our disposal. Our consciousness only lights up a small portion of the cave in which we huddle against the night. We are aware that there is a great deal 'left over' which resists formulation and remains a mysterious other. We then extend our perceptual and conceptual grids or projections. We subjectivize the unknown and attempt to make it amenable. Religion is where human beings experience and objectify this aspect of the world. Some religions, like Buddhism, fully recognize this as a projection; others, like theism, cling to the objectification while claiming that this objectification is necessary as the best we can do.

There is a still another version of the grid model that is extremely influential in Religious Studies and which, like Sierksma's, has at its root a theory of the relationship of consciousness to culture. It is the view that the conceptual schemes by means of which any conceivable human experiences are organized are 'social constructions'. The assumption here is that the 'world' any human being inhabits and takes for granted is experienced through a complex lattice composed of language, categories, representations, rules and typifications provided by culture. In traditional societies, religions are usually a part of this socially constructed lattice, normally functioning to provide a sense of absoluteness to the grid. In complex civilizations, they can be relatively autonomous symbolic forms, related in complex ways to the cultural grids just as science is.

One need only reflect on these various projection theories to realize that it is difficult if not impossible to generalize about them, and further, that one cannot relevantly criticize any of them without dealing with the theory in which the term 'projection' is embedded. There are, first of all, definitional questions concerning religion. Are religions defined substantively or functionally? Is it, for example, a necessary condition that religions involve interaction with superhuman beings? There are also general questions concerning the nature of these theories themselves. In what sense, for example, can these theories claim to be explanatory at all, and how do these 'explanations' compare with or meet the criteria of explanations in the social-scientific disciplines? Or again, are these non-religious explanations of religion necessarily reductionist? What, in fact, is reduction? In what sense, for example, is a psychological or sociological explanation of religion different in kind from the kind of explanation implicit in those descriptions of religious experience given by religious believers themselves in so far as they claim that these experiences are the result of an encounter with superhuman beings?[12]

More important, perhaps, are the epistemological issues raised by the theories. Freud's and Russell's theories, for example, are based on what the philosophical textbooks label 'naive realism', the assumption that the mind has direct access to the structures of reality and that natural science is the paradigm of knowledge. Religious beliefs are particular beliefs and generated from within and, hence, false. Grid theories like Nietzsche's, by contrast, are based on a more complicated epistemology. They assume that since a judgement is the attribution of a predicate (which is itself dependent on some classificatory scheme) to a subject (which can only be picked out by means of the rules of that scheme), it borders on unintelligibility to ask whether a grid as a whole is true or false. Conceptual schemes may be applied or utilized, be successful or unsuccessful for certain purposes, but they cannot be said to be true or false. They constitute the very framework within which 'true' and 'false' can be meaningfully employed.

Given this conception of religion as grid, it is not accidental that it has become especially attractive to some religious apologists. It makes possible the apologetic strategy of admitting that religions are projections but of depriving that term of any pejorative meaning.[13] Furthermore, the apologist can argue, as we have seen, that it is illegitimate to invoke the categories of truth or falsity with respect to religion. A religion, like a world-view, is a total framework and one can only choose to 'dwell in' such a framework. One can only adopt or reject a grid. The test of a world-view is not whether it corresponds with reality, a phrase that is meaningless, but whether it makes possible certain kinds of attitudes, experiences and interpretations.

III

It is against this background that I would register my own reservations about the strategy Prof. Hertzberg's adopts in his paper. I believe that it is a mistake, first, to assume that Feuerbach and Russell have the same view of religion 'as a projection of fear and wishes' and, second, I do not think that his analysis of wishful thinking takes us very far in criticizing any important theory of projection, certainly not Feuerbach's. What we have in Russell, as we also have in Freud's *Future of an Illusion*, is, at best, a village atheist's 'crackerbox' opinions about religion and these opinions are based on neither a sophisticated knowledge of religion nor a deep theory of some kind about the mind. By contrast, what we have in Feuerbach's *Essence of Christianity*, as Marx Wartofsky has shown in his magisterial book, is, first of all, a complex theory of self-differentiation, concept formation and consciousness derived from Hegel's *Phenomenology of Mind*.[14] Second, it is a detailed examination of Christian doctrine and practice which reflects, as Karl Barth has noted, an intimate familiarity with the Bible, the Church Fathers and the theology of Luther.[15] Desire and wish, it is true, play important roles in this theory – fear, incidentally, rarely does – but to ignore the larger theoretical context which defines the meaning of these terms as well as the detailed analyses of the role these desires play in actual Christian doctrine and practice is both to misunderstand and to trivialize his thought. One might as well first argue that Hegel's Philosophy of Spirit, in which the concept of desire plays a central role, is simply a more complicated version of Bertrand Russell's commonplace remarks on wishful thinking and then conclude that one can for this reason dismiss them both.

It is a rarely observed fact that Feuerbach actually seldom used the German term *projektion* but, rather, a host of terms, some technical and some informal, that his English translator, George Eliot, rendered in English as variations on the single verb form 'to project'. Moreover, the most often employed of these German terms, 'to objectify' (*Vergegenständlichung*) and 'to externalize' (*Entaüsserung*) are technical Hegelian terms which have important connotations which the English verb 'to project' does not have. The idea these terms express, in short, was a technical-philosophical one, and readers unfamiliar with the Hegelian background will not only be puzzled by the conceptual affinities these term have with others – for example, alienation – but will largely misunderstand them.

It is no more easy to summarize briefly Feuerbach's argument in *Christianity* than it is Hegel's *Phenomenology of Mind*, especially so since some of it will strike modern readers as arcane, for example, the argument that self-consciousness in the strict sense is consciousness of the infinitude of consciousness or that human predicates are 'absolutes'.[16] But basically the argument is that the self comes to self-consciousness in encounter with or over against other conscious selves. The condition of the possibility of self-consciousness is consciousness of another subject for whom I am an object. The I, so to speak, emerges over against another Thou. But as this self-differentiation is made, the self also comes to realize that it shares common predicates with this other Thou; that both of them are members of a species. It is the distinctive nature of human consciousness, Feuerbach argues, that it can make its own essential predicates an object of thought. Animals, to be sure, may possess a degree of consciousness but not species consciousness, and it is this species consciousness that makes thought and abstraction possible as well as the possibility of imagining oneself in the place of another.

Although informed readers will recognize this theme in Hegel's

Phenomenology, Feuerbach's argument contains some original elements. He insisted that the self-differentiation of the I was mediated through a bodily encounter with the other and not merely through consciousness. The Thou is perceived to be another because it is embodied. The other stands over against the I and physically limits it. Consequently, it is this encounter with an embodied other that mediates the awareness of nature in general. Unlike Hegel's Absolute, which produces the otherness of nature as the first 'moment' in its own process of development towards full self-consciousness, Feuerbach's human spirit first becomes aware of the otherness of nature in and through its encounter with a sensuously perceived Thou:

> The first object of man is man. The sense of Nature, which opens to us the consciousness of the world as a world, is a later product; for it first arises through the distinction of man from himself.[17]

This argument is accompanied by another which, when translated from the arcane language of nineteenth-century idealism, anticipates those contemporary cognitive theories underlying some grid theories of projection. It goes something like this. How any given organism relates to the world is a function of its own distinctive cognitive apparatus. Each type of organism has its own unique 'species perspective', on the world, so to speak. It has its own species-specific world of experience. The bird has a different 'world' from the fish and the spider.

Feuerbach then argues that how any subject necessarily relates to its objects tells us a great deal about the objective nature of that subject. Moreover, he argues that since the organism's distinctive nature determines how the world appears and is for it, it takes these predicates as 'absolutes', because they are the conditions of all possible experience. Moreover, they are perfections because, when fully exercised and used, they bring health and happiness.[18] Since Feuerbach believes that reason, will and feeling are the essential predicates or perfections of the human species, then consciousness can be said to be 'self-verification, self-limitation, self-love, joy in one's perfections'.[19]

Once the process of self-differentiation occurs and the self becomes latently aware that it is a member of the species whose essential predicates are 'absolute' and 'perfect', the isolated self is both enraptured by this perfection of the species idea and is aware that the individual I is an inadequate representation of it. The individual person yearns and longs for 'the perfect type of his nature'.[20] Implied in this yearning is the desire to be free from the limitation and sufferings imposed by natural necessity, including the necessity of death. The individual is driven by the will to live and to flourish (*Glückseligkeitstrieb*), which is to say, to realize its perfections. In the grip of this *Glückseligkeitstrieb*, the imagination, which is in the service of the feelings, seizes on the essential predicates of consciousness – reason, will and feeling – and transforms them into a transcendent divine being. The I imagines a perfect Thou in which all the perfections are realized.

This perfect divine being, which synthesizes in itself all human perfections – perfect knowledge (omniscience), perfect will (omnipotence) and perfect love (omni-benevolence) – not only serves certain cognitive desires, for example, the desire to have some explanation for the world, but, above all, the basic existential need to be recognized for what one is and, nevertheless, loved unconditionally. The Self emerges out of the I–Thou relationship in which, as Hegel taught, the need for recognition is fundamental. But the infinite Thou guarantees an unconditioned and unqualified recognition, an infinite love. God, in short, is the notion of the species transformed by the imagination into a perfect exemplar of the species which satisfies the basic human desire to be recognized and loved.

I do not intend here to endorse this argument, although I would argue, it can be and has been reformulated in ways that are plausible.[21] I merely intend to point out that it is only in this wider philosophical context that we can intelligently discuss what 'wishing' means in Feuerbach's theory and how he believes it functions in religion. To the degree that one can generalize about Feuerbach's view of desire it must be seen as rooted in the desire of the individual to be free from the limitations of nature, especially death, and the desire to be loved or recognized by another Thou. Religion is so powerful, Feuerbach believed, because it serves both of these fundamental desires. And Christianity is the absolute religion, he argued, because it is built on the basic premiss and revelation that the infinite Thou recognizes and loves the human species and will grant it its basic desire to be immortal like Him.

Feuerbach, unlike Russell, did not simply state that religion springs from wishing. Rather, by analysis and extensive quotations from the Church Fathers, Catholic and Protestant theologians, he demonstrated that these two desires are found in the Christian doctrine of the Incarnation, a doctrine which means several things. It means, first of all, that God 'has a heart', that He is a loving and merciful being and that religious people are only interested in a divinity that loves them and can help them. Second, the doctrine means, as many theologians have argued, that Jesus Christ is the very image of God, which is to say, that 'Man was already in God, was already God himself, before God became man, i.e., showed himself as man.'[22] Christians, Feuerbach argued, want above all a personal God. But for ordinary believers, the doctrine of the Incarnation has meant primarily that God was willing to suffer for the welfare of human beings, that out of love for humanity He was even willing to renounce his own divinity or Godhead. In this doctrine, as Luther saw, there is contained the faith that God values humanity more than his own being.[23]

It is important to emphasize again that Feuerbach did not just assert these things about Christianity but that he attempted to show that actual Christian doctrine and practice manifest them. Consequently, the greater part of his book deals with specific Christian doctrines, such as the Incarnation, the Logos, the Trinity, creation, providence and immortality, as well as practices like prayer. The pattern of his argument is itself interesting. Typically he argued, first, that those divine attributes dear to the religious mind are human attributes writ large; second, that there is an incompatibility between the traditional metaphysical attributes of God and the anthropomorphic attributes derived from personal feeling, an incompatibility Pascal and many other philosophical theologians have also noted.[24] And finally, he argued that it is to the anthropomorphic attributes which the ordinary Christian believers inevitably cling, a claim he justifies by looking at traditional and popular Christian prayers and hymns.

It is only in this context that one can usefully raise those questions about the role of wishful thinking which Hertzberg raises. Feuerbach believed, for example, that the belief in providence is one of the most fundamental Christian convictions because it assures the individual subject that God is interested in his or her welfare. Providence, he wrote, 'expresses the value of man, in distinction from other natural beings'.[25] Is this not a Christian wish? But in Christianity, this doctrine is closely connected to the doctrine of creation, on the one hand, and miracles, on the other. Since the doctrine of providence assures the individual that a personal loving deity has his/her welfare as its highest good, any being that can successfully secure this welfare must also have power over nature. This divine being must be able to raise us from the dead, if necessary. Consequently, the Christian doctrine of creation out of nothing is the corollary of the belief in a personal deity that can resurrect us rather than the resurrection being an inference drawn from the doctrine of creation. Can it be denied that the Christian hope in the resurrection is a wish? And if so, what are its presuppositions?

The doctrine of miracles is only an extension of the same belief in providence. It is, so to speak, the proof of providence. The belief in providence expresses the deepest wish of the faithful that God will care for them; miracles assure us that this wish can come true in an instant. It assures us that God is sovereign over nature and can set aside its laws, can interrupt the path of necessity. Luther, whom Feuerbach believed to be the most profound of Christian theologians, defined faith, as Kierkegaard did, as confidence in the possibility that God can do anything and everything to assure the well-being of the Christian subject. And Feuerbach often quoted the Protestant Reformer again and again to this effect:

> God can do everything, but only wishes to do good. . . . God is omnipotent; therefore He wishes us to ask for everything which is useful to us. . . . Since He (God) is omnipotent, what can I lack which He cannot give me or do for me? Since He is Creator of heaven and earth and Lord of all things, who will take anything from me or harm anything of mine? Indeed, how will all things not be for my benefit and serve me if the one to whom they are all obedient and subjected grants goodness to me?[26]

Because Feuerbach believed that the 'secret of theology is anthropology' he is frequently accused of being a reductionist. This term, I would argue, is itself ambiguous, but if it entails that Feuerbach paid no attention to the consciousness of religious believers themselves and their self-interpretation, this accusation is false. On the contrary, he argued that he differed from other demythologizers just because he attempted to do justice to what religious believers themselves say and believe. He was not primarily interested in the metaphysical discourse of theologians and their attempts to minimize the anthropomorphism of ordinary faith. Rather, he was interested in what believers themselves say and do. For example, against one of the earliest attempts to distinguish between an historical Jesus and a dogmatic Christ Feuerbach wrote:

I do not inquire what the real, natural Christ was or may have been in distinction from what he has been made or has become in Supernaturalism; on the contrary, I accept the Christ of religion, but I show that this superhuman being is nothing else than a product and reflex of the supernatural human mind.[27]

It is because Feuerbach did not appeal to wishful thinking in general but to the actual wishes of ordinary Christians expressed in their central doctrines and prayers that his interpretation of Christianity continues to disturb his readers even today. He was not a village atheist like Freud and Russell but, as Karl Barth noted, a lover of theology, albeit an unhappy lover:[28] 'my one purpose, one intention and idea', he once wrote, 'is religion or theology and everything connected with it . . .'[29] His serious critics, as Karl Barth has also noted, will have to come to terms with his exegesis and his analysis. 'Why', Barth asks, 'has Christian theology not seen these things earlier and better than Feuerbach, things that it certainly must have seen if it really knew the Old and New Testament? Its negligence of the Christian hope . . .?'[30] The same question might be posed to philosophers of religion.

Notes

1. Quoted by David Baken in *The Duality of Human Existence* (Chicago: Rand-McNally, 1966), pp. 38f.
2. Peter L. Berger, *The Sacred Canopy: Elements of a Sociological Theory of Religion* (Garden City, NY: Doubleday and Co., 1967). Fokke Sierksma, *Projection and Religion: An Anthropological and Psychological Study of the Phenomena of Projection in the Various Religions*, trans. Jacob Faber, Foreword by Lee W. Bailey (Ann Arbor, MI: UMI Books on Demand, University Microfilms International, 1993).
3. Even generalizations such as these are dangerous. Even though Carl Jung thinks religious symbols are generated from instinctual structures (archetypes), he does not characterize them as either delusions or illusions.
4. Sigmund Freud, *Totem and Taboo: Some Points of Agreement between the Mental Lives of Savages and Neurotics*, trans. James Strachey (New York: W.W. Norton, 1950).
5. 'Nothing I have said here against the truth-value of religions needed the support of psychoanalysis; it had been said by others long before analysis came into existence.' Sigmund Freud, *The Future of An Illusion*, trans. W.D. Robson-Scott, revised and newly edited by James Strachey (New York: Doubleday Anchor Books), p. 60.

6. The use of the term 'projection' in this fashion exploits certain linguistic associations inherent in the classical use of the verb 'to project', such as 'to cast' and 'to throw'. We can see a contemporary example of this in the reasoning of the English translators of Martin Heidegger's *Sein und Zeit*. Heidegger used the German term *Entwurf* to convey his view that the distinctive feature of *Dasein* is to categorize its experience in terms of its practical projects. The mind, he argued, does not apprehend essences but conceives of the world in terms of its instrumental purposes. The English translators argue that the connotations of the verb *'entwerfen'* are best conveyed by the English verb 'to project' because this word has been linked not only with 'throwing' but with the more abstract mental process of designing or sketching, as when we say that a geometer projects a curve upon a plane. Martin Heidegger, *Being and Time*, trans. John Macquarrie and Edward Robinson (New York: Harper and Brothers, 1962), p. 185, n. 1.

7. Gordon Kaufman, *The Theological Imagination: Constructing the Concept of God* (Philadelphia: Westminster Press, 1981), pp. 32f. See Terry Godlove's criticism of this extension of conceptual scheme to include religion in the light of his own acceptance of Donald Davidson's rejection of an intelligible distinction between schema and content. *Religion, Interpretation, and Diversity of Belief: The Framework Model from Kant to Durkheim to Davidson* (Cambridge: Cambridge University Press, 1989).

8. Clifford Geertz, *The Interpretation of Cultures* (New York: Basic Books, 1973), p. 90.

9. See Ernst Cassirer, *An Essay on Man: An Introduction to a Philosophy of Human Culture* (Garden City, NY: Doubleday Books, 1944), ch. VII.

10. Friedrich Nietzsche, *The Will to Power*, trans. Walter Kaufmann and R.J. Hollingdale, ed. with commentary by Walter Kaufmann (New York: Random House Vintage Books, 1968), paras 470–93.

11. Friedrich Nietzsche, *Twilight of the Idols* in *The Portable Nietzsche*, selected and translated, with an introduction, preface and notes, by Walter Kaufmann (New York: The Viking Press, 1954), p. 483.

12. See Wayne Proudfoot's argument that the descriptions of religious experience by believers implicitly contains an explanation of that experience. *Religious Experience* (Berkeley: University of California Press, 1985), pp. 216–27.

13. As an example, see Peter Berger's argument that mathematics is a human projection but that it applies to experience. *A Rumor of Angels: Modern Society and Rediscovery of the Supernatural* (Garden City, NY: Doubleday Anchor Books, 1969), pp. 46f.

14. Marx Wartofsky, *Feuerbach* (Cambridge: Cambridge University Press, 1977). Wartofsky argues that the book is so difficult for a lay reader to understand because Feuerbach, for complex reasons, decided not to spell out or develop the epistemological arguments that are so crucial to it. Consequently, the book can be read at both a popular and a more sophisticated level. At the latter there is an argument regarding how concepts are formulated in religion and philosophy. But since this is never spelled out, the reader has to reconstruct it.

15. Barth has written that Feuerbach's knowledge of the Bible, the Church Fathers and Luther 'place him above most modern philosophers' and that 'no philosopher of his time penetrated the contemporary theological situation as effectually as he, and few spoke with such pertinence.' 'An Introductory Essay', in Ludwig Feuerbach, *The Essence of Christianity*, trans. George Eliot, with an introductory essay by Karl Barth and a Foreword by H. Richard Niebuhr (New York: Harper Torch Books, 1957), p. x.

16. Feuerbach, *The Essence of Christianity*, ch. 1.

17. Ibid., pp. 82f.

18. One finds the same notion in the young Marx's 'Economic and Philosophical Manuscripts' in which the presupposition of his argument is that any system that deprives the worker of the exercise of his/her essential powers is alienation. See Karl Marx, *Early Writings*, trans. Rodney Livingstone and Gregor Benton and intro. by Lucio Colletti (New York: Random House Vintage Books, 1975).

19. Feuerbach, *The Essence of Christianity*, p. 6.

20. Ibid., p. 280.

21. See Wartofsky's reconstruction of the argument in his *Feuerbach*, ch. VIII. I have myself attempted to reconstruct it after suggestions by Alexandre Kojève in his *Introduction to the Reading of Hegel; Lectures on the Phenomenology of Spirit*, assembled by Raymond Queneau, ed. by Allan Bloom and trans. James H. Hichols, Jr (Ithaca, NY: Cornell University Press, 1969). See my forthcoming *Feuerbach and the Interpretation of Religion* (Cambridge: Cambridge University Press).

22. Feuerbach, *The Essence of Christianity*, p. 50.

23. Ibid., pp. 53f.

24. See the criticisms of Process philosophers and theologians such as John Cobb, Charles Hartshorne and Schubert Ogden, among others.

25. Feuerbach, *The Essence of Christianity*, p. 105.

26. Luther quoted by Feuerbach in *The Essence of Faith According to Luther*, trans. and with an introduction by Melvin Cherno (New York: Harper & Row, 1967), p. 57. Noting Feuerbach's repeated appeal to Luther, Karl Barth observed, 'Now, after Feuerbach, one may no longer repeat these things from Luther without some caution.' See 'An Introductory Essay', in Feuerbach, *Essence of Christianity*, p. xxiii.

27. Feuerbach, ibid., p. xli.

28. Barth in 'An Introductory Essay', in Feuerbach, *The Essence of Christianity*, p. x.

29. Ludwig Feuerbach, *Lectures on the Essence of Religion*, trans. Ralph Manheim (New York: Harper & Row, 1967), p. 5.

30. Barth in his introductory essay in *The Essence of Christianity*, p. xxc.

Part Three
Psychoanalysis and Religion

5

Psychoanalysis as Ultimate Explanation

John Deigh

Atomism offers ultimate explanations of the sensible events and processes of the physical world. It holds that such events and processes are ultimately the work of unseeable atomic particles of matter whirling about and colliding with each other in the void. Similarly, psychoanalysis offers ultimate explanations of human conduct and the conscious thoughts and feelings it manifests. It holds that such conduct, thought and feeling are the work of the subject's unconscious mind, the thoughts and wishes it contains, and the inherited drives from which they derive their psychic force. To be sure, the analogy between atomism and psychoanalysis is imperfect. The explanations of the former are reductive, those of the latter causal. But this difference does not spoil the parallel. In either, the theorist, drawing on similarities and differences he observes in the behaviour of the objects or people he studies, posits states and activities of things that no one can perceive to explain sensible events and processes or conscious thoughts and feelings. Both thus follow the same form of abductive argument in reaching their theoretical conclusions. Both follow the same pattern of scientific theorizing and hold out their results as ultimate explanations of the phenomena they study.[1]

To say that these explanations are ultimate, however, is only to say that within their respective theories, physics, in the one case, psychology in the other, they bring to an end the answers those theories give to questions about what explains the phenomena the theories cover. In other words, nothing about atomism or psychoanalysis *per se* precludes further explanation of these phenomena from outside those theories. Of course, atomism originated as a thoroughgoing materialism, and as such it precludes any explanation of physical phenomena outside of physical theory. But one can accept atomism without being a materialist, a point that goes back at least to Aristotle's observation that Democritus and his followers ignored the question of original motion. Psychoanalysis too sprang from a materialist conception of the mind. Freud, as is commonly remarked, looked forward to the day when neurophysiology would explain the operations of the unconscious that psychoanalysis uncovered. Hence, it would be even harder to misunderstand the restricted sense in which psychoanalytical explanations are ultimate. They are ultimate within psychology but are in no way meant to be the last word on why we act, think and feel as we do.

None the less, there is no denying their import. As ultimate explanations within psychology, they oppose some of the most entrenched doctrines about the human spirit in Western thought, and as products of scientific theorizing, they have a claim to being advancements in our understanding of mental phenomena. Consequently, the more one credits this claim, the more one will see psychoanalytic explanations as part of the general ascendancy of the natural sciences over those traditional ways of understanding the world and man's place within it that dominated intellectual life before the rise of modern science and that still influence our thinking. These older ways include, above all, the predominant spiritualist philosophy of Christian belief. And while the psychoanalytical critique of religion is typically identified with its uncovering of the Oedipal and neurotic character of religious myth and ritual, its opposition to doctrines about man's distinctively spiritual nature that are central to the Judaeo-Christian tradition may represent an even profounder challenge to religious belief.

Psychoanalysis, of course, has had plenty of detractors both inside and outside the natural sciences. Its methods and the theoretical harvest they have yielded remain controversial. Its founder and his followers and heirs continue to attract obloquy. Yet despite these objections and attacks, its acceptance in intellectual and academic circles has been sufficiently broad and enduring to establish it as a major force in pushing the claims of natural science into areas of thought previously reserved for philosophical and religious systems. Its claim to having advanced our understanding of mental phenomena has been given sufficient credit to render its explanations among this century's most influential arguments against the once-prevailing doctrines of Western philosophy and Christian belief that exclude certain forms of human thought and activity from the natural world.

How cogent an argument they make against these doctrines is the topic of this study. In raising the issue, however, I do not mean to dispute the claim of psychoanalysis to having advanced our understanding of mental phenomena. That the theory represents an advance in psychology, particularly an advance over the earlier theories in the field that offered accounts of human thought and activity as entirely products of natural forces, can be conceded. For the question that interests me is whether psychoanalysis, Freud's theory in particular, successfully answers the powerful objections that defenders of doctrines opposed to such naturalism have raised and that none of these earlier theories seems able to answer satisfactorily. It is easy, I think, to conclude from the differences between these earlier theories and Freud's that his does. Yet I will argue, to the contrary, that despite the advance Freud's theory represents, it does not. The spiritualist doctrines that argue against seeing all human thought and activity as natural phenomena, however far out of favour they may now have fallen, remain unrefuted by this most influential representative of the natural sciences.

I

The doctrines I have in mind concern, above all, the thought and activity that distinguishes human beings as moral agents. Intuitionist doctrines about the super-sensibility of value, Christian doctrines about the divine character of conscience and libertarian doctrines of free will are prime examples. While such doctrines – let us call them doctrines of human exceptionalism – belong to various systems of religious and philosophical thought, they share the idea that something about man's moral powers, his intellect, his sensibilities, his will, sets him apart from beasts. The difference the idea supposes between the two kinds of creature is this. Beasts belong completely to the natural world. They are creatures whose thoughts and behaviour are entirely products of natural forces. While human beings have an animal nature in common with beasts and thus much of their thought and behaviour is similarly a product of natural forces, they also, unlike beasts, possess a moral personality in virtue of which their thoughts and behaviour have a moral quality and as a result of which not all of those thoughts and behaviour are attributable to natural forces. Human beings, therefore, do not belong completely to the natural world. No one has expressed this idea of the profound difference between man and beast more powerfully than Rousseau:

This passage from the state of nature to the civil state produces quite a remarkable change in man, for it substitutes justice for instinct in his behavior and gives his actions a moral quality they previously lacked. Only then, when the voice of duty replaces physical impulse and right replaces appetite, does man, who had hitherto taken only himself into account, find himself forced to act upon other principles and to consult his reason before listening to his inclinations. Although in this state he deprives himself of several of the advantages belonging to him in the state of nature, he regains such great ones. His faculties are exercised and developed, his ideas are broadened, his feelings are ennobled, his entire soul is elevated to such a height that, if the abuse of this new condition did not often lower his status to beneath the level he left, he ought constantly to bless the happy moment that pulled him away from it forever and which transformed him from a stupid, limited animal into an intelligent being and a man.[2]

Freud, as I indicated above, was not the first major thinker to depart from these traditional doctrines of human exceptionalism. He was not the first to treat the moral thought and behaviour of human beings as wholly natural phenomena. Unquestionably, some Ancient Greek deserves the honour: Epicurus perhaps, or Aristotle, or someone even earlier. In any case, Hobbes and Spinoza, in the seventeenth century, and Hume, in the eighteenth, presented theories of human psychology on which all human thought and behaviour, and so *a fortiori* all moral thought and behaviour, were explicable by principles of nature. Their theories differed importantly from Freud's, though, in that they represented mental phenomena, which is to say, thoughts, feelings, desires, imaginings, and the like, as states of a single, undivided subject. Hobbes took this subject to be the whole person instead of the mind or soul of a person, for his materialism made him sceptical of talk of minds and souls. Spinoza, by contrast, took it to be a human mind, but for him the human mind was the same thing, under a different aspect, as the human body, so special division of the human mind made no sense on his system. And Hume too took the subject of mental phenomena to be a mind, but for Hume the mind was just a convenient fiction, something we invent to unify the disparate images and feelings succeeding one another in what James later famously called the stream of thought. Consequently, none of these great thinkers had a conception of the mind as a divisible realm of thought. None entertained the hypothesis, at the heart of Freud's theory, that the mind was divided into separate regions or domains tensions between which produced various thoughts and behaviour including the thoughts and behaviour that spring from man's moral powers.

Indeed, until Freud, the conception of the mind as divided into separate domains belonged principally to rationalist theories of moral psychology that represented reason as pitted against appetite and passion. Such theories went hand in glove with the traditional doctrines of human exceptionalism, which is, of course, not to say that every believer in such doctrines subscribed to one or another of these theories or that every subscriber to the latter believed the former. Still, because reason has, since the Greeks, been regarded as an essential human trait that distinguishes humans from other animals, representing it as possessing ideas and power that do not come from nature and thus as a counterforce to appetite and passion has been a common theoretical strategy among those who do believe these doctrines. Plato's moral psychology is no doubt the example that will first come to mind. But a slew of modern rationalist theories, capped by Kant's ethics, exemplify the strategy as well.

This strategy, it is important to note, amounts to more than distinguishing reason from appetite and passion. In particular, it amounts to more than taking them to be distinct mental faculties. Hume, after all, included such distinctions in his theory, but the distinction he made between reason and passion, for instance, merely followed his fundamental distinction between ideas and impressions, thoughts and feelings, and did not entail the sort of opposition that suggests a conception of the mind as divided into separate domains. Specifically, it did not entail that reason and passion ever opposed each other as forces. By contrast, the rationalist distinction entailed such opposition because rationalists attributed to reason the power to influence its possessor's will. Thus on rationalist theories of moral psychology conflicts between reason and passion consisted in the opposition of motivational forces, each striving to determine the will. Moreover, these theories further divided reason from passion by holding that ideas and principles peculiar to the former were essential to its operations but inessential to the latter's. Passion, according to these theories, could be excited and prolonged solely by sensory experience or its mnemonic residue, whereas reason required ideas and principles peculiar to its domain, even when it operated on materials furnished by the senses, memory or imagination.

Many of these ideas and principles were, to be sure, ideas and principles of logic. But not all were. Rationalist theories also included in the domain of reason the fundamental ideas and principles of morality. Indeed, their inclusion was essential to the theories' account of reason's power to influence the will. For that influence had to be transmitted through practical thought, and these ideas and principles were the materials of practical thought that effected the transmission. Thus, the theories typically counted among the ideas and principles peculiar to reason ideas of goodness and perfection, whose presentation before the mind could pull the will in the direction of their realization, and principles of right and wrong, the recognition of whose authority could restrain one's impulses to pursue pleasure, power, sexual union and other objects of appetite and passion. It was then sufficient for completing the strategy of using these theories as groundwork for doctrines of human exceptionalism to deny that human minds came into possession of these moral ideas and principles through the workings of nature. This denial implied that reason operated independently of natural causes when it influenced the will and, therefore, that the moral thought and behaviour attributable to these operations lay beyond the reach of natural science.

Clearly, what makes rationalist theories of moral psychology well suited for grounding doctrines of human exceptionalism is their division of the mind into two or more distinct domains of activity at least one of which is the domain of reason. Moreover, the division's suitability for grounding these doctrines matches the suitability of a conception of the mind as undivided for developing theories that oppose these doctrines. It should be no surprise, then, that traditionally the disputes between the doctrines' exponents and opponents turned on questions about the structure of the human mind.[3] Thus the conflicts of feeling and motive that rationalists took as evidence of the mind's having distinct domains were for thinkers such as Spinoza and Hume no different from any other instance of mixed emotions or competing impulses. That is, while these latter thinkers recognized experiences of being both drawn towards and repelled by the same object, they denied that such experiences ever amounted to more than the simultaneous arousal of desire and aversion in view of the prospective pleasure and pain associated with the object. Likewise, while they recognized experiences of being torn between two objects of interest, they denied that such experiences ever amounted to more than the simultaneous arousal of competing desires in view of the prospective pleasure that the consummation of either would bring. In other words, they saw in none of these experiences evidence of a motivational force that could not be reconciled with the mechanisms by which the prospects of pleasure and pain influenced the will or with comparably reactive mechanisms by which primitive urges and emotions exercised a similar influence. Unconvinced that such a force existed, these thinkers saw nothing to warrant a conception of the mind as divided.

Against their views, rationalists could and did appeal to the common experience of exerting oneself contrary to the attractions of some prospective pleasure or the repulsions of some prospective pain.[4] Thus they argued that the awareness of a power within oneself to resist these influences, an awareness, they maintained, that anyone of sound mind had, was evidence of a motivational force that was not reducible to a desire for pleasure or an aversion to pain. Nor was it reducible to any similarly reactive mechanism, such as a survival instinct, a maternal instinct or a herd instinct. For this power of which anyone of sound mind was aware, so their argument continued, was the power to set oneself on a course of action in conformity to ideas of good ends or principles of right action that, as ideas and principles of reason, were not reducible to ideas of pleasure and pain or expressions of instinctual demands. Consequently, no matter what the reactive mechanism one supposed, it would still be such that, on experiencing the impulse to action it produced, one could exert this power in an effort to restrain oneself from acting on that impulse. Hence, to the extent that abandoning belief in one's having such a power was difficult, the rationalists' argument for conceiving of the mind as divided was persuasive. And given that, in their traditional debate with anti-rationalists such as Hume, the latter's conception of the mind as undivided was identified with naturalism, a persuasive argument for a conception of the mind as divided translated into a persuasive argument against naturalism. It translated, in other words, into a persuasive argument for a doctrine of human exceptionalism.

II

Freud's theory changed the significance of this debate. Once the theory took hold, conceiving of the mind as divided no longer signalled belief in human powers that went beyond the natural world.

Because Freud's conception of the mind was at once different from the rationalists' conception and part of a naturalistic programme in psychology, it broke the traditional connection between the question of the mind's structure and the question of its place in the natural world. Whereas the rationalists' conception, in the way it represented the mind as divided, corresponded to a distinction between what was unique to human beings and what was common to both them and beasts, Freud's, in its representation of the mind as divided into a conscious and an unconscious domain, did not. Neither being conscious nor being unconscious was to be understood as solely a property of human minds. A beast's mind too could have both a conscious and unconscious domain. A dog too could be conscious of its surroundings when awake and have dreams when asleep. Freud's conception, in other words, unlike the rationalists', offered no hook on which to hang a doctrine of human exceptionalism.

To the contrary, in Freud's view, all mental states and activity, whether those of human minds or the minds of other animals, belonged to the natural world. All were appropriate objects of study by natural science. His distinction between the mind's conscious states and activity and its unconscious ones was, then, as he presented it, a major contribution to that study. Yet owing to complications and changes in what he wrote about the mind's different domains, how this distinction and so his division of the mind are to be understood is, in fact, a problematic question, a question with multiple answers. As a result, determining with what success Freud explained mental states and activity as natural phenomena, determining, that is, the cogency of his theory as an argument against doctrines of human exceptionalism, requires sorting through the different answers the question has.

The problem arises because Freud, as he readily acknowledged, used the term 'unconscious' ambiguously.[5] On the one hand, he used the term as a synonym for latent. An unconscious thought in this sense was a thought that existed but was not, as we say, present to the mind. Accordingly, the subject had the thought and might even have been influenced by it, but was none the less unaware of it. On the other hand, he used the term as a synonym for repressed. An unconscious thought in this sense was a thought that was kept latent by a force that opposed its becoming present to the mind. Such opposition, moreover, was necessary because the thought expressed a basic drive – it represented an instinct, as Freud put it

– and being invested with the force of that drive, would not have remained latent unless its force were blocked. In other words, an unconscious thought, on this second use, unlike the first, was the site of conflict between two inner forces: the instinctual force that powered the thought and a counterforce, the repressing force, that kept the subject unaware of this powerful thought. On the first use, then, which Freud called the descriptive use, being conscious and being unconscious were contradictory properties in the sense that, if a thought was conscious, then it was not unconscious, and conversely. By contrast, on the second use, which Freud called the dynamic use, being conscious and being unconscious were not contradictory properties in this sense. For on this dynamic use the term 'unconscious' did not apply to latent thoughts that were unrepressed. Freud called such thoughts 'preconscious' instead, and in introducing this term he affirmed an implicit ambiguity in his use of the term 'conscious' that corresponded to the ambiguity in his use of the term 'unconscious'. Clearly, then, whether one takes these two terms in their descriptive sense or in their dynamic sense will affect how one conceives of the two domains into which he divided the mind.

Specifically, if one takes the terms in their descriptive sense, one will conceive of the domains as mere containers of mental states or areas of mental activity, whereas, if one takes the terms in their dynamic sense, one will conceive of the domains as parts of a whole each of which is in tension with the other. The question, of course, once these two conceptions are distinguished, is how well-suited each is to a naturalistic programme in psychology. Are the reasons for seeing Freud's way of dividing the mind as unsupportive of doctrines of human exceptionalism as sound if one applies the second conception in understanding that division as they are if one applies the first? That they are sound on the first conception is clear since a conception of the domains as containers or areas applies to both the minds of beasts and those of humans. At the same time, this conception, because it follows from taking the terms in their descriptive sense, has no explanatory power. Hence, only the second conception grounds the characteristic explanations of psychoanalysis. Only the second yields explanations of thoughts and behaviour as the products of inner conflict.

On this second conception, however, the soundness of the reasons for seeing Freud's way of dividing the mind as unsupportive of doctrines of human exceptionalism is unclear since it depends on the nature of the forces in virtue of which the two domains, on this conception, are in tension with each other. Specifically, the more sophisticated the agency of repression, the harder it will be to suppose that this force operates in the minds of beasts as well as in human minds and thus the easier it will be to find in Freud's way of dividing the mind support for a doctrine of human exceptionalism. To be sure, even if repression were unique to human beings, this would hardly mean that psychoanalysis was committed to some doctrine of human exceptionalism. None the less, as long as its account of repression left open the possibility that its motivational force did not qualify as a natural force, one could not say that the conception of the mind as divided that psychoanalytical explanations required was well suited to a naturalistic programme in psychology.

At first glance, this may appear to be an idle worry. Looking at Freud's mature account of repression, one could easily conclude that the operation consisted of mechanisms that were not peculiar to the human mind.[6] Thus, on this account, repression is initially a reaction to anxiety. The anxiety alerts the subject to a preconscious or barely conscious thought that is invested with instinctual force and that threatens much greater distress should the subject become fully aware of it and thus compelled to acknowledge it. Repressing the thought is the subject's means to relieving this anxiety and avoiding the much greater distress it signalled. Accordingly, whatever attention the thought had initially received from the subject is withdrawn; its traces forgotten; and the thought is then blocked from again becoming conscious or nearly conscious. In this way the subject gains an immunity from the anxiety and the danger it signalled, though renewed exertions of repressive force are necessary to retain the immunity. And of course, the gain may have costs in the illnesses and disturbances that psychoanalysis, using this account of repression, famously explained. But these need not concern us here. What is worth noting instead is that, on this account, repression is a reaction to anxiety on a par with someone's reacting to anxiety that signals great and imminent danger in his surroundings. There is a difference of course, since the latter reaction could produce flight to a place of safety, a means of escape that is unavailable to the subject of the former. But this difference is due to a difference in the circumstances of the danger – an anxiety-provoking thought, after all, cannot exist independently of its subject while a burning building, say, can – and therefore does not make repression any more peculiar a reaction to anxiety than flight.

In either case the core mechanism is a common phenomenon of animal life.[7]

The conclusion follows, however, only if recognition of the danger the anxiety signals and the manner of its removal do not entail any peculiarly human endowment. The analogy, that is, between anxiety that signals danger in one's surroundings and anxiety that signals a dangerous thought argues for understanding the motivation and operations of repression as no different from those of flight or other animal reactions to perceived dangers only if recognizing the dangerousness of the thought and gaining immunity from it through repudiation and amnesia do not entail ideas or principles peculiar to the human mind. For if they did, the worry over whether the motivational force of repression was a wholly natural force would remain. To determine, then, whether they do, we must discover what it is about a repressed thought that, on Freud's account, explains why it would cause great distress in the person who had it if he were to become fully aware of it and compelled to acknowledge it. And to find the answer, we will have to look beyond its being invested with instinctual force, for Freud did not think every preconscious or barely conscious thought that is invested with such force caused anxiety sufficient to trigger repression. To find the answer, we must look instead at the thought's content. There we will discover what makes the thought seem so dangerous.

Freud himself indicated as much by characterizing exertions of repressive force as a kind of censorship one exercised as a way of keeping oneself ignorant of hateful and frightening wishes that one harboured. These wishes were thoughts of what would gratify the instinct with whose force they were invested, and the instincts Freud had in mind were powerfully erotic and destructive instincts which, given the normal familial context of infancy and early childhood, bound the child to its parents. Thus, the corresponding wishes were typically sexual and lethal wishes whose complete gratification, were it really possible, would be the stuff of tragedy. Incest and parricide were Freud's most important examples. What makes the wishes seem so dangerous to the subject, then, is the nature of the acts that would gratify them. Fulfilling these wishes means transgressing barriers erected to preserve relations with the most important figures in the subject's life, personages on whom he depends for protection and nourishment. Hence, repudiating and expelling the wishes and vigilantly blocking their return becomes necessary to ward off the extreme threat to his welfare and life they represent. Here it is plain how the content of the wishes makes them seem so dangerous. What is more, the recognition of danger and the removal of its source that initiates and constitutes repression seemingly contain ideas that are peculiar to the human mind. Surely, to see an act as a transgression and to repudiate the wish to engage in such action imply a kind of moral understanding of one's universe and sense of what is good and evil in it that is beyond the ken of beasts. Freud's account of repression, once it is fully fleshed out, thus leaves open the possibility that the motivational force of repression, owing to some of its components, did not qualify as a force of nature.

III

To make headway, at this point, we must move past Freud's account of repression and the conception of the mind on which it was originally based. Neither will ultimately answer our question about the cogency of psychoanalytical explanations as arguments against doctrines of human exceptionalism. To find answers we must consider yet another conception of the mind as divided that Freud developed. This conception corresponded to a sense in which he used the terms 'conscious' and 'unconscious' that differed from the descriptive and the dynamic senses we have already considered. On this third use, which Freud marked by the abbreviations Cs. and Ucs., the terms stood for distinct systems of thought and activity within the mind. Cs. named the system of perception and reflection, whose processes were intelligent and, with the acquisition of language, subject to principles of logic.[8] Ucs., by contrast, named the system of thoughts and wishes that gave direct expression to instinctual demands and whose processes reflected the unruly play of instinct and was for that reason completely alien to logic. Repression, which was an activity of the Cs., had a significant role in distinguishing the two systems, but it was not the sole criterion of that distinction. As a result, Ucs. included more than repressed thoughts, though it did not include preconscious ones. This third conception of the mind, then, was equivalent to neither of the other two. By allowing Freud to attribute to the mind unconscious thoughts that, while more than merely latent, had never undergone repression, it gave him more room to explore the work of the instincts outside of the theory of repression.

Eventually, though, Freud came to realize the inadequacy of even this conception for explaining all of the unconscious thought and activity, in the descriptive sense of 'unconscious', that he conceived of as more than merely latent. In particular, he realized that this third conception was as ill-equipped as the second to explain how the forces of repression themselves could be unconscious. As a result, he abandoned his use of 'conscious' and 'unconscious' (and the abbreviations Cs. and Ucs.) as names for the domain from which repression issued and the domain in which repressed thoughts and wishes were found and replaced them with 'ego' and 'id'. This change, moreover, was not just a matter of relabelling. Freud had for some time been working out ideas about the operations of the ego while only loosely identifying it with the system of perceptual and reflective thought that the abbreviation Cs. stood for. Renaming this domain 'the ego' thus enabled him to consolidate these newer ideas with his older ideas about repression and psychosexual development, and this consolidation produced an even richer conception of the way the mind was divided.

For our purposes, the most important result of this consolidation was the addition of an internal agency of morality and value, the super-ego, to this systemic or, as Freud came to call it, structural conception of the mind. The super-ego, Freud explained, develops out of the ego as a result of the processes, occurring in infancy and early childhood, by which the ego acquires personality. And though he sometimes described the super-ego as a 'grade in the ego', he mostly treated it as a distinct domain of the mind.[9] Thus, on this structural conception, the mind was divided into three distinct domains, and interactions among these domains, primarily those in which the ego mediated between the other two, became the basis of psychoanalytical explanations.

The addition of an agency of morality and value answered a long-standing complaint against psychoanalysis, that in concentrating on diseases and perversions of the mind, it ignored man's higher nature. Freud thought this complaint was unfair, both as a matter of accuracy and as a matter of proper scientific methodology. For one thing, he pointed out, 'we have from the beginning attributed the function of instigating repression to the moral and aesthetic trends in the ego.'[10] For another, he argued, a science must grow piecemeal according to the evidence it finds and should not be expected to lay out a complete theory all at once:

So long as we had to concern ourselves with the study of what is repressed in mental life, there was no need for us to share in any agitated apprehensions as to the whereabouts of the higher side of man. But now that we have embarked upon the analysis of the ego we can give an answer to all those whose moral sense has been shocked and who have complained that there must surely be a higher nature in man: 'Very true,' we can say, 'and here we have that higher nature, in this ego ideal or super-ego, the representative of our relation to our parents. When we were little children we knew these higher natures, we admired them and feared them; and later we took them into ourselves.'[11]

Clearly, this development in Freud's theory brings to a head the question of how cogent psychoanalytical explanations are as arguments against doctrines of human exceptionalism. The addition of the super-ego promises both to resolve our earlier worry about the nature of repression's motivational force, since it enlarges Freud's account of repression in a way that speaks directly to that worry, and to answer the rationalist objections to naturalist programmes in psychology I described above, since it supplies an explanation of the kind of inner conflict on which those objections were based. Whether it fulfils these promises, however, depends on how well the operations of the super-ego, as Freud characterized them, explain man's moral agency and on whether that explanation is sufficient to show that such agency is entirely the product of natural forces.

For the most part, Freud characterized the super-ego's operations as supervisory, restrictive and punitive. The model was that of a harsh and biting conscience, which operated as a moral guide and disciplinarian, instructing its possessor on matters of right and wrong, opposing his wishes and desires when they prompted wrong action, and plaguing him with criticism and blame if he ignored that opposition. Indeed, Freud frequently identified possession of a super-ego with possession of a conscience, though his considered view was that conscience was only one of the super-ego's principal functions.[12] A second function was that of holding up ideals by which its possessor could measure how admirable his life and personal qualities were. This function lay mostly in the shadows of Freud's writings on the super-ego, and it was only in one of his last works that he explicitly distinguished it from conscience. There he drew the distinction by reintroducing the term ego ideal, a term he had previously used interchangeably with super-ego, and giving it the narrower meaning of *idealfunktion*.[13] The distinction then enabled him to discriminate between affects of conscience and affects of self-appraisal, the sense of guilt and the sense of inferiority, in particular, and others, following his lead, have used it to distinguish between the emotions of guilt and shame and to explain how these emotions complement each other.[14] In these distinctions, both Freud's and his followers', one can see how Freud's theory incorporates into its explanation of moral agency ideas of goodness and perfection as well as principles of right and wrong. Conscience preserves and enforces the latter; the ego ideal maintains the former. Hence, the two kinds of practical judgement to which rationalists ascribed the motivational force of reason in its struggles with appetite and passion each have a place in Freud's account of the super-ego.

In that account, these two kinds of judgement are differentiated exactly as the two functions to which they correspond are differentiated. The chief differentia in either case is the motivational force driving the operations that define those functions. The operations of conscience owe their motivational force to aggressive drives; the operations of the ego ideal owe theirs to sexual drives. And these drives are then traceable, according to Freud, to the basic instincts of destruction (or death) and Eros. Consequently, on Freud's theory, judgements of morality and value have motivational force that is traceable to these basic instincts. How these judgements come to have such force, how a person's conscience and ego ideal become vehicles of these basic instincts, are questions whose answers are found in the way Freud explained the formation in the young child of a super-ego. The main theses of this explanation are well known. They describe the process by which the child internalizes parental figures as a way of resolving severe emotional conflict in its feelings towards its parents, a conflict that invariably arises out of the normal familial circumstances of early childhood. Thus, to the extent that this explanation covers the essentials of the phenomena and is plausible, Freud explained the moral agency distinctive of human beings.[15]

This explanation, moreover, offers an account of the kind of opposition between distinct domains of the mind that rationalists regarded as opposition between the force of reason and the forces of appetite and passion. Accordingly, such opposition is understood as a conflict between the forces of the super-ego and the forces of the id. The latter derive from the basic instincts and, in the cases that match what rationalists described as excitations of appetite and passion, are experienced as the impulses and urges of primitive desires and emotions. The former originate in the very same instincts, but because they operate in the super-ego and power its agency, they can oppose primitive desires and emotions that are invested with the same instinctual force. They are, then, experienced as dictates of conscience or aspirations of the ego ideal. And just as the rationalists characterized the opposition between the force of reason and the force of passion as a struggle for the determination of the will, so Freud characterized the opposition between the forces of the super-ego and the forces of the id as a struggle for complicity of the ego. In this way, Freud's theory explains the experiences of inner conflict on which rationalists based their objections to earlier naturalistic theories. In so far as these experiences require divisions within the mind to be satisfactorily explained, Freud's theory represents a significant advance over these earlier theories.

IV

This advance notwithstanding, we cannot yet conclude that Freud succeeded in showing that man's moral agency was entirely a product of natural forces. Indeed, we could not draw this conclusion even if we accepted as unproblematic and well-supported his account of the super-ego's operations. To be sure, if the spurs of a strict conscience or the aspirations of an ego ideal, which these operations explain, supplied the only motivational force that the judgements of morality and value distinctive of our moral agency ever had, the conclusion would follow from his account of them. But whether these spurs and aspirations exhaust the possibilities is still an open question. Perhaps children, as they grow up and receive a moral education that fits them for adulthood, develop capacities for acting on ideas and principles whose force as motives cannot be attributed to the operations of the super-ego. Developing such capacities would not, after all, be inconsistent with one's still being subject to the strictures of conscience or the pressures of high ideals; it would not, that is, be inconsistent with one's having a powerful super-ego. What it would mean, though, is that the operations of the super-ego were not the only sources of moral motives. Freud's theory excludes this possibility by assuming that moral development subsequent to the formation of a super-ego involves nothing more than enhancement and modification of this agency's operations. But this assumption is hardly uncontroversial. Freud's explanation, let us grant, is a complete and compelling account of the sources and workings of moral motives in young children. But whether it is a complete and compelling account of the sources and workings of moral motives in human beings, whatever their age or level of maturity, is another matter.

The moral development of a young child consists not only of internalizing parental figures but also of learning from direct instruction what sort of conduct is praiseworthy and what sort will not even be tolerated. In receiving this instruction the child learns the language of right and wrong, good and bad, responsibility and punishment, and so forth, as well as the specific norms and values that are communicated through the use of this language. And in learning the language, along with these norms and values, the child learns how to think systematically about right and wrong and how to deliberate to conclusions about what ought to be done. If the acquisition of these cognitive powers brings, as it should, a new understanding of oneself and one's relations with others, perhaps it brings new capacities for motivation as well. Or perhaps the self-understanding we develop in acquiring these cognitive powers requires that we understand what moves us in circumstances in which we act after deliberating to a conclusion about what ought to be done as thoughts whose motive force originates in our own affirmations and exertions.[16]

Freud, it is important to note, ignored this aspect of a child's moral education. Indeed, sometimes, it seems, he wrote as if the cultural transmission of norms and values were entirely a matter of each generation's acquiring the personality traits of previous generations through the unconscious processes of personality development that his theory described.[17] Of course, if judgements of right and wrong, good and bad, had motivational force solely in virtue of their being invested with instinctual force, as Freud believed, then the acquisition of the cognitive powers those judgements imply would affect only how that force was channelled and directed and not how it originated. In this case, it would make sense for someone whose interest was in the germination of moral agency and not in its flowering, who thought that the former and not the latter contained the ultimate explanation of the agency's activity, to ignore the way learning the language of morality and value increased a child's cognitive powers of moral judgement. But the belief that such judgement has motivational force solely in virtue of its being invested with instinctual force is not philosophically innocent. It implies a controversial thesis about the nature of moral judgement, a thesis that contradicts but does not refute rationalist theses about the nature of such judgement. In other words, Freud's explanation of the moral agency distinctive of human beings argues against doctrines of human exceptionalism only by assuming as a premiss a thesis that contradicts propositions about the nature of moral judgement on which rationalists traditionally based those doctrines.

Freud, of course, did not have a philosophical theory of moral judgement. He was not directly engaged in the modern debate about its nature. As a psychologist, however, he held views about voluntary action and human motivation that, though they may not have committed him to any recognized, affirmative position in this debate, did implicitly commit him to opposing a range of such positions. He held, in particular, the view that the springs of all voluntary actions were motives whose force originated in biologically basic instincts,[18] and the anti-rationalist commitment implicit in this view is unmistakable. Among other things, the view includes, as a special case, Freud's belief that the judgements of right and wrong, good and bad, have motivational force solely in virtue of their being invested with instinctual force. Thus it directly opposes the rationalist's thesis that one's understanding of the ideas of goodness and perfection and the principles of right and wrong alone give rise to the motivation to act on judgements of value and morality in which those ideas and principles are applied. Freud held this view about the instinctual origins of the springs of all voluntary action not because he had evidence to support it. Nor did he reach it from reflective considerations on the philosophical questions it raised. Rather, the view was a fixed point in his work. He used it as a guide to interpreting the observations he made and to constructing theoretical schemes that greatly increased the explanatory power of those interpretations. As a fixed point, however, its probative value – and thus the probative value of the explanations that proceed from it – is limited.

This limitation is itself instructive. Consider the conflict that arises when one realizes that the demands of one's conscience are excessive. On the one hand, one feels a need to obey these demands yet, on the other, one concludes, having recognized their unreasonableness, even arbitrariness, that one ought to resist them. One's judgement thus opposes the forces of one's super-ego. On Freud's theory, if this judgement comes from a greater understanding of reality – in this case, inner reality – and of the adjustments one must make to reduce its harshness and achieve some measure of happiness, as presumably it does, its motivational force is the force of the ego's initiative in negotiating peace among the id, super-ego and the requirements of reality.[19] The fixed point we have noted in his theory then requires that this force originate in some basic instinct, and Freud, as befits his genius, advanced a remarkably fertile hypothesis that explained the instinctual sources of the ego's initiative in such matters.[20] At the same time, nothing beyond the fixed point argues for applying this hypothesis to the example of a mature individual recognizing the irrationality of a felt need and judging, as a result, that it ought to be resisted. Nothing in the theory beyond its own anti-rationalist commitments, therefore, argues against a rationalist understanding of the conflict presented in this example.

Leaving these anti-rationalist commitments aside, we could instead explain the motivational force of the individual's judgement as the result of his deliberating from certain general values and principles the understanding of which he had acquired in developing his powers of practical reason. Accordingly, we would understand the conflict between the force of the individual's judgement and the force of his overbearing conscience as arguing against the view that the springs of all voluntary actions are motives whose force originates in biologically basic instincts. We would understand it, that is, as the rationalists understood the conflicts on which they based their objections to naturalistic theories of moral psychology. Thus, to the extent that the explanation is persuasive, it represents a forceful objection to Freud's theory. To the extent that it is persuasive, Freud's theory, like its predecessors, fails to answer satisfactorily the objections of the rationalist school.[21]

Notes

1. See Freud's 'An Outline of Psycho-Analysis', *The Standard Edition of the Complete Psychological Works of Sigmund Freud*, gen. ed. James Strachey (London: Hogarth Press, 1969), vol. 23, pp. 196–7.
2. *The Social Contract*, trans. Donald Cress (Indianapolis: Hackett Publishing Company, 1987), Book I, ch. VIII.
3. An important exception to this is Descartes, who both insisted on the essential unity of the mind and subscribed to doctrines of human exceptionalism. This position required that he exclude all mental

phenomena from the natural world and correspondingly deny that
beasts had minds. To simplify our discussion, I ignore this Cartesian
position. Its thesis about the mindlessness of beasts long ago doomed
it to the graveyard of dead philosophical views.

4. See, e.g., Thomas Reid, *Essays on the Active Powers of the Human Mind*,
    essay IV, ch. VI; and Immanuel Kant, *Critique of Practical Reason*,
    trans. L.W. Beck (Indianapolis: Bobbs-Merrill, 1956), p. 30.
5. See, e.g., 'The Ego and the Id', *Standard Edition*, vol. 19, pp. 13–15.
6. Using Freud's mature account is, admittedly, anachronistic. By the
    time Freud offered it, he had abandoned the second conception in
    favour of the three-fold conception that represented the mind as
    divided into Ego, Id and Super-ego. I use the mature account none
    the less because the exposition is much easier and more comprehen-
    sible. To present the earlier account, on which anxiety was a conse-
    quence rather than an initiator of repression, requires expounding
    Freud's views about transformations and distributions of libidinal
    energy, and this would make the exposition unnecessarily compli-
    cated. Nothing in the difference between these two accounts, as will
    be seen below, affects my argument.
7. See Freud's remarks on the 'automatism of the pleasure–pain prin-
    ciple' in 'New Introductory Lectures on Psycho-Analysis', *Standard
    Edition*, vol. 22, pp. 89–90.
8. Freud did not consistently use the same abbreviations for this sys-
    tem. Sometimes he used Cs., other times Pcpt-Cs. Sometimes he dis-
    tinguished a preconscious system Pcs. from Cs., other times he treated
    them as one system, using Cs. (Pcs.) to indicate the merger. See, e.g.,
    'The Unconscious', *Standard Edition*, vol. 14, passim; and vol. 19, pp.
    13–27.
9. Ibid., vol. 19, p. 28.
10. Ibid., p. 35. And also, 'Since we have come to assume a special agency
    in the ego, the super-ego, which represents demands of a restricting
    and rejecting character, we may say that repression is the work of
    this super-ego and that it is carried out by itself or by the ego in
    obedience to its orders'; vol. 22, p. 69. Cf. 'Inhibitions, Symptoms
    and Anxiety', vol. 20, p. 94.
11. Ibid., vol. 19, p. 36.
12. Ibid., vol. 22, p. 60.
13. Ibid., pp. 62–6.
14. See, e.g., Gerhardt Piers and Milton Singer, *Shame and Guilt: A psy-
    choanalytic and a cultural study* (Springfield, Ill.: Charles C. Thomas,
    1953), Part 1, ch. 3; and Richard Wollheim, *The Thread of Life* (Cam-
    bridge, Mass.: Harvard University Press, 1984), ch. 7.
15. For details of this explanation and a discussion of problems internal
    to Freud's exposition, see my 'Remarks on Some Difficulties in Freud's
    Theory of Moral Development', *International Review of Psycho-Analysis*
    11 (1984), pp. 207–25.
16. The possibility is contained in P.F. Strawson's distinction between
    participatory and objective standpoints and can be traced back to
    Kant's doctrine of the two standpoints, that of nature and that of

freedom. See Strawson, 'Freedom and Resentment', *Proceedings of the British Academy*, 48 (1962), pp. 1–25; and Kant, *Groundwork of the Metaphysics of Morals*, trans. H.J. Paton (New York: Harper Torchbook, 1964), pp. 124–6.

17. *Standard Edition*, vol. 22, pp. 66–8.
18. See 'Instincts and Their Vicissitudes', *Standard Edition*, vol. 14, pp. 118–20.
19. Ibid., vol. 22, pp. 75–8.
20. Ibid.
21. An earlier draft of this essay was discussed at the Claremont Graduate School's sixteenth annual conference on the philosophy of religion. I am grateful to the conference's participants and audience for their comments. I have benefited, in particular, from Ilham Dilman's comments in his paper and in conversation. I have made some revisions in response to them.

6

Psychoanalysis as Ultimate Explanation of Religion

İlham Dilman

FREUD'S CONCEPTION OF RELIGION
AND THE GOD HE REJECTS

I want to ask what psychoanalysis can make of religion and whether it can help a patient in his religious, spiritual problems. In Professor Phillips' words: can it regard gods or demons as ultimate – as 'last things'?[1]

Deigh points out, quite rightly, that Freud's view of ethics is on the whole negative. I shall put the sense in which this is so briefly and in my own words. Human beings in their very nature are selfish and aggressive; morality is a product of a culture that is alien to human nature and opposed to it. It is imposed on us in opposition to our nature. It has the advantage of making communal life and co-operation possible, but at a cost to the individual. Even when it is no longer externally imposed, it is still imposed on the individual by a part of him which sides with it: the super-ego. It is thus a force of repression and any belief to the contrary – that is, the idea that moral qualities are to be admired for what they are in themselves – a deception. For morality prevents us from being ourselves. Since, however, it is nevertheless beneficial in that it regulates human conduct in community life, the only way to be moral without self-deception is to see through the pretensions of morality and accept its strictures voluntarily. This, then, is an enlightened choice as opposed to a surrender.

Freud thus allows the possibility of being both moral and oneself at the same time. But he makes morality into something one at best tolerates. He can see nothing in its values – theoretically, not personally – to which one can give one's heart without being duped. I have argued elsewhere[2] that Melanie Klein and other psychoanalysts, some of them influenced by her writings, have broken part of this mould in which morality is regarded as alien to human nature and have argued that there are forms of morality which contain something much more positive than Freud was able to allow.

Freud's views on religion are in many ways similar to his views on morality, except that he does not find in religion even the re-deeming features he finds in morality. The most he can find there is that religious belief helps to 'make tolerable the helplessness of man'[3] and 'succeeds in saving many people from individual neuro-ses'.[4] Religions may have evolved from totemism to monotheism, Freud points out, but they remain rooted in infantile fears and needs. To hold religious beliefs is thus to be deceived in a double sense. It is to hold beliefs which at best cannot be substantiated; it is to give credence and allegiance to something for which there is no rational support. Second, it is to give in to wishful thinking and remain wedded to infantile fears and insecurities and to infantile ways of dealing with them. So if one is to grow up, shoulder re-sponsibility for one's life and be oneself, one has to see through one's religious beliefs, if one has any, and shed one's religion. There is no reason for reaching a willing accommodation with religion, as there is in the case of morality, for religion can only serve the irra-tional and infantile side of one's personality.

Thus the only kind of sense Freud can see in any religion is the kind he sees in the obsessional behaviour of his neurotic patients. When he speaks of the 'hidden significance of obsessive neurotic practices' he means their role in the individual's mental and emo-tional balance, maintained in the face of various psychological strains and stresses. They serve a purpose there, though they are otherwise a nuisance and an encumbrance. The aim of psychoanalytic treat-ment here is to make what constitutes the strains and stresses in question accessible to the patient, so that he can face them and work on them. When they are lessened he will be able to dispense with his neurotic obsessional acts and so be free of the handicap they constitute. They thus have a role, a purpose, in his mental economy; that is, in his ability to maintain a balance with a mini-mum degree of pain. But they have no sense or significance *in them-selves*. Similarly, Freud sees no sense in religious beliefs and practices which he compares with neurotic practices, speaking of religion as a mass neurosis, a 'universal obsessional neurosis'.[5] Their sense in religious terms for Freud is a cover-up. The difference between the two is that neuroses are individual elaborations whereas religions are cultural products. They are taken up by the individual because they respond to existing needs which are widely shared.

This is the general picture, and I see little point in elaborating on it. It follows that the ultimate explanations of the religious practices and beliefs, the religious fears, anxieties and self-criticisms of religious patients in analysis will be in non-religious terms – in terms of what they do for the patient, including what they help him avoid facing in himself, and so what they are a response to in him.

Now it is perfectly true that any part of the patient's conduct and beliefs, however genuine, can be so treated in analysis, and legitimately so. For instance, an analysand whose politeness is perfectly genuine may nevertheless help him avoid certain forms of confrontation with people in the face of which he may feel helpless. It may be important for the analysand to confront this helplessness in his analysis in order to work on what lies behind it and deal with it. When, therefore, his analyst points out that his politeness serves him to evade it he may think that his analyst is suggesting that his politeness is not genuine, that it is a defensive posture. But this need not be the case. He may be genuinely polite, yet his politeness may serve a purpose which is not *his* purpose, not even unconsciously, though he benefits from it in terms of his mental economy. In such a case he will not lose his politeness in analysis; all he will lose will be what makes him lack confidence in standing up for what he believes in certain circumstances. Indeed, he will now be able to do so firmly, straightforwardly, but still with politeness.

The trouble with the patient's religious convictions and the actions which come from them is that no such possibility exists for them in Freud's view. They *cannot* be genuine without the analysand being duped. So, in the course of an analysis that is progressing, they have to be analysed away – that is, given Freud's conceptual orientation. My question is whether there is something about psychoanalysis, which after all is Freud's brainchild, which makes this impossible. I shall argue for a negative answer: that is, that psychoanalysis does not have to analyse away a patient's religious beliefs – not when they are genuine.

Before doing so, however, let me point out by way of a relative mitigation that there is this much truth in what Freud says about religious belief. What he says does not have to be true. On that score he is wrong and displays a mind closed to the possibilities of sense in religions. Indeed, he is blinded by his professional preoccupations to what religions are in their variety, to the way they represent and emphasize the significance of, express and enable believers to respond to what is important to them as human beings in the life of their culture. This said, there is an element of truth in what he says: people do give their allegiances to their religion – say, to Christianity – out of non-religious needs. It is well known in Christianity that many people's attachment to its beliefs have their source, at least partly, in the compensations and consolations they find there – very much as Freud describes these. It is also true that for some people the objects of their religious beliefs become a focus for their infantile feelings and attitudes.

Many recognize this fact. Bonhoeffer, for instance, responds to it as follows: 'The only way to be honest is to recognize that we have to live in the world even if God is not "there". Like children outgrowing the secure religious, moral and intellectual framework of the home, in which "Daddy" is always there in the background, "God is teaching us that we must live as men who can get along very well without him".'[6] Freud teaches us that 'abandoning religion must take place with the fateful inexorability of a process of growth'.[7]

The religion to be abandoned is the one Bonhoeffer also rejects: 'we have to live in the world even if God is not "there".' Simone Weil puts this by saying that the God she believes in manifests Himself in the world by His absence. Freud's God encourages infantile dependence; that is why Freud thinks that such a God must be abandoned if people are to grow up. But Bonhoeffer's and Simone Weil's God cannot be faulted in this way. The dependence which the believer in such a God accepts as part of his belief has nothing infantile about it. It is interesting to note that Freud's prejudice is matched in those who think that psychoanalytic therapy encourages a childish attitude in the patient and that the mature attitude towards one's problems is to deal with them oneself *instead* of seeking psychoanalytic help. What such a view fails to recognize is that what the analyst helps the patient to learn in analysis is precisely to shoulder responsibility for his problems. Thus those who take such a view of psychoanalytic therapy are as blind to the possibilities within it as Freud was to the possibilities within Christianity.

I am suggesting that Freud's interest in the 'pathological' in a broad sense made him see it where it exists unseen, but equally where it does not exist. His perception was Janus-faced; he saw what others missed, but it made him lose sight of distinctions which in his position it was important for him to be sensitive to.

I said that there is an element of truth in Freud's view of religion. We could say that he was rejecting a certain view of Christianity, on personal as well as intellectual grounds, without however being able to see the possibility of alternative views to which his objections might not have applied. He was rejecting a scientific or metaphysical view of Christianity, at least partly on intellectual grounds. He was rejecting a religion of compensation and consolation and advocated the courage to face reality without reliance on crutches. He did not see that Christianity does not have to be opposed to his values – at any rate not to all of them. I should like to note in this connection Freud's ideal of independence, towards which he believed psychoanalysis must work, was in part itself a reaction-formation to the kind of dependence he disliked. It has given way for many analysts to what Fairbairn[8] calls 'mature dependence'. This is obviously more in tune with the Christian belief of our dependence on God.

AN ALTERNATIVE CONCEPTION BY A
PSYCHOANALYST: RYCROFT'S GOD

I now turn to the question of whether psychoanalysis has to remain wedded to Freud's view and estimation of religion: religious belief and religious truth. My answer is that it does not, and various writers have tried to disengage it from those views. I want to consider one such attempt in a paper by Charles Rycroft.[9] I shall take what he says as my starting point.

Rycroft was originally given the title 'The God I Want'. He explains that in these words he was invited to speak about the God he can make sense of, give his heart to, believe in, and thus to speak *personally* – to speak for himself as a person who has been trained as a psychoanalyst. In this sense, we should recall, there was no God that Freud wanted, since the only God he could think of was one from which he turned away in disdain. Rycroft says: 'the God I want will have to be someone who never came into Freud's field of vision – at least when he was writing about religion'.[10] 'I do not want Him as a father-figure [he writes], nor as a mother-figure. . . . And even if I did want a God who restored me to childhood, my professional conscience would not allow me to endorse such a wish'.[11] On this point Rycroft is in moral agreement with Freud.

Rycroft also says: 'I do not want Him to explain the universe for me or to invoke Him as a First Cause or Prime Mover . . . I do not . . . want a God who will provide me with a cosmology, and I am, therefore, dispensing with Him in the role for which until recently he was most often wanted'.[12] Rycroft takes 'cosmology' in the sense in which the cosmology of Christianity in the Middle Ages has since been superseded by scientific astronomy. 'In the cosmological sense God is, to my mind, dead'.[13] But this is not the only sense in which some of the claims Rycroft has in mind can be understood. For instance, understood in a spiritual sense, there need be no conflict between the claim that God created the universe and the so-called big bang theory of the universe. It is clear that Rycroft here is rejecting a metaphysical conception of God.

So far what Rycroft says is negative: 'the God I do not want'. His positive statements are, to my mind, too general and ambiguous. The God they portray is rather pale; his features are too general to be able to sustain the depth of spirituality of which the Christian God can be the focus. Still, I think we can agree on this much, that Rycroft is looking for Him in the right direction in so far as it is one which is diametrically opposed to the direction in which Freud found the God he rejected. What he says is that belief in God can be an 'affirmation of love' and he identifies the God he wants with love.

Such a God is not an object, in the widest sense of the term, nor is He a foil for the projection of the believer's fears and wishes. He does not offer consolation for the believer's weaknesses or compensation for his pains and frustrations. Rycroft sees a certain parallel between the idea of God as an object, a God whose attributes are the properties of such an object, and the ideas of the mind as a substance and of Freud's unconscious as a region in that substance. In such a conception the unconscious is invested with causal powers whose operations bypass the individual as an 'intentional agent'. 'There is . . . a growing body of literature which suggests that there may be something intrinsically paradoxical about the enterprise of applying the scientific method to human beings . . . and that the point of psycho-analysis may lie not in its capacity to elucidate the causes of human behaviour but in making sense of it.'[14] This is a point he has developed in a paper entitled 'Causes and Meaning'.[15] In the present paper he suggests, similarly, that the existence of God is not, or at any rate need not be, a hypothesis about the existence of an object for the believer, one that is causally responsible for what befalls us as well as everything else we find in life.

Rather, a belief in God, at least the one that makes sense to him, helps the believer to make *sense* of life – of what is to be met there, of the pains, frustrations and deprivations to be found there, of the good and evil that is part of that life which ends in death – a sense, not an explanation, one that calls for a certain kind of *response*.

Rycroft does not elucidate the character of the response, but he says that it comes from that side of the believer which gives him the capacity to give himself to others, to attend to them in their distress, to forgive them their trespasses, to share their joys in gladness. For belief in his God, he says, is the affirmation of just such a love. When this kind of religious belief in someone in analysis is genuine, he says, it is not subject to analysis, for there is nothing further about it which can be analysed. It is an expression of the kind of love it affirms having become part of the person, of his having made it his own. In such a case the love in question does not exist in dissociation from the person's will, it is not in conflict with any egocentric side to him, it is not used to stave off anything unwelcome. In other words, there is no inner division within the person to be made accessible through analysis for it to be healed by inner work so the analysand can come to greater wholeness.

Let me note, in passing, the parallel between this and what Melanie Klein says about the fate of the Freudian super-ego in a successful analysis. When the patient's morality has its source in the super-ego it is subject to analysis. For, she agrees with Freud, the super-ego is a part of the self divided from the rest and standing in the way of its autonomy. When, however, the patient makes his morality his own the super-ego changes into a 'genuine conscience' and the patient himself changes in the process, attaining greater wholeness in himself. There is then nothing further for the analysis to say about it.

The kind of religious belief which Rycroft tells us he can make sense of is an expression of such wholeness, because the kind of love of which it is an affirmation, when it is genuine, is the very *antithesis* of what turns a person on himself, puts him at the centre of his considerations, eclipsing from him other people's full reality. It is in just the kind of engagements which such love makes possible that the believer finds a meaning in life which is independent of his own successes and failures. It is precisely this capacity for love that enables him to outgrow what is egocentric in him and thus to find greater wholeness.

Rycroft compares Freud's God, whose attributes are what the

believer *projects* onto him, with the psychoanalyst as a transference figure in analysis. Projection is a form of dissociation, defensive in character: the patient externalizes what belongs to him and relinquishes responsibility for it. He both expects everything from such a figure and also feels himself under its power and so fears it. Analysts are familiar with this attitude towards themselves in their patients. Rycroft contrasts a God who is the focus of the believer's projections with a God belief in whom is an 'affirmation of love', so that one who believes in Him is, in his belief, at one with himself in the kind of love his God stands for. Since in this oneness the believer finds wholeness, Rycroft says that 'integrity, wholeness, health and insight . . . may be recovered either by psychoanalysis or by communion with God'.[16] By *health* he means what results from the healing of splits or divisions that are endemic to a person's very mode of being. The *insight* of which he speaks is, I think, the kind of knowing of what matters to one, and so of what to do in situations which pose problems for one, a knowing of what to make of things which affect one personally, of how to respond to them. It is a form of knowing which involves a person in his wholeness and which cannot be separated from the person. As such it belongs to his affective orientation. Rycroft contrasts it with intellectual apprehension and scientific knowledge.

He speaks of the language of religion as 'the subjective, metaphorical language of insight' and contrasts it with what he calls 'the objective language we use when dealing with the impersonal'. He does not say much to clarify this contrast, but what I can extract from what he says comes to the following. In its everyday sense *insight* is not confined to religion or psychology. It means grasping a truth directly, cutting through what commonly blurs, diffuses or deflects thought. 'Metaphorical' is not, I think, the word Rycroft wants for the language that conveys the kind of insight he has in mind. For what is expressed in metaphors can be expressed in literal terms. Some philosophers and theologians who, like Rycroft, thought of religious language as metaphorical wanted, in the name of clarity and directness, to replace metaphor with literal speech and ended with an attenuated sense of what is expressed in that language. I shall argue in the following section that Rycroft's account of the God he wants suffers from this kind of attenuation. Such 'demythologizing', as it has been called, is as unfeasible in religion as it is in poetry. What is needed for those for whom the language in question poses problems is *clarification*. Its equivalent in the case of poetry is literary criticism. What Rycroft seems to have in mind when he characterizes the language of religion as 'metaphorical' is precisely the parallel he finds between religious language and the language of literature: the way each speaks about life and the kind of perspective it conveys which people can take into their lives.

The word 'subjective', which others have used in this connection like Rycroft, is equally misleading. It suggests a kind of free for all in which anyone can understand what he likes. What I think Rycroft wishes to convey is that the assent to what is true here, in the insight which one comes to, must come from the person. In the case of scientific truth a person properly puts his feelings aside as irrelevant. Reason, in the sense of what counts as good reason here, and evidence, override the person. *Anyone* who understands what is in question has to go along with it. Such reason is *impersonal*, it bypasses the person so that assent to the truth is dictated by the object. Hence the term 'objectivity' used in connection with science and the kind of knowledge that belongs to it. Indeed, there is a sense in which the objective person does not affirm the truth; he simply puts himself at the disposal of what is impersonal, namely reason and evidence. The person who does so where life, art, morality and religion are concerned has no insight and simply conveys what is second-hand. Nietzsche describes him as 'the objective man' to which George Eliot's Casaubon constitutes a very good example. As his wife Dorothea is to discover to her great disappointment, the wisdom she thought he had is a sham, and he has nothing to give or share with her.

It is in this sense that religious, in the sense of spiritual, truths are *personal*. I think 'personal' is a less misleading term than 'subjective'. One who is detached, and in that sense takes an objective stance, cannot have access to the wisdom or insight one can find in it. Here 'whether I like it or not what it says is true' is an evasion. If my belief is a delusion or my lack of belief is a form of blindness, there can be no removal of the blindness or delusion without my changing *in myself*. What leads you to assent to a particular religious belief may be perfectly clear to me intellectually; but unless it engages me *in myself* the way it engages you, and no doubt others as well, I cannot give my assent to it, I cannot in all honesty call it 'true'.

Assent to religious truth is thus not a matter of the intellect alone. Here the intellect has to be part of the person, that is to be at one with and work through his feelings – feelings he has made his own. He cannot subordinate himself, his feelings, to the intellect, as in the sciences. Such subordination in one's responses to life would amount to a form of dissociation – to be noticed particularly in academic circles where the intellect is overvalued. T.S. Eliot[17] praised the metaphysical poets, of which John Donne is one, by saying that they had their intellect in their fingertips. In other words, their intellect was accessible to them even when they wrote about matters of passion and sensuality; it was not dissociated from their sensibility. Such a dissociation would have left their sensibility impoverished, and their response, when they brought in the intellect, would have been 'cerebral' or 'mental' in the sense in which D.H. Lawrence uses these terms. In either case it would have been fatal to their poetry.

Rycroft also mentions T.S. Eliot and argues that a religion that is in competition with the sciences, and so emulates them, encourages a dissociated conception of God. So he says that the God of such a religion is not the kind of God he personally wants. He does not want such a God for others either. He thus rejects a *rationalist* conception of God for encouraging such a dissociation: 'I am placing God in the realm of feelings', and thus in the realm of the personal.[18] Only such a God engages the believer as a whole.

CRITIQUE OF RYCROFT: THE PSYCHOLOGICAL AND THE INDIVIDUAL

I have tried to articulate the kind of conception of God Rycroft develops when conveying what kind of God he can make sense of personally, as someone who has been trained as a psychoanalyst – and that means as someone who has changed in himself in the course of a personal analysis and has learned from its insights. I have tried to make the best of what I have found in what he says, reading between the lines in the light of my knowledge of psychoanalysis and my acquaintance with the writings of such analysts as Melanie Klein, Winnicott and others who have developed Freud's work and tried to rectify its various faults.

It is clear that the God Rycroft wants and speaks about is, or at any rate is meant to be, a *spiritual* as opposed to a *metaphysical* God. It is further also clear that his opposition to a metaphysical God is both conceptual and spiritual, and also, he says more than once, professional – and I take it he means psychological. He says, 'the God I want would not ordinarily be recognised as one; or, to put it . . . more honestly, I do not want a God in any sense in which that word is ordinarily understood.'[19] This, of course, depends on what is meant by 'ordinary' and on how what anyone's understanding amounts to is assessed. Here I remember some words by Simone Weil to the effect that if you want to know what kind of God, say a judge, believes in, look at the words he speaks when he sentences a criminal in court, not at what he says in church. Rycroft should be sympathetic to these words. He goes on: 'some kinds of God have become unavailable to me, since my professional training and conscience would compel me to interpret them as wish-fulfilling illusions'.[20] A God who guarantees that if one is a good boy all one's sufferings will be compensated and all one's good deeds will be rewarded at some future date would be an example. Rycroft is at one with Freud about the kind of God he rejects.

I want to return, briefly, to the question why Rycroft thinks that the God he wants 'would not ordinarily be recognized as one'. Partly, I think, because Rycroft is unable to make any sense, except a metaphysical one, of the theological claims made about God, His attributes and what he has in store for the good and the bad. As such he rejects them. Consequently, what he is left with does not seem to him to agree with the God ordinary Christians believe in as described in the traditional terms of Christian theology. This is one reason. But, in any case, there is indeed a natural tendency to give a metaphysical twist to the sense of these traditional terms, just as there is a natural tendency to think of man's soul as a little invisible bird within, which will be released and fly away into another world at death.

Such metaphysical conceptions which, as Wittgenstein said, arise when language is like an engine idling, can and I suspect have in fact become part of a tradition shaping ordinary religious conscious-ness in Christianity. I mean, they assume a life of their own and give Christianity a worldly twist. It is, I think, primarily from this *worldly* strand in Christianity that Rycroft tries to detach his con-ception of God and the God he wants. It is *this* worldly God, in metaphysical clothing, which it seems many Christians believe in, that Rycroft has in mind when he speaks of the sense in which God is 'ordinarily' understood by Christians.

What about Rycroft's God? How far does Rycroft manage to put Him in a pivotal position in a spiritual life? After all, someone may sincerely say that his God is love and this may not be very different, in logic, from saying of someone that his God is power or money, in the sense that he attaches supreme importance to these things, indeed worships them in the way he lives. This is hardly what one would call a religious conception of God – not even in a worldly sense. Does he belong with people who erect an altar to power, surround it with certain rituals, have a special language in which it is given new connections and assumes a particular significance in the light of these connections? Similarly for love. Anyway, the question is, what kind of love?

To be fair to Rycroft, when he speaks of love and its affirmation, he needs to be understood in a context, by now well known in psychoanalysis, where human love is seen as subject to growth in depth and quality with the development of the individual, and where its 'mature' varieties are explicitly connected with such moral notions as remorse, forgiveness and gratitude. In what I have said I have myself taken this as understood and have made it explicit where it is implicit in what Rycroft says. I have in fact connected mature love with growth out of egocentricity. But what is the notion of 'maturity' involved here? As Rycroft points out, 'psychoanalysts do not always agree as to what is meant by maturity'.[21] At any rate until that is made clear and more substance is given to the love affirmed by indicating the position the person affirming it gives it in his life and the connections it assumes there, its spiritual character is bound to remain vague. Does the respect which belongs to it give the life of those towards whom it is directed a sacred character? After all, respect on its own, though a moral notion, is not a religious concept as such. This applies equally to the things with which Rycroft connects love, if only implicitly: gratitude, forgiveness and the rest. More is needed to turn it into a religious notion and to make its affirmation into a religious belief.

Rycroft has a sympathetic critic in me. For I am prepared to agree that a particular individual who does not speak the language of God, of the God of Christ, may nevertheless, in the course of his life and unknown to him as such, have gone through the fire of the love of God – just such a God. In him the expression and affirmation, in particular contexts, of a love that can be seen by others to shine in its purity, may well amount to, for those who speak the language of Christianity, a love of and belief in God. He can, that is, be attributed such a belief, but only by those who speak the language in question. It is in that language that such a belief and its object is identified. It is from such a language that Rycroft stands too much at a distance when portraying the God he wants. No wonder he says that his God is very different from the Christian God as *ordinarily* understood. In trying to distance himself from that language as 'ordinarily understood' he distances himself from that language altogether and so loses sight of the connections it makes between the love affirmed and various things in the life of the culture to which the person affirming it belongs – seen from a particular perspective.

The result is that he finds himself confined to express these connections, not surprisingly, in psychological terms. We have already seen that he likens the religion he can make sense of to psychoanalysis: in its language, its use of myths, in its placing of the individual at the centre of its concern. It could be said that religion is palatable to him through the insights of psychoanalysis. Thus he says, for instance, that the God he wants, both for himself and for others, is one who would annul the dissociation of sensibility which a rationalist conception of God accentuates – annuls it by an act of synthesis.[22] He seems to value and want it for its therapeutic and, perhaps, also its moral character. He writes, we have seen, that 'integrity, wholeness, health and insight . . . may be recovered, either by psycho-analysis or by communion with God'.[23] No doubt, this is true. But in psychoanalysis wholeness is, or at any rate may be, the object of the enterprise. In religion that is not so, and the wholeness which the believer finds there is a bonus. Perhaps there is a sense in which this is also true in psychoanalysis. For one of the lessons which the analysand may learn in his analysis is that wholeness, like happiness, cannot be sought directly. Having learned this lesson the analysand may be able to give himself to his analysis unconditionally and so begin to move towards the wholeness which has so far eluded him. Nevertheless there is still a sense in which the analysand may be said to be seeking the kind of wholeness which is at least one of the objects of the therapy.

In any case, is spiritual wholeness the same as the wholeness sought in therapy? Rycroft himself is uneasy about the identification of the one with the other. He writes that he may have laid himself open to the charge that in what he says he suggests that 'the religious quest can be restated in terms of health, depression and the manic denial of depression'.[24] Such an accusation would, I think, be unfair. But it still remains true that he tends to run together the spiritual and the psychological. 'Health, which is both a medical and a religious concept may be defined in terms of . . . the attainment of an inner state of wholeness'.[25]

I agree that 'health' is a normative concept in both connections, but that in itself does not make the medical and the religious concept of health the same. At most one can say that just as, as the saying goes, a healthy mind can only be found or, perhaps, is normally to be found, in a healthy body, so similarly, spiritual health does not exist entirely in separation from mental or psychological health. At any rate I am inclined to think that although they are not identical, the spiritual does not exist in limbo from the psychological; they interpenetrate one another.

Plato identifies spiritual health with goodness, and goodness cannot be explained in psychological terms without destroying it or giving it a corrupt aspect. What I mean is that there cannot be a psychological answer to the question, 'what makes him good?' or 'why is he good?' For if one thinks – as indeed Freud did – that goodness is something towards which a person's psychology disposes him, then one downgrades it, one turns it into something else. If I may put it like this: what makes a person good is the goodness in him or the goodness to which he comes in his development as an individual. What makes him good is what the goodness that finds expression in his life and actions means to him. This is, of course, another way of saying that his goodness, when it is genuine, can have no psychological explanation. One may even say that it is the way that love, the concern and compassion he feels for others, work in his life. We may say that it is this that makes him good. But then there is no psychological question to be answered as to what makes him compassionate or what gives him a loving nature. At most, if it is something to which he has come, we can say how he has come to it.

It still remains true, however, that to attain goodness a man must overcome certain psychological barriers in himself and in doing so turn around in himself. A convincing portrait of goodness in a person needs to be psychologically convincing as well. This is something any great novelist knows. Some people have argued, for instance, that in *The Idiot* Dostoyevsky has not succeeded in giving a convincing portrait of goodness or saintliness in his portrayal of Prince Myshkin. A convincing portrait of goodness would have to be in terms of a psychology that leaves the good man open to goodness. In such a portrait we have to see a psychology that does not stand in the way of goodness engaging him at the deepest level, one which leaves him free to respond in ways that are an expression of goodness. The freedom which his psychology thus gives or allows him does not, of course, explain his goodness. Otherwise it would not be *he* who is good; whatever he would be as a result would not be genuine goodness. If he is genuinely good, that goodness must come from *him*, not from his psychology.

For Plato[26] a person who is alienated from goodness by the evil he has done, or by his indifference, lacks spiritual health. I have argued elsewhere[27] that the remorse such a person feels in the first case is an expression of self-division. This is not controversial. But I have also argued that the indifferent man for whom goodness holds no attraction and means nothing is someone who in his egocentricity has not come to himself. Although he may not be divided in himself, he lacks the kind of wholeness which comes from the kind of engagement with life, and this involves other people in one way or another, which the egocentricity of evil or of indifference to goodness prevents. If I am right (and this is the subject of an ongoing controversy between Professor Phillips and myself[28] to which he will soon receive a new contribution from me), then the link between Plato's notion of spiritual health and Rycroft's notion of psychological wholeness is closer than we may at first think. Indeed, it may turn out that the idea that a patient's spiritual health is of no concern to his analyst, since it falls outside the province of psychoanalytic therapy, conceived of on a medical or quasi-medical model, is a misconception.

PSYCHOANALYSIS, RELIGION AND THE INDIVIDUAL

I shall return to this question presently. Rycroft agrees with what I said about the way goodness and the spiritual lies beyond psychological explanation. He says that the God he wants 'must be immune to interpretation' – that is, to psychoanalytic interpretation. He says that such a God 'cannot be one who either recreates for me the blissful security of childhood or who compensates me for the bliss which I perhaps never enjoyed'.[29] The ideas that all religious beliefs are interpretable, that they are the product of wishful thinking, etc., that the super-ego is the most one can find of 'what people call the "higher" things of human life',[30] that all thinking is rationalization, all love is transference, belong to the excesses of Freudian thinking. None of these is an integral part of the psychoanalytical framework. I have called them 'philosophical froth'. This is not to deny that Freud advanced these ideas in perfect seriousness. Many psychoanalysts after him have taken them seriously enough to wish to try to rectify Freud's excesses while remaining faithful to his insights. They have also added their own insights to those of Freud while developing psychoanalytical thinking. Rycroft is one such psychoanalyst.

Thus where a patient's religious beliefs are sincere and genuine, I do not see what the purpose of psychoanalysing them would be. I do not believe that an analyst whose mind is free from prejudice and indoctrination would attempt to do so. Someone will tell me, 'But psychoanalytic training is a form of indoctrination, what else can it be, it is bound to stand in the way of the development of wisdom.' I would remind him that the same has been said of religious training. Let us suppose that a genuinely religious patient has religious problems and he brings them to analysis. A psychoanalyst to whom the religious ideas of the patient are alien and who cannot sympathetically enter into his problems obviously cannot help the patient. If he is wise, he would have the good sense to appreciate this and stand aside as far as those problems are concerned.

This is not to say that there may not be room for psychoanalytical work in investigating the psychological surroundings of these problems. Imagine a similar situation with a patient who has genuinely philosophical problems: Why does he shilly-shally with them so? Why does he evade getting down to serious philosophical work on them, dramatizing his difficulties? A person may in his work face deep philosophical problems which are difficult to resolve. The way he stays with them, the way they absorb and trouble him, may be a measure of his seriousness. But, in someone else, what appear to be such seriousness may, on closer acquaintance, turn out to be something quite different. He may be an 'eternal student' with his problems, capitalizing on them by keeping them alive. This could be true even when he is genuinely interested in the matters that give rise to these problems. I give this as one example of the intermix between the genuine and the 'pathological'.

To return to the patient with genuine religious problems. If his analyst can enter into them, he can be of help in discussing them with his patient in the way that a wise counsellor would. It would be enough for him to listen to and give the patient his full attention as the patient talks. It is sometimes forgotten that listening, what I am inclined to call 'active listening', that is, listening to which the analyst puts himself in the attention he gives to his patient, constitutes a good part of psychoanalytic therapy. The analyst intervenes with interpretations generally when the patient is not himself in what he says, hides something or is deceiving himself in what he says. In the case of the patient who talks about his religious problems, even where he is perfectly genuine in his religious beliefs, other aspects of his personality do not have to be excluded from the discussion or analysis. For, as I said, they may turn out to have a bearing on his religious problems.

Besides, a person's religious and moral beliefs, when they are genuine, like his love for someone when it is sincere, come from him, they are 'his' in the strong sense of that term. I mean they do not just happen to be what he believes because he was brought up that way; he has made them his own. I do not mean anything necessarily dramatic by this: in the process of his growth and development they have become his. In them his whole way of being comes to be involved. Why should we rule out *clarifying* what his love of God or his love of his friend or lover engages in him, what part of himself he gives to the loved one, with what part of himself he responds to what concerns him? Such clarification is not something alien to analysis and may even deepen the patient's convictions and feelings. It may, of course, reveal that things are not quite what they seem, and then the scrutiny may open up problems for the patient from a consideration of which he may move one way or another in himself, changing in one direction or another.

I want to return now to a question I wanted to say more about at the end of the previous section. Rycroft writes: 'Those who have had a religious upbringing will tend to affirm [their love] in religious terms, while those who have had a secular upbringing will do so in secular terms, but I doubt whether those who affirm in one mode differ essentially from those who do so in the other'.[31] Here Rycroft is not taking sufficiently seriously the difference which the language one speaks makes to the way one sees things, to the significance they assume for one, and so to one's problems. He does not take sufficiently seriously the difference it makes to the feelings one can express in that language and so to the feelings one is capable of expressing in situations to the significance of which it contributes or which it shapes in the perspective it gives us on them. I have already said that whether the love someone affirms has a spiritual role in a person's life shows in how he speaks about things.

This said, it is, of course, possible for someone who has had a secular upbringing to have a love in him which makes such a difference to his responses to people and give him such an outlook on things that it amounts to what a Christian may call a love of God. The problems such a person may meet when he faces the ingratitude and even betrayal of those he loves and has made sacrifices for, or the suffering and death of loved ones, however he expresses himself, are spiritual problems. He may, for instance, feel discouraged, hurt, feel on the verge of losing hope and giving up. His very vision of things may start tottering, his belief in goodness may begin losing certainty. He may wonder whether he has been a fool.

Some people will speak of these as 'psychological problems'. A psychoanalyst may classify them as such and see them as emanating from 'depression'. Yet there may be a close affinity in what he has to say about them and what a deeply religious person does. I was first struck by this a great many years ago when in *The Brothers Karamazov*[32] I was reading a chapter in which Father Zossima was exercising his healing powers. Some peasant women who understood the language of faith had come to see him. One of them – I am speaking from memory – had lost her little boy and her life had come to a standstill. Father Zossima spoke to her only a few words that addressed her emotions and went right to the root of her problem. He told her to cry and not be consoled, but to remember that her little boy was in heaven with the angels. He touched and blessed her and she, thanking him, left greatly calmed.

With his words Father Zossima led her to a position, in terms of the perspective of her feelings, to which someone else in a similar situation may be led, or herself come to, in a personal analysis. 'Do not be consoled' here means 'Do not let anything – any consideration – stop you grieving or hurry you. Grieve and be patient.' 'Your little boy is in heaven with the angels' is meant to convey to her that though he has been wrenched from and taken outside her physical reach, he is being cared for, he has not been abandoned. In terms of her feelings he is not outside the reach of her care. She can think of him as flourishing; what she wants for him is being granted. 'You feel you have lost a piece of your flesh, of yourself, of your life; but you are still connected. In your grieving you think of him with love. In that love he will be restored to you: he will continue to live in your feelings. Though you will always continue to miss him you will find the wholeness you had with him and lost with his death. At present you feel you have nothing and no one to give of yourself to; but in time when you can think of your boy as well again, when your love will have healed him in your feelings, you will find other things in life to engage your love, to give yourself to.

Indeed, in that engagement you will be faithful to your boy, faithful in your very love for him. In this way you will find peace and your life will begin to move again. But now stay with your pain, it is the pain of love, and keep faith with your grief in patience.'

I have put in secular terms and without any psychoanalytic jargon what Father Zossima conveys to the peasant woman in the language of her faith and what a patient in a similar situation may find out in her personal analysis with a Kleinian psychoanalyst. I quoted Rycroft's words: 'those who have had a religious upbringing will tend to affirm [their love] in religious terms, while those who have had a secular upbringing will do so in secular terms', but what they express comes to the same thing. I was critical: not any such affirmation amounts to a belief in a spiritual God, and the language of religion makes a difference to the love that a person comes to in his life. On the other hand, there is something right in what Rycroft says. Grief at the loss of a loved one is a universal phenomenon and the insight which Christianity brings to it is not the unique possession of Christianity. One finds it in what psychoanalysts have written about grief, and a patient can come to it in his analysis.

Let me make it perfectly clear that I was not suggesting, in secular terms, an analysis of the religious terms used by Father Zossima in what he said to the peasant woman – an analysis of the language of heaven and the angels. These terms have a great many connections in the language of Christianity and Father Zossima relied on only a few of these in what he said to the woman whose grief he addressed. I was only suggesting what they convey in that limited context. I agree with Rycroft that in such a particular context the insight conveyed by them is not confined to Christianity.

This is, of course, very far from Freud's view that the language of religion is the language of a mass illusion, one in which people are deceived – deceived about life or the world and deceived in and about themselves.

CONCLUSION: RELIGIONS AS PRODUCTS OF HUMAN CULTURE

The question put to the Claremont Conference on the Philosophy of Religion, as I understand it, is: Are psychoanalysis and religion incompatible? Can a psychoanalyst leave his patient's religious beliefs, when they are genuine and sincere, alone? Is there anything about psychoanalysis that would prevent the psychoanalyst from understanding his patient's religious beliefs and religious problems in their own terms. *Ultimately*, do they have to be something else for him?

My answer to this question in its final version has been: for Freud they have to be something else in their *final* analysis, but not for psychoanalysis. I have tried to indicate why this had to be so for Freud and why it doesn't have to be so for psychoanalysis. I have tried to bring this out through a consideration of a paper by Rycroft, a recent psychoanalyst, imaginative and independent in his views. My consideration has been at once sympathetic and critical. In this paper he does not speak about religions in the plural, but about the God he can make sense of in the religion in which he has been brought up, namely Christianity. The religion he speaks about is above all a spiritual religion and he finds no incompatibility between belief in such a religion and the psychoanalytic investigation of his personality on the part of the believer. Indeed, he finds a close parallel between the kind of insight a person can come to in religious belief and in psychoanalysis. I have been concerned to make up my mind about how far he is right.

At the beginning of this paper I subdivided the question about the *ultimate explanation* of religion in psychoanalysis into two: (1) that of a patient's or analysand's religious beliefs, and (2) those of a particular religion. I have not discussed the second question. The beliefs of a religion belong to a particular culture. Freud recognizes this and still advances a *psychological* explanation for their existence and their content. Rycroft does not touch on this question. But obviously the *clarification* of the content of the beliefs of a religion, where they raise problems of understanding, belongs to philosophy and calls for a particular kind of sympathy and imagination. Even then there are additional problems: What are we to take to be the content of these beliefs? As held by *whom*? For Christians do not agree among themselves, and the differences between them are not wholly differences in what they *say*, that is, differences in the accounts they give of their beliefs. Where are we to look for what may be called the tradition when those who belong to it disagree among themselves? I think the best thing to do is to note the various possibilities within the tradition, or at any rate those that interest one, and to consider them individually. This comes nearest to what I have done.

Returning to the question of explanation, I said that where individual beliefs are genuine there can be no psychological explanation of them. One can, of course, ask: how has some particular person come to hold these beliefs? But, obviously, there must be a special context for this question to make sense: for instance, how did he come to hold these beliefs when he has had a specifically secular upbringing? Sometimes the answer may be psychologically relevant; it may throw light on the person's psychology.

Similarly for the cultural question: why did the people of Israel come to hold such-and-such religious beliefs? Why has this kind of religion developed at such-and-such a time among these people? One can ask a similar question about psychoanalysis too: why did psychoanalysis develop in Vienna at the turn of the century? These are historical questions about cultural developments. But the answer to them, whatever it may be, in no way undermines the worth of the ideas in question or the truth which people find in the beliefs they acquire within the framework of these ideas.

To touch, finally, on an idea which engenders much misunderstanding and raises people's hackles. To say that any particular God, any God whom anyone believes in, belongs to a religion, and any religion belongs to or is part of a culture and, in that sense, a product of culture and, therefore, of complex historical, sociological and physico-geographical circumstances, is not to say that God is man-made; that is, is a human creation. It is not to say that the reality of the God, for instance, sincere Christians believe in is an illusion, as Freud says for similar reasons.

God is no more an invention than our language and our moral values are. The world in which we live, the human world, is to a large extent the product of the language we speak, and the realities that form part of this world, including the reality of physical things and phenomena, are internal to this language. This does not mean that physical things do not exist independently of us, the speakers of that language. Our language certainly exists independently of the individuals who speak it. Far from our language, including the religious language or languages which people speak, being an invention of those who speak it, it is we, its speakers, who are what we are, human beings, in the language we speak, and we find our individuality in that language. The reality of God and of particular moral values, for those who believe in them, is radically different from the reality of physical things. But this is not to say that these things are in any sense less real, that their reality is a fiction or an illusion.

In any case I have not affirmed or denied the reality of any God here. I said that the God of a particular religion has reality for those who belong to that religion and believe in him. It is not an illusion, as Freud claims. In a similar vein I said that there are many different gods. This in no way contradicts the Christian or Muslim who says, 'There is only one God.' The statement 'there are many gods' is what one may call an *observation statement* which I make as a philosopher. A sociologist or anthropologist could have made the same statement. It has an 'objective status' in the sense I have explained. In contrast, 'there is only one God', is a *personal statement*, a 'confession', made from within a particular religion. If the person speaking it were to say to me, 'the other gods, or so-called gods, to which you refer are false gods, illusions', again he would not have said anything that I should wish either to contradict or to affirm.

As a philosopher I am in the business of *clarifying* what I observe – for example, beliefs belonging to a particular religion working in and changing the lives of those who affirm them, the lives, that is, of those speaking the language of that religion: how do they understand these beliefs and what do they mean to the believer? I am not in the business of affirming or denying any of these beliefs. These are two very different things.

Notes

1. See D.Z. Phillips, 'Ten Questions for Psycho-Analysis', *Philosophy*, vol. 68, no. 264 (April 1993), p. 188.
2. Ilham Dilman, 'Psycho-analysis and Ethics: Some Reflections on the Self in its Relationship to Good and Evil', in *Commonality and Particularity in Ethics*, ed. Lilli Alanen, Sara Heinämaa and Thomas Wallgren (London: Macmillan, 1996).
3. Sigmund Freud, *The Future of an Illusion*, trans. W.D. Robson-Scott (London: Hogarth Press, 1949).
4. Sigmund Freud, *Civilisation and its Discontents*, trans. James Strachey (London: Hogarth Press, 1949).
5. Sigmund Freud, 'Obsessive Acts and Religious Practices', *Collected Papers*, vol. II (London: Hogarth Press, 1950).
6. Quoted in John Robinson, *Honest to God* (London: SCM Press, 1966), pp. 38–9.
7. Freud, *Future of an Illusion*, p. 76.
8. W.R.D. Fairbairn, *Psycho-analytic Studies of the Personality* (London: Tavistock, 1952).
9. Charles Rycroft, 'On Continuity', *Psycho-Analysis and Beyond* (London: Chatto and Windus, 1985).

10.   Ibid., pp. 283–4.
11.   Ibid., p. 283.
12.   Ibid., p. 282.
13.   Ibid.
14.   Ibid., p. 286.
15.   Charles Rycroft, 'Causes and Meaning', *Psycho-Analysis and Beyond* (London: Chatto and Windus, 1985).
16.   Rycroft, 'On Continuity', p. 290.
17.   T.S. Eliot, *Selected Essays* (London: Faber & Faber, 1972).
18.   Rycroft, 'On Continuity', p. 284.
19.   Ibid., p. 291.
20.   Ibid.
21.   Ibid., p. 288.
22.   Ibid., p. 284.
23.   Ibid., p. 290.
24.   Ibid., p. 282.
25.   Ibid., p. 288.
26.   Plato, *Gorgias* (London: Penguin Classics, 1973).
27.   See Dilman, 'Psycho-analysis and Ethics: Some Reflections on the Self in its Relationship to Good and Evil'.
28.   See ibid. and Phillips' response in the same volume: 'Ethics and Humanistic Ethics'.
29.   Rycroft, 'On Continuity', p. 283.
30.   Sigmund Freud, *New Introductory Lectures on Psycho-Analysis*, trans. W.J.N. Sprout (New York: W.W. Norton, 1933).
31.   Rycroft, 'On Continuity', p. 282.
32.   Fyodor Dostoyevsky, *The Brothers Karamazov*, vol. I, trans. Constance Garnett (London: Everyman, 1957).

Part Four
Religion as a Social Construct

7

Sources of the Self's Senses of Itself: A Theistic Reading of Modernity

Stephen Mulhall

THREE SELF-INTERPRETATIONS

As a set of directions for reading the text it precedes, the Preface to Charles Taylor's *Sources of the Self* could be improved on, particularly in its presentation of the relationship between Part I and Parts II–V of that work:

> The book . . . begins with a section which tries to make the case very briefly for a picture of the relation between [senses of] the self and moral [visions], which I then draw on in the rest of the work. Those who are utterly bored by modern philosophy might want to skip Part I. Those who are bored by history, if by some mistake they find this work in their hands, should read nothing else.
>
> (SS, p. x)

On this account, Part I constitutes a purely philosophical investigation and Parts II–V a purely historical one: the latter draw on a conceptual blueprint which the former outlines and attempts to justify, but the blueprint can be assessed independently of its narrative realization, and the narrative can be comprehended without grasping its conceptual architecture. *Sources of the Self* is thus written for two distinct audiences; however, many of its readers are members of both, and in this sense, it comprises two self-contained books.

In fact, the idea that conjoining philosophy and history is a matter of taste is undermined not only by other methodological passages in the book but also by the experience of reading it. Clearly,

131

much of the strength of Taylor's philosophical claims that internal relations exist between conceptions of the good and conceptions of the self, community and narrativity can be evaluated without referring to his subsequent historical account, which presents the development of certain aspects of Western culture as a series of developments in this loose conceptual package. But that account is not just an application or illustration of an independently meritorious logical analysis; for Taylor's methods of forging the connections he wishes to make in Part I are not always what one might call 'purely argumentative'. When, for example, he claims that conceptions of the self cannot be divorced from conceptions of society and of narrativity, the basis of his claim is much less obviously rigorous. For it amounts to the articulation of a metaphor or picture of selfhood, one in which the self inhabits moral space and so requires orientation – a good map (that is, evaluative frameworks which define the shape of the qualitatively higher, and which can only be derived from interaction with other selves), and knowledge of where it is on that map (where it stands in relation to the good, whether its life is leading it towards or away from the good, and so to an understanding of its life as a story unfolding within moral space). Taylor gestures towards other philosophers who have argued for such conclusions (e.g., Wittgenstein, Heidegger, MacIntyre), but he rests his own case solely on the resonance of his picture of selfhood. And although he develops that picture with clarity, elegance and control, those interested solely in modern analytical philosophy are not likely to acknowledge such discourse as having recognizably philosophical rigour, while those who *are* prepared to acknowledge its rigour will recall that the true significance of any picture lies in its application. Consequently, if Taylor can provide a historical narrative of Western moral culture whose organizing principle presupposes the truth of his philosophical conclusions and which can provide analytical illumination of a sort that compels conviction from its readers, he will greatly enhance the plausibility of those conclusions.

If, however, Parts II–V provide important support for the conclusions of Part I, the full import of that 'purely historical' narrative will entirely be lost for any reader who skips the 'purely philosophical' prolegomenon. For some of the claims that the prolegomenon advances generate methodological principles which make the idea that Parts II–V are a purely or primarily historical narrative (however organized) entirely untenable. One such claim is perhaps

Taylor's most famous contribution to philosophical anthropology – his Heidegger-derived notion that human beings are self-interpreting animals, creatures whose experiences, identity and nature are not specifiable independently of their interpretations of it. The content and scope for further refinement of those interpretations are in turn determined by the range and structure of the vocabulary available for their articulation; and that vocabulary is itself necessarily drawn from the prevailing webs of interlocution that make up the human being's culture and society. Since, on Taylor's view, moral argument is one fundamental aspect of human self-interpretation, it too must draw on whatever conceptual resources are available in contemporary culture; accordingly, identifying the present content of the interrelated conceptions of self, society, mode of narrativity and vision of the good which form the framework for any moral discourse whatever will be the best way of charting our present resources for moral self-interpretation. From this perspective, tracing the development of that loose conceptual package over time is simply one perspicuous way of clarifying the full range of conceptual resources available in contemporary culture, of increasing our awareness of the webs of interlocution that define the moral space of modernity within which we must orient ourselves in so far as we wish to be moral agents at all.

Thus, the 'purely historical' narrative of Parts II–V is in fact a ground-clearing exercise for the business of contemporary moral self-interpretation; it is an essential prolegomenon to any substantive contribution to moral thinking and moral argument. And Taylor himself stresses this second self-interpretation at several points in his historical account, when the self-interpretation that the Preface foregrounds is safely distant. For example, when (in Chapter 12) he defends himself against the accusation that his historical narrative betrays an excessively idealist conception of the motors of cultural change, he declares his project to be not a history of ideas, but an elucidation of the appeal of the various elements of the modern identity via an analysis of what their appeal originally was, as articulated by their best and most influential advocates. And in the book's concluding pages, he reiterates that its goal is 'to clarify my portrait of the modern identity' (SS, p. 499).

Even this second self-interpretation does not, however, take us to the heart of Taylor's 'historical' enterprise. Once again, we must remind ourselves of a claim Taylor advances in the supposedly detachable Part I of *Sources of the Self*, a claim about the nature of

practical reasoning. As part of his general attack on naturalist epistemology, he rejects the idea that moral arguments ought to be
modelled on those employed in natural science, and in particular
that they should aim to avoid anthropocentric bias by prescinding
entirely from our moral reactions, so that they might in principle
convince people who share absolutely none of our basic moral
intuitions (and, at the limit, even those who do not share our basic
commitment to morality). For what makes those reactions distinctively moral is that they can be articulated in terms of some particular ontological account of the human beings that are their objects;
and such accounts are not detachable from the reactions they support, because they articulate claims that are implicit in the reactions
themselves. Accordingly, to prescind from those reactions would
be to prescind from the very topic of the argument and from the
terms within which such argument can alone be conducted. Abstracting from all our moral reactions is not the route to a commendable moral objectivity, but a recipe for losing touch with
morality altogether; it amounts to changing the subject, not gaining
perspective.

In reality, practical reasoning is not a matter of establishing that
some position B is absolutely correct, correct regardless of who we
are, or where and when we find ourselves, or what our considered
moral views may be; it is rather a reasoning in transitions. Its concern is with comparative rather than absolute propositions; its aim
is to establish that position B is superior to some other position A
by demonstrating the epistemic gain conferred by the transition
from A to B. It attempts to show that the move resolves a specific
contradiction or confusion in A, acknowledges the importance of a
factor which A screened out, or something of the sort – in short, it
presents the transition as error-reducing; and attempts to contest its
validity taking the form of proposing rival interpretations of possible transitions from A to B, or vice versa.

Of course, in making and contesting such interpretations one must
address the moral perspective of one's interlocutor, but this does
not amount to question-begging; for the only alternative – abstracting from the specific texture of her experience and viewpoint – will
ensure that one's arguments lack conviction and even (at the limit)
intelligibility for her. More generally, moral objectivity is achieved
not by a global abstraction but by neutralizing perspective-specific
responses for substantive rather than formal reasons; we aim to
transcend (her or our) petty jealousies, egoism, thraldom to some

particularly traumatic experience not because they are her (or our) responses but because they are jealous, egoistic and enslaving – because their particular nature distorts or obliterates other, more worthy, moral responses. Correctly identifying any given response as distorted and another as insightful is not, of course, easy; but it *can* be done, and in roughly the way we achieve a better purchase on perceptual knowledge – not by giving up on our perceptual capacities altogether but by concentrating, taking more care, and generally employing those capacities with greater vigilance.

In effect, then, Taylor's account of practical reasoning is rooted in – is an aspect of – the essentially interlocutory and narratival structure of human life: reasoning about the good is a matter of one person engaging with a specific other or others about how best to understand the unfolding story of a specific life. As Taylor puts it:

> This form of argument has its source in biographical narrative. We are convinced that a certain view is superior because we have lived a transition which we understand as error-reducing and hence as epistemic gain. I see that I was confused about the relation of resentment and love, or I see that there is a depth to love conferred by time, which I was quite insensitive to before. But this doesn't mean that we don't and can't argue. Our conviction that we have grown morally can be challenged by another. It may, after all, be illusion. And then we argue; and arguing here is contesting between interpretations of what I have been living.
>
> (SS, p. 72)

Each component of his loose conceptual package is thus implicit in his account of practical reasoning; the account is an application, as well as a part, of the package as a whole. But its essence lies in its emphasis on narrative as the primordial medium of rationality; for that raises the possibility that the historical narrative developed in the subsequent Parts of *Sources of the Self* should itself be understood as an instance of practical reasoning.

In other words, the purpose of this narrative is definitely not purely historical – it is not a matter of tracing the diachronic progress of the conceptual package synchronically identified in Part I. But neither is it purely a preparation for practical reasoning, a form of analytical stage-setting necessary before moral argument proper can begin. That self-interpretation is not, and cannot be, the whole story, because the endeavour of which it is an interpretation takes the form of telling a story; it amounts to a narrative of the development of Western culture, a particular interpretation of its present as the outcome of a series of conceptual transitions in the past, and so as the jumping-off point for certain further transitions in the future. In short, it offers one possible genealogy of our culture, a biography which will inevitably present some of the transitions it has experienced as error-reducing and some as error-enhancing; but any such biography must itself be told from a particular moral perspective, and its representation of the epistemic worth of any given transition will inevitably be contestable, arguable. To present any such transition in this narrative form amounts to making a judgement on its epistemic worth; and to make such a judgement is not to prepare the way for, but rather full-bloodedly to engage in moral argument. In short, the business of Parts II–V of *Sources of the Self* is continuous with the concerns of Part I. The difference between them is not the difference between philosophy and history, and not that between the logical and the cultural geography of morals; it is the difference between meta-ethics and ethics.

THE MORAL MAP

According to Taylor's meta-ethic, any attempt to justify a given range of moral commitments will inevitably involve articulating and developing a particular conception of the status and nature of human beings; and in so doing it will identify a certain range of moral sources – something (or things) of fundamental value which help constitute the good for human beings, and the love of which empowers human beings to do and to be good. His moral cartography, his mapping of the terrain for fruitful contemporary ethical argument, therefore has three aspects: to identify himself with a certain range of moral values, to specify the general lineaments of the conception of the self which underlies them, and thereby to unearth those moral sources by attention to which individuals might succeed in living a life which is informed by, and so will further the implementation and development of, those values.

The first stage is most sketchily delineated, but its general purport is clear. Taylor takes it that a certain set of moral ideas which developed from the Enlightenment still forms 'the horizon of our moral outlook' (SS, p. 394). This includes a moral imperative to reduce, alleviate and even to end suffering; a recognition of the centrality of freedom to human well-being; a commitment to justice, typically understood as the protection of human rights; and a concern for democratic equality. These values, according to Taylor, are universal – not just in the sense that it appears no longer possible for governments, institutions or individuals in the West publicly or seriously to disavow them (although they can, of course, fail to live up to them), but also in that they are held to have global application – to require implementation in every branch of the family of nations.

How, then, might one defend these ideas as appropriate to their objects? What ontology of the human is implicit in our commitment to such wide-ranging and demanding moral ideas? In Taylor's view, a very specific conception of human beings as selves, as individuals whose sense of their own identity has three fundamental facets: inwardness, an affirmation of ordinary life and an expressivist conception of nature as manifest within as well as around them.

The modern notion of inwardness involves going beyond a view of oneself as one creature among others, and beyond a concern for one's own material well-being, to a more radical reflexivity encapsulated by the adoption of a first-person viewpoint. By this, Taylor means focusing our attention on the way the world is for us, attempting to experience our experiencing of that world rather than the world itself; his debt to Nagel's conception of what it is like to be a self-conscious agent of some kind is obvious (and, it might be thought, damaging). Taylor argues that this emphasis on radical reflexivity was introduced by Augustine and passed on to Descartes – versions of the *cogito* argument are central to the thought of both; and it generates a sense of the self as able to determine its own standards of validity, in contrast with the earlier objectivist conception of an ontic logos to which human subjects must conform. It also encourages the development of a conception of the self as radically disengaged: for Descartes, rational self-mastery means abstracting from our ordinary embodied way of experiencing reality, taking an external perspective on our bodies and our desires as well as the material universe, and thereby viewing both as domains of potential control by instrumental reason. This conception, Taylor claims, lies behind the quintessentially modern emphases on disciplines of sexual, economic and moral self-control in accordance with internally generated and justified standards. Thus, the contemporary compulsion to picture the self from a third-person perspective appears as a paradoxical consequence of attempts to accord priority to the first-person perspective.

The affirmation of ordinary life originates in the Reformation period, with the rejection of the prevalent Catholic view of the sacred; Protestants denied that sacramental rites or membership of a clerical or monastic order brought individuals closer to the divine – God was as close to laymen in their everyday working and family lives as He was to monks and priests, and these ordinary human realms of production and reproduction were seen as sacred to just the degree that their participants engaged in them with the correct attitude. This initially reinforced a disengaged stance towards the world, since that correct attitude amounted to a detachment from earthly pleasures and the treatment of created things as instruments rather than ends in themselves. However, when puritan conceptions of original sin were first diminished and then discarded, it became easier to affirm wider ranges of human desires and needs as good in themselves and so as worthy of fulfilment; and in such a context, morally worthy behaviour became focused on the maximization of pleasure and avoidance of suffering for all human beings. Sentiments of benevolence thus became central in the writings of Shaftesbury and Hutcheson, where they retain a theological role as the human way of contributing to the plans of Providence; but this Deist notion of a providential order is later rejected by utilitarians, who understand nature as a neutral interlocking domain of beings (ourselves included) whose structure we must master in order to acknowledge our own purely physical nature and maximize the fulfilment of our natural desire for pleasure. However, although this naturalist version of instrumentalism understood itself as thereby freed from *any* reliance on qualitative distinctions, Taylor argues that it retained an emphasis upon Deist life-goods (self-responsible reason, the worth of ordinary desires and benevolence) and thereby rejected modes of behaviour which failed to further these ideals.

Deism also opened up a line of development which contradicted the instrumentalist utilitarian conceptions of benevolence and of nature. For the importance it assigned to moral sentiments as *normative* of right action helped to make examination of one's feelings a reason-independent mode of access to what is good; and the contemplation of nature began to be seen as a means of conducting such self-examination, a way of eliciting noble sentiments and so discovering powers and capacities within us which instrumental reason represses. This in turn leads (through Rousseau) to the Romantic conception of nature as an independent locus of value: these feelings are seen as the voice of nature speaking through us, and recovery of contact with them is a recovery of contact with the spirit of nature in us. Simultaneously, however, Romantic express-ivism added a new depth of inwardness to the human self; for if we can only fully know ourselves by articulating and so realizing that depth of feeling, then our individuality is definable only through creative self-expression. According to Taylor, it is this which under-lies contemporary fascination with the artist, and our tendency to assign spiritual worth to her work; the artwork has become an epiphanic locus of the manifestation of something of the utmost spiritual significance.

These three facets of the modern identity are presented as under-pinning the range of values Taylor isolates as distinctive of moder-nity. For example, the affirmation of ordinary life, and the resultant emphasis on benevolence, find expression in the idea of the allevia-tion of suffering; whereas the inwardness of the self-determining subject has generated a new emphasis on personal freedom and universal justice. But the modern conception of the self also makes available a wide range of moral sources. First, of course, there is God: the precise form of His relationship to the human race and the cosmos might shift over time and according to which religious tra-dition we examine, but love of Him plainly remains a constitutive and empowering idea in the lives of millions. But a central aim of Taylor's narrative was to show how alternative moral sources arose in Western culture; and he groups these under two heads or fron-tiers of exploration.

> The first lies within the agent's own powers, those of rational order and control initially, but later . . . it will also be a question of powers of expression and articulation. The second lies in the depths of nature, in the order of things, but also as it is reflected within, in what wells up from my own nature, desires, senti-ments, affinities.
>
> (SS, p. 314)

Learning to be the disengaged subject of rational control is accom-panied and powered by a sense of our dignity as rational agents; and although this dignity was originally placed in a theistic per-spective (by Descartes, Locke and Kant), in so far as the powers from which it derives lie within us, the basis for a non-theistic morality is there. And similarly, although a theistic notion of a providential order incubated the idea of nature as a vast network of interlocking beings working towards the conservation and fulfilment of its parts, once that order and its fulfilment were understood in purely natural terms, the stage is set for Nature itself to be the prime moral source.

In short, the multiple facets of the modern conception of the self go hand-in-hand with multiple moral sources; and this evolving multiplicity creates the space for several families of ethical stances or positions, each offering a way of underpinning the distinctive moral commitments of modernity. Thus, in competition with broadly theistic conceptions of humanity, we can see, for example, a naturalism of self-responsible freedom and Romantic expressivism. Each has its own version of the available moral sources, its own empowering conceptions of human beings and of nature: the former focuses on disengaged reason and the evolutionary epic of nature, the latter on the creative imagination and the inner depths of the natural world. Of course, these conceptions are not fixed: they are explored in more depth and refined or otherwise altered by those who propound them. Neither are they self-contained: there have been attempts to combine elements from more than one of these families (Marx's marriage of naturalism and expressivism being one influential example). Moreover, not everyone in contemporary times is living by recently evolved versions of them – a point that is particularly pertinent with respect to those who cleave to theistic conceptions of the good. By mapping out these complexities, Taylor attempts to show that the terrain of contemporary moral argument is both limited and yet tolerant of profound divergence.

EXPLORING THE THEISTIC FRONTIER

So much for the stage-setting aspect of Taylor's narrative. But I claimed earlier that his account also amounted to a performance on that stage – to a substantive exercise in moral argument; and this may seem implausible, given two important elements of that account. First, Taylor stresses the multiplicity of moral sources and conceptions of self, society and narrativity that are available in contemporary Western culture. For him, part of the predicament of modernity is that influential families of these available conceptions of the good tend to repress the moral sources on which they none the less draw. For example, certain utilitarian versions of the ethic of benevolence are based on a vision of nature as a neutral domain of which human beings are simply one more part, and so regard themselves as freed from any commitment to specific life-goods or evaluative frameworks, and so as free from the obligation to articulate or justify them. Since Taylor regards such self-interpretations as damagingly mistaken (for no recognizably moral stance can be free of such an obligation), it is a central part of his project to recover the conceptions of the good that are thereby repressed and thus to restore a measure of self-understanding and self-empowerment to those inhabiting his culture. But this exercise in overcoming repression inevitably impresses the reader with the sheer variety of moral stances among which she might choose, rather than helping to narrow down that choice.

Second, Taylor repeatedly emphasizes that he regards the task of defending a particular position on the terrain he has mapped out as a separate task which he will execute later, if at all. In the Preface, he says that 'the whole study is . . . a prelude to our being able to come to grips with the phenomena of modernity in a more fruitful and less one-sided way than is usual. I didn't have space in this already too big book to paint a full-scale alternative picture of these phenomena. I will have to leave this . . . to later works' (SS, p. x). He ends his book by saying, 'my goal here is less to contribute to the debate than it is to clarify further my portrait of the modern identity' (SS, p. 499). And in the midst of his narrative, after identifying as fundamental the question whether our best self-interpretation involves acknowledging the significance of human life and whether this is best explained in immanent or theistic terms, he flatly states that 'all this remains to be argued out' (SS, p. 342).

A closer examination of the portrait Taylor paints will, I hope, make it clear that these self-interpretations are at best misleading; but they do help to identify the type of moral stance which Taylor at least wishes to expound in putative later works – for they make it clear that his commitment is to a theistic grounding for our demanding moral values. For example, when asking whether a non-theistic explanation of the significance of human life is tenable, he says that his 'hunch is that the answer . . . is "no". It all depends on what the most illusion-free moral sources are, and they seem to me to involve a God' (SS, p. 342). And in his concluding pages, when expressing the hope that the highest of our spiritual aspirations need not lead either to mutilation or to destruction, he writes: 'It is a hope that I see implicit in Judaeo-Christian theism . . . and in its central promise of a divine affirmation of the human, more total than

humans can ever attain unaided' (SS, p. 521). My question, therefore, becomes: What, if any, aspects of Taylor's portrait of modernity actually contribute to, rather than simply preparing the ground
for, the claim that our best self-interpretation must involve God?

According to Taylor's own analysis of practical reasoning, identifying any moral self-interpretation as our best available account
means proving its superiority over its present competitors – showing either that a move away from it to any of them involves an
epistemic loss or that a move to it from any of them involves the
greatest epistemic gain. We must demonstrate that such a move
will, for example, resolve a confusion or remove a contradiction or
acknowledge the importance of a factor screened out in other available accounts. So, any attempt to defend a theistic grounding for
the values of modernity (which amounts to defending the claim
that God is the most illusion-free moral source available to us) must
demonstrate that making a transition to that account from any of its
present rivals would be an error-reducing one. And Taylor's supposedly stage-setting account of the contemporary moral terrain
appears to construct just such a demonstration. The argument is
carried forward on three interlinked fronts, on each of which a
historical claim underpins and cloaks a conceptual or epistemic one.

The first such front is opened in Taylor's study of the process of
secularization which Western moral culture underwent after the
Enlightenment. As we have seen, according to his account, this
involved the emergence of two new frontiers of moral exploration
(the dignity of self-responsible reason and the goodness of nature),
which then became available as secular alternatives to the theistic
perspective within which they originated. Any attempted explanation of this particular aspect of secularization must therefore ask:
What made the mutation of theistic variants of these moral sources
into secular ones not only possible but necessary? Taylor's answer
is clear: 'when and to the extent that it seemed to people that these
moral sources could only be properly acknowledged, could only
thus fully empower us, in their non-theistic form. The dignity of
free, rational control came to seem genuine only free of submission
to God; the goodness of nature, and/or our unreserved immersion
in it, seemed to require its independence, and a negation of any
divine vocation' (SS, p. 315). Taylor then attempts to justify this
claim in his account of the rise and decline of Deism in the face of
the challenge posed by the radical Enlightenment and Romantic
expressivism. In other words, this part of his historical narrative

attempts to establish that the cultural transition away from theism and towards secular moral sources occurred because it was perceived to be an emancipatory, illusion-destroying and so an error-reducing one.

But it is also intended to establish that this perception, however understandable it might have been at the time, was itself illusory – that this secularizing transition really resulted in a variety of epistemic losses. This second strand of argument is manifest in Taylor's repeated emphasis upon the theistic roots of each of the three aspects of the modern identity that he delineates, and each of the two new frontiers of moral exploration that he identifies. Indeed, it is not too much to say that the ground-plan of his entire historical narrative is subordinate to establishing these points. By starting his account of the inwardness of the subject with Augustine, he makes it clear how much of the Cartesian turn towards the self – down to a reliance on a version of the *cogito* argument – was centrally prefigured in the Christian tradition; and he couples this with a reminder that the powers underpinning the dignity of free, self-responsible human agents were originally articulated as God-made and as part of the divine plan for the cosmos. His account of the origins of modernity's affirmation of ordinary life roots it in the theological underpinnings of a schism within Christianity. And he presents the secular conception of the natural world as a self-contained system of interlocking beings as having developed from a vision of nature as providentially ordered, while our sense of nature as an independent locus of value is shown to be rooted in the same Reformation-based reinvigoration of the scriptural doctrine that God as creator affirms life and being as good.

This architectonic implies two substantive moral conclusions. First, it establishes that every element of modern secular understandings of the self and of moral sources is not only perfectly compatible with, but potentially central to, a theistic perspective on human reality. And second, it forces us to consider whether the supposedly secular mutations of those original theistic conceptions might none the less still be drawing on theistic spiritual sources.

This question forms the sub-text of Taylor's discussion of radical Enlightenment in Chapter 19. He locates its genesis in a rejection of Hutchesonian Deism, one that denies the Deist picture of the relation of the cosmos and the human race to God while retaining a commitment to Deist life-goods – particularly their ethic of benevolence (a human impulse which they denounce Deists for hindering by their superstitious idolatry). Since naturalist versions of Enlightenment humanism utilize a materialist picture of nature as an order of interlocking beings, they tended to think themselves committed to denying the reality of evaluative frameworks. But this makes them incapable of articulating the vision of the good which empowers their commitment to benevolence; and since some such vision is required to make sense of their lives, they are placed in the position of drawing on the moral sources of the very theistic perspective against which they define their own position. In short, the utilitarian combination of reductive ontology and moral impetus compels such naturalism to be parasitic on that which it most violently opposes, at once deriving its affirmation through the rejection of an alleged theistic negation of nature (its words of power mainly consisting of polemical passages in which religion is denounced as erroneous, superstitious and fraudulent) and modelling that affirmation upon the Christian notion of *agape*.

Of course, Taylor's claims here constitute an *ad hominem* argument, their force restricted to versions of Enlightenment humanism that mistakenly combine a reductive ontology with moral commitments; and Taylor never denies – indeed, he traces with some care – the gradual working out of naturalist articulations of secular moral sources, centring on the dignity of self-responsible human freedom, for example. But a variant of the same form of argument has a more general application; and the ground is prepared for it by Taylor's continual stress on the demanding nature of the moral values that he takes to be definitive of modernity. In his account of our commitments to the relief of suffering, the provision of universal justice and respect for freedom, and so on, he constantly emphasizes the universality of their application, and so the strain under which they place us. And this strain is not, or not simply, a psychological one:

> The question which arises from all this is whether we are not living beyond our moral means in continuing allegiance to our standards of justice and benevolence. Do we have ways of seeing good which are still credible to us, which are powerful enough to sustain these standards? If not, it would be both more honest and more prudent to moderate them.
>
> (SS, p. 517)

For Taylor, this question highlights a central distinction between theistic and non-theistic moral sources: the latter, unlike the former, are inherently contestable. The point is not that theism is immune to contestation as to its truth; its opponents are all too likely to regard it as false, and as degrading and unfortunate for humans even if it were true:

> But no one doubts that those who embrace it will find a fully adequate moral source in it. The other two sources suffer a contestation on this score. The question is whether, even granted we fully recognize the dignity of disengaged reason, or the goodness of nature, this is in fact enough to justify the importance we put on it, the moral store we set by it, the ideals we erect on it.
>
> (SS, p. 317)

On Taylor's view, it is this sense of threatened inadequacy, this fear that in committing ourselves to the values of modernity on a purely secular basis we might be living beyond our moral means, that turns these two sources into frontiers of exploration – spaces within which continually renewed attempts are made to articulate those sources in ways that will put that fear to rest. But these attempts have unearthed as many reasons to judge that fear well-grounded as to dismiss it out of hand.

This issue is central to the third front of historical exploration opened in Taylor's later chapters. There, he recounts the work done by Schopenhauer, Dostoyevsky, Nietzsche and Freud in revealing the murky depths of human motivation in order to remind us of several reasons for doubting the adequacy of non-theistic moral sources. For that work suggests that we can no longer believe in the Enlightenment's idealized, optimistic vision of nature as unproblematically empowering benevolence, or as moving us to extend help to those who lack the full health and strength of the normal human creature, or in our acts of benevolence themselves as unproblematically loving and selfless. And in the same chapters, he also attempts to show that theistic moral sources do still have this necessary power. He points to the careers of individual believers, such as Mother Teresa and Jean Vanier; but he also stresses throughout his account of the nineteenth and twentieth centuries the degree to which crucial extensions in the reach of our moral ideas of justice and benevolence – ranging from the anti-slavery movement in England to the civil rights movement in America – were headed by Christians and significantly empowered by religious beliefs (cf. SS, pp. 399–401).

We therefore find that Taylor's historical narrative presents us with a multiplicity of reasons for coming to one particular conclusion about the epistemic gains and losses involved in the transition from theistic to secular moral sources. If secular moral sources are parasitic on theistic ones and incapable of bearing the burden of empowering the full range of modern moral ideas, whereas theistic sources can bear this burden and can also acknowledge versions of the sources on which secular moral visions exclusively rely, then we have strong reason for thinking that the cultural transition away from theistic sources amounted to a significant epistemic loss. In short, theism is our best available moral account.

But which theism? Taylor can hardly imagine that the way to recover our epistemic losses is to return to theism in the forms in which it was originally rejected; any such attempt to turn back the clock is doomed to failure. And as he himself emphasizes, contemporary theism constitutes a family of positions, a frontier of moral exploration within which there is much synchronic and diachronic divergence, and at least as much contestation as there is between theistic and non-theistic positions; so even if this frontier can provide us with the best available moral account, we need to know which of them it is. Unsurprisingly, however, Taylor's historical narrative makes his answer to this question tolerably clear.

Two features are essential to anything Taylor will be prepared to recognize as our best available theistic account: it must give a central place to the concept of grace, and it must dispense with any reliance on any notion of a human-independent ontic logos. The importance of the first requirement forms the subtext of Taylor's account of the origins of modernity's distinctive affirmation of the ordinary in the Reformation. He ends his discussion of Locke's work as the inspiration of Deism by emphasizing that the place of mystery in Lockean religion shrinks to the vanishing point, and with it the place of grace. For if the good of man to which God calls us becomes more and more available to human rational scrutiny, it also becomes more and more encompassable with human powers. In the pre-Lockean tradition as Taylor defines it, there were

two ways in which the human natural good was seen as needing supplementation by grace: (1) God calls humans to something more than the natural good, to a life of sanctity, which involves participation in God's salvific action. This takes us beyond the excellences defined by the natural good. In the language of

Thomism, beyond the natural virtues stand the 'theological' ones – faith, hope and charity. (2) Human will is so depraved by the Fall that humans require grace even to make a decent attempt at and perhaps even properly to discern the natural good, let alone go beyond it.

(SS, p. 246)

Most Christian theologies contained versions of both (1) and (2), but they varied radically according to which was dominant. If (1) dominates, then grace perfects nature rather than destroying it; where (2) dominates, there is suspicion and hostility even to the pursuit of the natural human good. As Taylor points out, both proponents of Deism and opponents of theism particularly criticized radical, hyper-Augustinian interpretations in which (2) dominated; but in so doing, they mistakenly thought themselves to have revealed the superfluity of any and all accounts of the need for grace, including versions in which (1) is dominant.

It is clear that, for Taylor, this is the point at which the baby has been jettisoned along with the bathwater. The opponents of theism have confused an attack on hyper-Augustinianism with an attack on all forms of religion, whereas the Deists have opened the way to a theistic account of the good that God wills for us which centres exclusively on natural good, and thus eliminates the need for grace at all. The implication is clear: in so far as the intra- and extra-theistic rejection of hyper-Augustinian suspicions of human nature and natural goods grounded the transition from theistic to non-theistic moral sources, it was based on a confusion, a failure to appreciate the existence of an attractive and powerful theistic account of the human good centred on a conception of grace in which it supplements human nature in the first rather than the second sense outlined above. And if he does not explicitly declare in these passages that such a theistic position will provide our best available moral account, he effectively does so in the concluding sentences of the book, where (as we have already seen) he talks of a hope implicit in 'Judaeo-Christian theism . . . and its central promise of a divine affirmation of the human, more total than humans can ever attain unaided' (SS, p. 521). In this brief articulation of his theistic vision, Taylor talks of a loving divine affirmation of human goods, and of faith in God as opening to us a source of hope not otherwise available to us – the hope that we might live up to our demanding modern moral commitments; and he thereby invokes the same

trinity of faith, hope and charity which Aquinas names as the theological virtues through which grace perfects (rather than rescues)
human nature.

The second requirement Taylor imposes on any adequate theistic
account of human reality flows from his core understanding of the
modern identity. What primarily distinguishes the self of modernity from its ancestors is its distancing from the Platonic notion of
an order of being that exists entirely independently of our perceiv-
ing it to be so – an order within which we can find our fulfilment
only in so far as we connect ourselves with it by right thinking and
right action, but one which constitutes a conception of the good, a
moral source, that is entirely external to us. The distinctively modern self, the self of inwardness and nature as inner voice, is one of
whom any vision of the good must be understood as at least in part
dependent for its existence upon that self's seeing it as good, or
otherwise helping to bring it into existence. Whatever order of things
is understood to be constitutive of the good is not, and can no
longer be, unmediated; we can no longer conceive of any such order
to which our access is not an epiphany wrought by the creative
imagination, refracted through the medium of someone's artistic
creation:

> The moral or spiritual order of things must come to us indexed
> to a personal vision. . . . Two important things . . . dovetail to lock
> us into this predicament, to render any unmediated order be-
> yond our reach: the detachment of the spiritual order from the
> order of nature we explore in natural science, which had to render
> the former problematic, is compensated for and complemented
> by our post-Romantic notion of the creative imagination. Both
> together spell the end of unmediated orders.
>
> (SS, p. 428)

This makes a certain subjectivism inseparable from all modern
manifestations of spiritual significance – including the theistic. We
can certainly distance ourselves from any substantive Romantic
emphasis on seeking the order of things within us, but we cannot
escape the mediation of our epiphany through the imagination; we
cannot sever the connection between articulation and inwardness.
Even when the content of our vision is resolutely transcendent, we
have to conceive of our articulation of it as the making manifest of
a personal refraction. This radically increases the risk of a fall into

self-centredness: if all modern epiphanies are indexed to a personal vision, it is tempting to transform them into celebrations of our own powers of creative articulation. But that is not an inevitable outcome. To say that there can only be refracted visions of the good does not mean that the content of all such visions must focus exclusively on the powers and depths of those capable of articulating them; it means only that what is manifested in such visions cannot be separated from the media which have been created to reveal it – that the spiritual content of the epiphany and its expressive form are internally related.

The proper meaning of these last formulations, and the connection between this feature and the roles of grace, become clearer in a five-page sequence at the heart of Taylor's discussion of the subtler languages of the post-Romantic Age. In it, he outlines a powerful and influential mode of response to the crisis of affirmation that he earlier identified with respect to the moral commitments of modernity – the feeling that recent insights into the darker side of human motivation and the natural world might have permanently discredited them as moral sources. The response is to deploy the Romantic idea of the creative imagination as having the power to transform base reality, so that we meet the crisis by transfiguring our own moral vision, and thus our stance towards the world and ourselves, rather than simply by a recognition of some objective order of goodness:

[T]he world's being good may now be seen as not entirely independent of our seeing it and showing it as good, at least as far as the world of humans is concerned. The key to a recovery from the crisis may thus consist in our being able to 'see that it is good'. The Judaeo-Christian origins of this whole notion ring in the phrase I've just used ... in the first chapter of Genesis, the goodness of the world is not something independent of God's seeing it as good. His seeing it as good, loving it, can be conceived not simply as a *response* to what it is, but as what *makes* it such ... what we have in this new issue of affirming the goodness of things is the development of a human analogue to God's seeing things as good: a seeing which also helps effect what it sees. This can mean, of course, that the self-attribution of this power is a resolutely atheist doctrine, the arrogation to man of powers formerly confined to God. This will be so with Nietzsche ... but this doesn't have to be so. One of the most insightful thinkers to explore this power is Dostoevsky, who sees it in a Christian perspective.

(SS, pp. 448–9)

Here, Taylor gives us a concrete example of the species of theistic vision with which he most closely identifies himself (cf. SS, p. 518), and of its most powerful non-theistic opposition. But his brief depiction of the Nietzschean perspective makes it clear that, for him, its power depends ultimately upon a paradox. As he summarizes it:

One of the things that makes a doctrine of our affirming power so necessary is just our commitment to an ethic of benevolence, which is why an inability to affirm the goodness of human beings can be threatening. But Nietzsche wins through to his total yea-saying precisely by jettisoning the ethic of benevolence, which is inextricably linked in his view with self-negating morality. He presents us with a cruel dilemma. Is it one we have to face?

(SS, p. 455)

Taylor's all but explicit answer is no: this prospect of self-mutilation can be overcome if we make the transition to the species of theistic affirmation of the human that Dostoyevsky represents.

Focusing on *The Devils* and *The Brothers Karamazov*, Taylor describes how 'one of Dostoevsky's central insights turns on the way in which we close or open ourselves to grace. The ultimate sin is to close oneself, but one's reasons for doing so can be of the highest . . . [But] the person who is closed is in a vicious circle from which it is hard to escape' (SS, p. 451). One example of this is Ivan Karamazov: he wants to give God back his ticket, to close himself off from the the world out of loathing for its unacceptable suffering; but such rejection seals one's sense of its loathsomeness and of one's own, in so far as one is part of it – and from this can only come acts of hate and destruction, which radiate out in a chain, a kind of negative apostolic succession (just as Ivan's nobility is shown to issue not in any positive actions in defence of the good, but rather in Smerdyakov's murderous crimes).

Dostoevsky . . . gives an acute understanding of how loathing and self-loathing, inspired by the very real evils of the world, fuel a projection of evil outward, a polarization between self and world, where all the evil is now seen to reside. This justifies terror, violence, and destruction against the world; indeed, this seems to call for it.

(SS, p. 451)

But in cutting themselves off from the world in order to avoid the humbling admission that they themselves are part of it and so of its evil, such noble nihilists also cut themselves off from the current of grace that circulates through the whole of creation. If they can learn to accept being part of that world, and so accept responsibility for its evils, they can come to see it as good in spite of those wrongs, and so to love the world and themselves.

Loving the world and ourselves is in a sense a miracle, in face of all the evil and degradation that it and we contain. But the miracle comes on us if we accept being part of it. Involved in this is our acceptance of love from others. We become capable of love through being loved; and over against the perverse apostolic succession is a grace dispensing one: from Markel to Zossima to Alyosha to Grushenka ...

(SS, p. 452)

Here, the Christian idea of people being transformed by the love of God, a love that they mediate to one another, is brought together with the modern notion of a subject who can help to bring about transfiguration through her stance to the world and herself. Dostoyevsky opposes the belief that human beings can affirm their dignity and worth in separation from the world; but he is not denying that dignity and worth, or the Romantic emphasis on the importance of the creative imagination. As Taylor points out, it is no coincidence that Dostoyevsky's most positive figures have to go through the experience of modernity; '[his] healing grace lies beyond the modern identity, not anterior to it' (SS, p. 452) – and Taylor's book is designed to urge the same transition on his readers.

ADDRESSING THE ARGUMENTS: FORM, CONTENT AND GENRE

I have now, I hope, achieved three goals. First, I have identified the broad lineaments of the theistic position with which I take Taylor to be identifying himself; second, I have traced the substantive considerations that he takes to demonstrate the epistemic gains that would accrue from making a transition to that position from either of its two contemporary competitors (a naturalism of disengaged reason, and Romantic expressivism – together with its modernist successors); and third, I have shown how his narrative of the historical twists and turns that have made these three frontiers our best available moral resources is inevitably also a deployment of certain of those resources in the service of that theistic position. It is now time to ask how one might wish to respond to their deployment.

First, it would be wrong to think that, because Taylor's argument for theism presupposes the meta-ethical assumptions outlined in Part I of *Sources of the Self*, it necessarily reduces the God for whose existence he is arguing to the status of a social construct, a mere human invention. His account of human beings as self-interpreting animals necessarily inhabiting moral space and so in need of orientation within it through linguistically and institutionally articulated moral frameworks and sources certainly entails that a theistic vocabulary (like any other) is a social construct; and it also entails that a belief in God would be inconceivable for anyone whose culture's webs of interlocution provided no vocabulary within which that belief might be given expression. But it does not follow that the Being whose nature is elucidated and whose existence is proclaimed in essentially social frameworks of evaluation is dependent on those frameworks for His nature or His existence. *We* may be dependent on them for an understanding of that nature and existence – we may require them if our form of life is to be theistic, if we are to orient ourselves properly towards God – but He does not.

To be sure, for Taylor, his theistic account must prove its truth by providing the best available articulation of our considered moral responses; but this requirement does not annihilate the essentially transcendent or super-human aspect of God's nature and identity. For Taylor is here simply emphasizing that our acceptance of any overarching or supreme good (any hyper-good), whether theistic or not, is connected with our being moved by it.

> We may accept something as good although we are relatively unmoved by it, because, at the lowest, we think very little about it . . . or because we revere and look up to established authority; or perhaps best, because we choose certain figures as authoritative for us, sensing in them that they are moved by something

authentic and great, even though we don't fully understand it or
feel it ourselves. But through all these complex chains of interme-
diation, the connection between seeing the good and being moved
by it cannot be broken. . . . [T]hose who give these goods their
energy and place in our lives, *they* felt them deeply.

(SS, pp. 73–4)

In other words, if the candidate account made no connection
with our moral intuitions, it should not and could not gain our
acceptance.

This intrinsic connection between seeing and feeling does not
amount to defining the validity of moral sources in terms of whether
or not we feel good about them; on the contrary, for Taylor 'we
sense in the very experience of being moved by some higher good
that we are moved by what is good in it rather than that it is valuable because of our reaction' (SS, p. 74). Here, he is just reiterating
that moral evaluation is strong evaluation – that discriminations of
right and wrong are not rendered valid by, but rather determine
the validity of, our desires, inclinations and choices; they allow us
to discriminate between our intuitions by rational argument, even
if the considerations then adumbrated must themselves connect with
some moral intuition. And the moral source which, in a given person's view, provides the best account of her experience need not be
something immanent to it; the fact that the considerations in its
favour are grounded in her moral experience does not prevent them
from invoking a being whose nature and mode of existence infi-
nitely transcends anything in her experience and understanding. To
think otherwise is once again to confuse the form and the content
of moral argument.

A similar confusion also fuels fears about Taylor's seemingly more
substantive claim that theistic conceptions in modernity are now
inescapably indexed to a personal vision; does not this entail that
all contemporary conceptions of God are inevitably person-relative,
and thus reduce God to a subjective construct? Once again, the
answer is no. When he claims that all such conceptions are indexed
to a personal vision, he does not mean that their validity is necessarily restricted to the person who articulated them, or that the
reality of the moral source they articulate is relative to the people
who endorse that articulation. He means rather that their articulation must, in some part, depend on the personal resources and
texture of the creative imagination through which they are mediated,

and that their content must be inflected by that fact. In short, he means that in modernity the medium and the message cannot entirely be separated.

But it doesn't follow from this that such personal visions can only have meaning or validity for the person who creates them. In so far as they are articulated in a language, they are in principle open to the comprehension of others; and in so far as they are articulated with the aim of deepening our understanding of a particular moral source, their creator has a vested interest in striving to avoid the merely subjective – formulations in which all that she is really talking about is herself or the idiosyncratic quirks of her experience. Taylor's picture is rather that such a thinker will look for formulations that articulate her own deepest intuitions and insights, and offer them in the hope that they will similarly resonate in the hearts and minds of her interlocutors; she will, in short, aim to provoke a confluence of subjective visions, an overlapping of personal resonances. What will then result is a genuine community of agreement; but one forged through, rather than by avoiding (in the manner favoured by scientists or logicians), the inflection of a personal perspective. And the content of the articulation on which such a community is based need not be immanent to the moral experience either of its creator or of those prepared to adopt her formulations; so any conception of God articulated in this way need not be any less transcendent than its pre-modern ancestors. On the contrary, if the articulation is to be recognizable as a theistic one, central aspects of the biblical and pre-modern vocabularies which have sustained religious belief in previous eras can at most be adapted, not rejected, when passed through the lens of our creative imaginations. In short, Taylor's claim here is simply that contemporary conceptions of God must be refracted through, not reduced to, the inwardness of individual vision.

Removing these objections to Taylor's enterprise does not, however, exhaust the anxieties to which it seems subject. Two matters in particular seem likely to generate far more penetrating criticisms of his argument: one relating to his treatment of Kierkegaard, and the other to his conception of the relation between philosophy and art (or, more precisely, literature). Both might be thought of as questions of genre – questions about Taylor's conception of the sort of enterprise in which he is engaged in *Sources of the Self*, about how it is to be understood as a species of writing or communication. The connection with Kierkegaard is implicit from the moment

Taylor develops his conception of practical reasoning as a reasoning in transitions. The emphasis this places on comparative rather than absolute judgements, combined with its reliance on the model of biographical narrative, implies that the proper locus of moral argumentation is the confrontation between one person and another. A party to a moral dispute speaks from a perspective defined by the moral intuitions that her best reading of her own experience has delivered, and speaks to the perspective of her interlocutor, attempting to engage with the detailed texture of that other's experience and life story; it is a confrontation between two resolutely first-person viewpoints. The competing notion that there might be a once-for-all, perspective-free, absolutely impersonal moral truth of any given matter is rejected in favour of something profoundly reminiscent of a Kierkegaardian perspective on the nature of human intercourse about morality.

This seems to me to be one of Taylor's most powerful invocations of the work of previous thinkers; but other aspects of his writing suggest that he has not fully grasped its import. For one of its implications is that we can neither impose nor discover any impersonal, objective hierarchy governing available moral perspectives and positions; if all judgements of their relative moral worth are indexed to a personal biography, then even when another moral agent is brought to agree with them, that agreement should be seen as the confluence of two individual perspectives rather than the joint recognition of a perspective-independent reality. Accordingly, when one party to a moral debate presents her reasons for advocating a certain transition, she should do so in a manner which acknowledges the personal experiential and intuitional roots of her argument. If she were to present them as impersonally decisive, the form of her discourse would imply a belief that pure logic dictates a certain perspective on the issue at hand, when the reality is that adopting or rejecting any ethical stance is a personal decision, an existential act, the responsibility for which one cannot avoid by sloughing it off onto logic.

These, of course, are considerations that are usually taken to be encapsulated in such Kierkegaardian notions as indirect communication and the leap of faith, and to underpin his deployment of pseudonyms throughout his writings on philosophy, ethics and religion. For a strategy of pseudonymity inscribes the meta-ethical position just outlined in the form as well as in the content of his writings, so that the former takes on and lives up to the demands of the latter – thus avoiding what one might call an existential contradiction. But given the obvious links between these issues and a conception of moral argument that Taylor explicitly adopts, it is disturbing to find that his exegesis of Kierkegaard is completely insensitive to these matters. First, he takes such texts as *Either/Or* to be aimed at establishing the objective superiority of the ethical to the aesthetic stance, and the objective superiority of the religious stance to both. We are told that 'Kierkegaard lays out the idea of an aesthetic transfiguration of life, only to trump it with a higher form, the ethical' (SS, p. 449), and that in his later writings, he 'evolved beyond this definition of the ethical, which came to be seen as a stage which was in turn trumped by the religious' (SS, p. 450). But if Kierkegaard had argued anything of the sort, he would have been making an objective, perspective-free judgement about morality – a comparative judgement, to be sure, but one presented as if it were true eternally and without regard to the personal biography and existential resolution of his readers, as if a clear perception of conceptual relations would alone be enough to demonstrate the truth of the judgement and bring about the adoption of the form of life it justifies.

Taylor's failure to identify this problem is not surprising, since there are passages of certain Kierkegaardian texts (particularly the *Concluding Unscientific Postscript*) that look as if they are presenting just such an argument; but that appearance is placed in question by the second aspect of Kierkegaard's work that Taylor entirely ignores – the fact that each such text is pseudonymously authored. The views Taylor regales us with are variously those of Judge William and Johannes Climacus (among others), the views of highly specific fictional constructs, about whose idiosyncratic perspectives and arguments we are thereby encouraged to make a personal judgement; but Taylor (along with most of the secondary literature in this area) unproblematically attributes them to Kierkegaard himself, and thus entirely overlooks both the evaluative distance that otherwise opens up between Kierkegaard's own views and those of his pseudonyms, and the fact that Kierdegaard's meta-ethical stance demands the construction of just such a way of establishing harmony between the form and the content of his writings.

This myopia in Taylor's self-understanding finds expression in passages of his writing entirely unrelated to his exegesis of Kierkegaard; it is registered most subliminally, but perhaps therefore most influentially, in his frequent, indeed all but uniform use of the first-person plural pronoun throughout *Sources of the Self*. The story he tells in the book is always *our* story: we have endured certain transitions, we find ourselves in certain predicaments, with certain resources available to us and so with certain options open and others closed, and we are offered one particular way of extricating ourselves from the difficulties created by our commitment to demanding moral values. This syntactic strategy generates an air of inclusiveness, of unproblematic unity, that may be either seductive or irritating according to taste; but whatever the reader's reaction on that score, it has an important two-fold effect. First, it constructs Taylor's interlocutors as a collective, a single, undifferentiated group rather than a set of individuals, each with her own biography, experience and intuitions; and second, it submerges Taylor himself into this collective, just another atom in the mass to whom he speaks rather than a particular individual, with a specific perspective on the matters at hand and a desire to convince other individuals of its rectitude for each of them. But a reader primed by Taylor's Kierkegaardian emphasis on moral argument as a confrontation between concrete individuals would surely expect some registration of that meta-ethical point in the form of Taylor's narrative. This need not mean adopting a strategy of pseudonymous discourse, but it should at least mean more use of the pronouns 'you' and 'I' – more acknowledgement from the author that he is speaking in the first person to persons who must respond in the same way.

  Taylor might reply by emphasizing that he is telling the biography of a culture, the transitions of a society or societies; and in so far as his readers are being addressed as members of that culture, then the first-person plural pronoun is surely the only correct one to employ. But his own conception of practical reasoning as an encounter between individuals makes any shift from the personal to the cultural level highly problematic. It would seem to require regarding the culture as if it were a person, a single organic individual; but if what matters in a moral argument is that one address the experience and intuitions of one's interlocutor with all the concrete detail and specificity that one can muster, then the very idea the one can so address a culture seems incoherent. In the end, Taylor's book is not read by his culture but by a given number of individual members of that culture. And if they are addressed only in so far as they are indistinguishable from all of their fellow members, then that address will tend not to engage with the real detail of their individual perspectives and experience; and its form will also tend to imply that the argumentation in which its narrative ineluctably engages constitutes an impersonal, supra-individual set of pro-theistic considerations which any member of the culture is logically obliged to accept and enact, rather than one route to an existential possibility that each individual must either accept or reject for themselves. In short, Taylor's reluctance to address his readers in such a way that the form of his discourse reflects its content may seriously damage his ability to prove his case and to live up to the insights he seeks to convey.

However, other considerations make Taylor unwilling to press home his account with the fullest vigour, considerations which also involve his sense of the genre to which his work belongs. They come through most clearly in the final chapter of his book, when he reiterates his belief that any contemporary attempt to articulate moral sources must be indexed to a personal vision, a vocabulary of personal resonance:

> This is true not only of epiphanic art but of other efforts, in philosophy, in criticism, which attempt the same search. This work, though it obviously fails of any epiphanic quality, falls into the same category. I have throughout sought language to clarify the issues, and I have found this in images of profound personal resonance like 'epiphany', 'moral sources', 'disengagement', 'empowering', and others. These are the images which enable me to see more clearly than I did before. They could, I believe, be the animating ideas of an epiphanic work, but that would require another kind of capacity. The great epiphanic work actually can put us into contact with the sources it taps. It can *realize* the contact. The philosopher or critic tinkers around and shapes images through which he or another *might* one day do so. The artist is like the race-car driver, and we are the mechanics in the pit; except that in this case, the mechanics usually have four thumbs, and they have only a hazy grasp of the wiring, much less than the drivers have.
>
> (SS, p. 512)

This is a startlingly self-contradictory passage. On the one hand, *Sources of the Self* is identified as being of the category of epiphanic artistic, philosophical and critical works, works designed to forge a vocabulary, indexed to a personal vision, for the articulation of moral sources. But on the other hand, it is doubly disqualified from that category in that it is deemed to be neither epiphanic nor capable of actually putting its readers into contact with the moral sources it articulates. And what seems to motivate this second, contradictory self-interpretation is not just a commendable modesty on Taylor's part, but also his interpretation of the relation between philosophy and criticism, on the one hand, and art on the other. For him, the philosopher is the mechanic or underlabourer, the artist is the driver or master builder; the former shapes concepts, arguments and insights which the latter then vivifies and renders life-giving in their turn.

Taylor's overt reason for making these claims is to declare that philosophy and criticism on his conception are not entirely hard-edged; neither his historical narrative nor his meta-ethical prologue are free of reliance on personal vision. But his Romantic elevation of the artist depends on a distinction that simply does not appear tenable within that meta-ethical perspective; for it presupposes that a vocabulary might have profound personal resonances that enable its creator and his interlocutors to see the nature and depth of certain moral sources more clearly than before, and yet not put them in touch with or help them to realize those sources. But if this vocabulary can enable its creator and others to see a moral source more clearly, then it already *has* put them in contact with it; there is no further step to be taken. From which it follows that the successful philosopher and critic, solely by virtue of her success, has and must have manifested the talent that Taylor wishes to assign exclusively to the artist. In this respect, good philosophy and good art require one and the same capacity.

In effect, Taylor has correctly identified an important but person-relative question and mislocated it as a discipline-relative one. For the author, the real question is not: am I an artist or a philosopher? but rather: am I capable of articulating a moral source in an inter-subjectively resonant way? And for the author's reader, the real question is not: am I reading a piece of philosophy or a work of art? but rather: do I find this personal vision resonant, convincing, empowering? In both cases, the answer to these questions may be no: the particular author may fail to make her articulation convey the power she believes her source to possess, or the reader may be unwilling or unable to be moved by it. But if so, the failure derives from a personal rather than a disciplinary limitation; it is not guaranteed simply because the author concerned is wielding, adapting or otherwise intervening in recognizably philosophical discourse.

It is as if Taylor were only prepared to acknowledge a partial and limited intrusion of the personal into the realm of moral philosophy – as if he still wished to retain a sense that moral philosophy, just because it is philosophy, is to some degree an impersonal, objective enterprise; and so he must regard a fully-fledged commitment to speak from a personal moral vision as necessarily taking the speaker outside the philosophical realm. As a consequence, *Sources of the Self* oscillates between being an impassioned articulation of a personal moral perspective and a dispassionate delineation of history, conceptual geography and the skeleton of a moral trajectory that is objectively compulsory for Western culture and its members. But Taylor's own intersubjectively resonant meta-ethical vocabulary implies that this conception of moral philosophy should be placed in question, and that the book of which this meta-ethical exercise is a part should rather have a form which more thoroughly eradicates any implication of the impersonal. In other words, what *Sources of the Self* may require is not supplementation by a personal moral manifesto but rather restatement in a form which makes it clearer that it always already was a personal moral manifesto. The correct response of a reader upon completing its narrative should thus be not 'More!', but rather, 'Once more with feeling!'

8

Doing Justice or Giving the Devil his Due

Peter Winch

> My ideal is a certain coolness. A temple providing a setting for the passions without meddling with them.
>
> (Wittgenstein, *Culture and Value* (1929) p. 2)

I am neither competent nor inclined to follow Dr Mulhall into the labyrinths of Taylorian exegesis. His own discussion is so closely entwined with his interpretation of Taylor that I find it sometimes difficult to discern how far he is agreeing with Taylor and how far not. Rather than try to disentangle these threads I shall take up certain issues arising from Mulhall's discussion and treat them largely independently, though distancing myself from time to time from certain emphases in Mulhall's paper that I find disturbing, or at least misleading. The subject which we were invited to discuss in this symposium was 'whether God is a social construct'. Mulhall's main explicit points on this theme are as follows:

- Taylor's position entails that 'a theistic vocabulary (like any other) is a social construct'.
- Belief in God is inconceivable for anyone whose culture's 'webs of interlocution' provide no appropriate vocabulary.
- It does not, however, follow that 'the Being whose nature is elucidated and whose existence is proclaimed' in such structures is dependent on them 'for his nature or his existence'. He goes on: '*We* may be dependent on them for an understanding of that nature and existence – we may require them if our form of life is to be theistic, if we are to orient ourselves properly towards God; but He does not.'

As I understand Mulhall, these are points concerning which he and Taylor are in agreement. Let me try to define my own attitude to them. First, the term 'social construct', very often used in this connection, but to my mind doubly unfortunate. On the one hand, 'construct' suggests something like an artefact, deliberately produced as a church (I mean a particular sort of *building*) is. On the other hand, 'social' suggests a co-operative venture the participants in which all agree on what they are trying to do; or, *à la* Durkheim, an activity carried out by a special sort of entity, Society.[1] Leaving other objections aside, both these suggestions seem to presuppose that religion, and also the God to whose worship religion is devoted, are quite unambiguously identifiable: whereas it seems obvious after a little reflection that there is just as much diversity and conflict between different kinds of religious tradition (often involving very different conceptions of God) as there is between religions on the one side and secular traditions on the other.[2] I agree, therefore, with Mulhall's objections to Taylor's liberal use of the first-person plural in reporting what 'we' think; I shall in fact later urge that he does not carry these objections far enough.

Putting the word 'construct' on one side for the time being, we have to distinguish the question whether God is a social phenomenon from the question whether *religion* is a social phenomenon. First, something about the formulation of this second question. Mulhall spells it out in terms of the availability of a certain *vocabulary*. This is certainly an important factor, but only one among many, including a large number of other modes of expression:[3] as gestures, facial expressions, rituals, the existence of holy texts, recognized forms of worship, established ecclesiastical offices, and so on. It is easy to see that all such factors have at least as substantial a social dimension as does a vocabulary. In some circumstances the existence of a particular vocabulary may not be important at all; and it is notorious that two people may use the same vocabulary with very different import:

> Actually I should like to say that in this case too the *words* you utter or what you think as you utter them are not what matters, so much as the difference they make at various points in your life. How do I know that two people mean the same when each says he believes in God? And just the same goes for belief in the Trinity. A theology which insists on the use of *certain particular* words or phrases, and outlaws others, does not make anything clearer (Karl Barth). It gesticulates with words, as one might say, because it wants to say something and does not know how to express it. *Practice* gives the words their sense.[4]

Keeping such considerations in mind, we may feel inclined to say that yes, religion is certainly (among many other things) a social phenomenon. In the same sense so are music, historiography, chess, patience (solitaire), the life sciences, physics, chemistry, social phenomena. Consider chemistry. Only in the context of the discipline of chemistry can one speak of, say, mercury as a chemical element. But from this, plus the fact that the discipline of chemistry is, in one of its aspects, a social phenomenon, it does not follow that either a given mass of mercury or indeed mercury *sans phrase* is a social phenomenon; nor can we conclude more generally that chemical elements are social phenomena from the fact that the term 'chemical element' has the meaning it does only in the context of (the social phenomenon of) chemistry. What would explain the existence of such an element as mercury I do not know; to find out I should have to go, perhaps, to a geophysicist. The sense of the question 'What explains the existence of chemical elements as such?' is obscure; I would take it to be asking what explains the fact that within chemistry one distinguishes as one does between, for instance, elements and compounds. The answer would presumably involve a good deal of talk about the general structure of chemical theory and perhaps about the history of chemistry. I should see little merit in the suggestion that, because chemical theory exists only within the framework of a social phenomenon (chemistry) and because the history of chemistry is the history of a social phenomenon, therefore chemical elements are social phenomena or even that therefore the concept of a chemical element is a social concept. And I do not find that it sounds any better if we substitute the phrase 'social construct' for 'social phenomenon'.

'God' is a term which has its home in religion, which (in one of its aspects) is a social phenomenon (or a complex of social phenomena). This does not mean or imply that *God* is a social concept, still less that God is a social entity. The existence of God does not depend on society any more than the existence of mercury, or more generally of chemical elements, depends on society. Just as one may ask how the concept of *mercury* came to be as it is, so one may ask how the concept of *God* (perhaps some particular concept of *God*) came to be as it is; in each case the answer would include a great deal of human history, but it would clearly be absurd to conclude that either mercury or God came to exist or to be as they are as a result of human history.

I do not apologize for spelling these things out in somewhat boring detail. Indeed, I think a great deal more such detail would be advantageous. The kind of issue we are concerned with suffers greatly from commonly being depicted in such broad strokes and from being argued in such great jumps. In terms of such broad strokes, it may look as though I must be agreeing with Mulhall when, speaking of God as 'the Being whose nature is elucidated and whose existence is proclaimed' in the socio-linguistic structures constituting religion, he points out that though 'we may be dependent on them [such socio-linguistic structures] for an understanding of that nature and existence, He is not thus dependent.' Of course, I certainly do not want to *contradict* him on this point, but nevertheless I am uneasy. Consider the Grand Canyon. There is a great deal of literature, talk, art, music,[5] etc., along with many official personages devoted to what one certainly might call (if one likes such language) 'elucidating the nature and proclaiming the existence' of the Grand Canyon. Yet the relation between these 'webs of interlocution' and the Grand Canyon is quite different from that between religious discourse and God. I do not doubt that Mulhall would agree with this; but the imagery contained in his way of speaking fatally suggests (to me at least) some such analogy. Moreover, it crucially fails to do justice to the insight that is expressed, albeit in exceedingly misleading terms, by calling religion, and even God, a 'social construct'. The term 'construct' here is a (muffed) attempt to acknowledge the importance of what one may call 'concept formation' in somebody's discovery of God. There is indeed a sense in which someone who discovers the Grand Canyon for the first time may be said to find that his picture of the world, of what is possible, has been revolutionized. Yet in another sense his pre-existing picture of the world already had room for the Grand Canyon. He had perhaps known other canyons, or had seen pictures of them; he knew what a mountain is and what a valley, etc. In other words, prior to his seeing the Grand Canyon he had the conceptual resources to understand descriptions of it; and having understood such descriptions he was in a position to 'know what to expect'.

Contrast the case of such a person with Huckleberry Finn, confronted with what he believes (or thinks he believes) to be his moral duty, to turn over his friend, Jim, the runaway slave, to his 'owner':

> It would get all around, that Huck Finn helped a nigger get his freedom; and if I was to ever see anybody from that town again, I'd be ready to get down and lick his boots for shame. That's just

the way: a person does a lowdown thing, and then he don't want to take the consequences of it. Thinks as long as he can hide it, ain't no disgrace. That was my fix exactly. The more I studied about this, the more my conscience went to grinding me, and the more wicked and low-down and ornery I got to feeling. And at last, when it hit me all of a sudden that here was the plain hand of Providence slapping me in the face and letting me know my wickedness was being watched all the time from up there in heaven, whilst I was stealing a poor old woman's nigger that hadn't ever done me no harm, and now was showing me there's One that's always on the lookout, and ain't a-going to allow no such miserable doings to go only just so fur and no further, I most dropped in my tracks I was so scared. Well, I tried the best I could to kinder soften it up somehow for myself, by saying I was brung up wicked, and so I warn't so much to blame; but something inside me kept saying, 'There was the Sunday school, you could a gone to it; and if you'd a done it they'd a learnt you there, that people that acts as I'd been acting about that nigger goes to everlasting fire.'

It made me shiver. And I about made up my mind to pray; and see if I couldn't try to quit being the kind of a boy I was, and be better. So I kneeled down. But the words wouldn't come. Why wouldn't they? It warn't no use to try and hide it from Him. Nor from *me*, neither. I knowed very well why they wouldn't come. It was because my heart warn't right; it was because I warn't square; it was because I was playing double. I was letting *on* to give up sin, but away inside of me I was holding on to the biggest one of all. I was trying to make my mouth *say* I would do the right thing and the clean thing, and go and write to that nigger's owner and tell where he was; but deep down in me I knowed it was a lie – and He knowed it. You can't pray a lie – I found that out.[6]

What did Huck find out? In the first instance something about the nature of prayer; but at the same time something about the nature of God ('He knowed it'). A more interesting question: what did his 'finding out' look like? Of course, Huck comes to this crisis with a lot of the ground already prepared. He has been brought up by the Widow Douglas and her sister Miss Watson and has certainly already acquired a considerable part of the vocabulary of religion. Here are some descriptions of that teaching given by Huck himself. Speaking of the Widow Douglas, he says:

After supper she got out her book and learned me about Moses and the Bulrushers; and I was in a sweat to find out all about him; but by-and-by she let it out that Moses had been dead a considerable long time; so then I didn't care no more about him; because I don't take no stock in dead people.

And, at greater length, of Miss Watson:

Miss Watson would say, 'Don't put your feet up there, Huckleberry'; and 'don't scrunch up like that, Huckleberry – set up straight'; and pretty soon she would say, 'Don't gap and stretch like that, Huckleberry – why don't you try to behave?' Then she told me all about the bad place, and I said I wished I was there. She got mad, then, but I didn't mean no harm. All I wanted was to go somewheres; all I wanted was a change, I warn't particular. She said it was wicked to say what I said; said she wouldn't say it for the whole world; *she* was going to live so as to go to the good place. Well, I couldn't see no advantage in going where she was going, so I made up my mind I wouldn't try for it. But I never said so, because it would only make trouble and wouldn't do no good.

   Now she had got a start, and she went on and told me all about the good place. She said all a body would have to do there was to go around all day long with a harp and sing, for ever and ever. So I didn't think much of it. But I never said so. I asked her if she reckoned Tom Sawyer would go there, and she said, not by a considerable sight. I was glad about that, because I wanted him and me to be together.[7]

Huck is taught by Widow Douglas and Miss Watson, first, a number of stories, of which he can make little, in connection with a rudimentary 'moral' training, of which and of the connection between which and the stories, he can also make little. I am reminded of Rush Rhees's wonderful response to an (only somewhat) more sophisticated version of the religious view of these ladies that if someone were to teach him that there existed a powerful being who would blast him to hell if he didn't behave as instructed, 'I hope I would have the decency to say, "Go ahead and blast".'[8] Huck himself in the moment of greatest depth in his initial response, gets close to that in his remark about wanting to have nothing to do with heaven if his friend Tom is not there.[9] It is also evident from his subsequent reflections that he has been initiated into a number of practices: prayer, Sunday school, for instance; and no doubt church-going and, one would naturally expect, how to behave when in church; the tones of voice in which it is appropriate to speak of certain 'holy' matters; and so on. In other words, he has access to a good deal of what I take Mulhall to mean when he speaks of the 'webs of interlocution' of religion.

Does this mean that he already has the concept of God? I don't quite know how I should answer that question. It would depend on the precise point one wanted to bring out, I suppose. If I were going to compare him, for instance, with a child of the same age who had had no kind of religious upbringing whatever, I might try to mark the contrast by saying he has the concept of God whereas the other one does not. I have no objection to putting the matter that way in those circumstances. On the other hand, I think I also want to say that there is a sense in which, at this time of crisis over what to do about Jim, he does for the first time seriously learn what it is to use the word 'God'. He can now apply this word in a way he was not able to apply it before. He might before have said, repeating what he had been taught, that you cannot pray a lie, but he would not have been able to mean it or, perhaps better, he would not have had the resources to understand the point of saying such a thing.[10] Perhaps there is some analogy here – though it cannot be pressed too far – with the situation of a blind person who has learned colour language and can recognize what makes sense and what does not in what other people say in this language and can also say a good deal herself. But there's also a great deal she cannot say; there are a great many circumstances in which she cannot apply colour language as other people do. Moreover, one feels inclined to say that these are precisely the applications of colour language that give it its point, that without them the concept of colour is, if you like, altogether lacking. This looks something like Huck's inability before the crisis to use religious language in certain ways as contrasted with the uses elicited from him by the crisis.

At any rate considerations like these seem to me to make talk of God as a 'social construct' much less attractive than it would be if we simply confined our attention to what Huckleberry Finn had already learnt at home. What he now learns in a certain sense *frees* him from a merely 'social' conception. Starting off from the thought that 'if I was to ever see anybody from that town again, I'd be ready to get down and lick his boots for shame', he comes to see that this is not the point, which is rather that: 'It warn't no use to try and hide it from Him. Nor from me neither.' It is the conception of God as all-seeing that he now sees the force of; its force is that, in relation to such issues as this one, it is not the view of society that matters, but the truth of the matter. At this stage Mark Twain still embeds Huck's understanding in irony of course. Huck misidentifies what God is showing him. He thinks He is merely pointing out Huck's hypocrisy, rather than revealing to him what he really believes: namely that the decent, 'clean' thing for him to do is to rescue Jim from his pursuers at all costs: an odd function, surely, for a 'social construct'.

I think here of the following remarks of Wittgenstein (from 1950):

> Life can educate one to a belief in God. And experiences too are what bring this about; but I don't mean visions and other forms of sense experience which show us the 'existence of this being', but e.g. sufferings of various sorts. These neither show us God in the way a sense impression shows us an object, nor do they give rise to conjectures about him. Experiences, thoughts, – life can force this concept on us.
>
> So perhaps it is similar to the concept of 'object'.[11]

That last sentence should clearly not be taken as meaning that 'perhaps God is a kind of object'. The point, rather, is that the concept of an object is not derived from 'experiencing objects' (perhaps by a process of 'abstraction'); and it would be misleading to characterize the use we make of the concept of 'object' by saying that 'we believe in the existence of objects'. Rather, the lives we lead, the problems we confront in dealing with our environments, the making of distinctions required for living a human life, etc., force this concept of an object on us: it is a concept that characterizes the grammar of all kinds of things we say, a *formal* concept in the language of the *Tractatus*. So with the word 'God'. It doesn't refer to a particular 'Being', the way we use it characterizes the grammar of all sorts of things we say: what we say, for instance, in dealing with experiences of loss, in expressing wonder at the beauty of things, or at certain kinds of conduct in others, or consciousness of deficiencies, and worse, in oneself, and so on. Such situations may elicit certain responses from me, responses that I do not choose but, perhaps, cannot suppress. It is important to remember here that the acquisition of a concept is not simply a matter of storing what one observes or experiences, but always includes an element of reaction.[12] And our reactions may be shaped by the language we have learned. It is important to put the matter in this way because, of course, people do use the word 'God' differently (in so far as they use it seriously at all), though within certain parameters of agreement sufficient to assure us that it is indeed the same word (and not just a homonym) that they are using. People do not all respond in the same way to the crises that life presents them with; for one thing the language of religion does not play a part in everyone's reactions; for another, even among those in whose responses it does play a part, it is not always the same part.[13]

In what I have been saying I may seem to be not very far distant from Mulhall, or even, perhaps, Taylor when he emphasizes (the words are Mulhall's) that conceptions of God 'are indexed to a personal vision', that 'their articulation must, in some part, depend upon the personal resources and texture of the creative imagination through which they are mediated, and that their content cannot avoid being inflected by that fact'. I suppose the emphasis here is on the 'vision' of an influential moral and religious teacher. To be sure there seems to me an over-intellectual bias in this formulation. The 'creative imagination' is certainly something to be emphasized where we are assessing the role of a great religious teacher, such as, say, St Francis. I think for instance of the poetry infusing the way he spoke of nature, the brilliance of such a phrase as 'Sister Death'. But St Francis would not have been the inspiring figure he was if he had been just a poet in that sense. It is the way in which he embodied this poetry in his own life that counts. It was wonderful for him to say of the lilies of the field, 'See how they praise God', but those words gained their quite peculiar resonance from the way in which Francis's own manner of praising God in his life so perfectly embodied the conception of 'praise' in which it was also possible for him to speak of the lilies as 'praising God'. And we can see something of what it meant to address Death as 'Sister' from what we know of Francis's own life and how he himself approached death. For all this something rather more than 'creative imagination' was necessary – immense courage, for instance. 'Practice gives the words their sense.' The point becomes all the more relevant when we remember that quite particular conceptions of God are embodied in the lives of inarticulate individuals with little claim to creative imagination; and when we remember that, much as such lives may owe to the example of great teachers, the existence and

greatness of such teachers itself only make sense against the (obscure) background of such lives.

I want to turn now to the two 'far more penetrating criticisms
of his [Taylor's] argument', which Mulhall identifies towards the
end of his paper. The first concerns Taylor's 'general relation to
Kierkegaard' and the second 'his conception of the relation between
philosophy and art (or, more precisely, literature)'. The four or five
pages in which Mulhall discusses the relevance of Kierkegaard to
Taylor's argument seem to me easily the best in his paper. I think
he is quite right in pointing out what he calls Taylor's 'myopia' in
not seeing how devastating a criticism of 'his frequent, indeed all
but uniform use of the first-person plural pronoun' is implied by
Kierkegaard's whole method of writing, especially, though not exclusively, his use of pseudonymous works.

The second of Mulhall's two criticisms of Taylor also seems to me
to raise a matter of great importance and I sympathize with a good
deal of what he writes; but I also have in the end considerable
misgivings about the position to which he is led. Mulhall's point of
criticism follows from the previous one about Taylor's insufficient
taking to heart of Kierkegaard. It is that his 'emphasis on moral
argument as a confrontation between concrete individuals' should
have led to a greater acknowledgement on his part 'that he is speaking in the first person to persons who must respond in the same
way'. I believe Mulhall is right in saying that Taylor's distinction
between 'setting the stage' for substantive moral argument and
actually speaking in one's own person from that stage is more problematic than he realizes and that 'he is in fact speaking in the first
person far more pervasively than is registered in his text'.

I also agree with him, though perhaps for different reasons than
his, that the difficulty here is not a difficulty concerning the 'genre'
to which one's work belongs – 'Is it philosophy or is it art?' I think
it hopeless to try to draw lines here, since there will be no agreement on where the line should be drawn and, perhaps more seriously, most of us individually will feel that there is something
arbitrary about trying to carve up 'disciplines' in this way. If it is
simply a matter of deciding to call a given work 'philosophy' or
'literature', one may legitimately wonder why this should matter.
What does matter, though, is that one should be clear about the sort
of appeal that is being made to one; particularly if what is at stake
is something as important as one's spiritual orientation.

It is at this point that Mulhall seems to me to miss something really important because, ironically enough, he too has not taken Kierkegaard sufficiently to heart. One may bring the point out by looking a bit more closely at the use made in this discussion of the image of the stage. Mulhall criticizes Taylor for trying to distinguish in his work between 'stage-setting' and (to use Mulhall's rebarbative phrase just once) 'stage-strutting', arguing that Taylor is under an illusion if he supposes that in his book he is merely arranging the stage and not speaking from it in his own voice. He seems to forget that to stand on the stage and speak in one's own voice is not the only, or even the most characteristic, use of the stage. One also stages dramas, in which *a diversity* of characters speaking in *different* voices are portrayed. Of course, sometimes plays are didactic and it is clear that the author is trying to promote a particular message of his own; but this is not always the case. One need only think of Shakespeare, for instance. The aim may be to portray as faithfully as possible a segment of life, without shying away from the possibility of there being irresolvable conflicts (not merely divergencies) which can only have a tragic outcome.

This last point, by the way, points to the main thing that is wrong with Mulhall's way of expressing the relation between differing moral and religious outlooks as so many 'perspectives'[14] which 'refract' a common reality. Tell that to the heretic tied to the stake and the Inquisitor ordering the fire to be lit! (Of course, there are plenty of other less extreme examples, but also many more equally extreme ones.)

I spoke a moment ago of the importance one may attach to 'the sort of appeal that is being made to one'. When one hears in the background of a didactic play, for instance, the sounds of an authorial axe being ground, one may feel resentfully that one is being got at, that one is not being honestly dealt with. The same thing, of course, may happen in other contexts. I should like here to quote Wittgenstein at some length:

Religious similes may be said to move on the edge of an abyss. Bunyan's for example. For what if we simply add: 'and all these traps, quicksands, wrong turnings, were planned by the Lord of the Road, and the monsters, thieves and robbers were created by him'? Certainly that is not the sense of the simile! But such a continuation is all too obvious! For many people, including me, this robs the simile of its power.

But more especially if this is – as it were – suppressed. It would be different if at every turn it were said quite honestly: 'I am using this as a simile, but look: it doesn't fit here'. Then you wouldn't feel you were being cheated, that someone was trying to convince you by trickery. Someone can be told for instance: 'Thank God for the good you receive, but don't complain about the evil: as you would of course do if a human being were to do you good and evil by turns.' Rules for life are dressed up in pictures. And these pictures can only serve to *describe* what we are to do, not *justify* it. Because they could provide a justification only if they held good in other respects as well. I can say 'Thank these bees for their honey, as if they were kind people who have prepared it for you'; that is *intelligible* and describes how I should like you to conduct yourself. But I cannot say: 'Thank them because, look, how kind they are!' – since the next moment they may sting you.

Religion says: *Do this!* – *Think like that!* – but it cannot justify it and, if it tries to, it becomes repellent; because for every reason it offers there is a valid counter-reason. It is more convincing to say: 'Think like this! – however strangely it may strike you.' Or: 'Won't you do this? – however repugnant you find it.'[15]

For this sort of reason Mulhall's advice to Taylor on how to clean up his act (so to speak!) seems to me catastrophically misconceived:

> what *Sources of the Self* may require is not supplementation by a personal moral manifesto but rather restatement in a form which makes it much clearer that it always already was a personal moral manifesto. The correct response of a reader upon completing its narrative should thus be not 'More!', but rather, 'Once more with feeling!'

The trouble is that Taylor's book seems to be, as it stands, only a very impure 'personal moral manifesto' as far as content is concerned, because it does indeed claim to give reasons – for instance, for preferring a religious to a non-religious view of the world; and 'for every reason it gives there is a valid counter-reason'. We hear, for instance, that religious 'sources' provide greater moral energy for benevolent acts than do non-religious 'sources'. Sometimes perhaps yes. But careful! the bees may sting you (inquisitors and heretics). Or again, there are other species of bee that may derive their moral energy precisely from opposition to the first sort (Jeremy

Bentham?). If there is going to be argument about such matters, then, to be above board, one must not conceal cases inimical to the conclusion one wishes to draw.

Now there does exist a philosophical tradition which has concerned itself precisely with the problem how to present moral or religious world-views in such a way that the passion behind them, which has to be evident if one is to recognize them for what they are, is clearly in view, along with the conception of the good that they embody, while at the same time equal justice is done to alternative and even hostile conceptions. Achieving this is a task of enormous difficulty, both at the technical level and also because of the moral demands it makes on the writer, who will of course him or herself have strong moral or religious commitments and will also be hostile to certain other possibilities.[16] A writer who described these kinds of difficulty as well as anyone I can think of was Simone Weil[17] whose admiration – not to say veneration – for the author of *The Iliad* may well have been a reflection of her realization how difficult she herself found it to do justice to ethico-religious views at variance with her own very passionately held ones.

The three philosophers who seem to me to have addressed most directly and successfully the problems involved in this sort of representation are Plato (writing in dialogue form), Kierkegaard (representing conflicting viewpoints pseudonymously) and Wittgenstein. In that last case I think particularly of the intricate interweaving of internal voices so characteristic of *Philosophical Investigations*, a technique by the way that expresses best, it seems to me, that the conflicting views are frequently to be found together in one's own breast. Part of the 'peace' that Wittgenstein thought philosophy should bring was a peaceful 'resolution' of such inner conflicts. My use of (single) scare quotes there is meant to indicate that precisely one of the main difficulties of achieving peace in such a context springs from an obscurity about what a word like 'resolution' can mean here.

Notes

1. Mulhall, of course, criticizes both these ideas in his final evaluation of Taylor.
2. This is not to deny that the diversities and conflicts will be different in the two kinds of case.
3. A very important dimension of such modes of expression is that they involve ways of distinguishing between authentic/sincere from inauthentic/insincere manifestations. This is a matter that is very difficult indeed to elucidate at all satisfactorily and I shall not attempt it here. I mention it because it is something to which we cannot do justice if we think in terms of 'vocabularies'. There are thought-provoking discussions of such issues in Wittgenstein's *Last Writings on the Philosophy of Psychology* and *Philosophical Investigations*, Part II, section xi.
4. Wittgenstein, *Culture and Value*, p. 85e.
5. At least vicariously. I am thinking of Disney's use of Bach in *Fantasia*, though I should not be surprised to learn of other cases.
6. Mark Twain, *Huckleberry Finn*, ch. XXXI (London: The Folio Society 1993), pp. 209f.
7. Ibid., pp. 4f.
8. In *Without Answers*. I quote from memory, my copy of this book having, alas, been misappropriated by an unscrupulous borrower.
9. Tertullian please copy!
10. And he would seem to share that lack with numerous contemporary philosophers – if one goes by the way they speak about the concept of God's *omniscience*.
11. Wittgenstein, *Culture and Value*, p. 85e.
12. For more discussion of this very important point see Peter Winch, *Simone Weil: 'The Just Balance'* (Cambridge and New York: Cambridge University Press, 1989), Chapter 4.
13. Cf. Wittgenstein's remark: 'The way you use the word "God" does not show *whom* you mean – but, rather, what you mean' (*Culture and Value*, p. 50e). (It is, of course, important to the sense of this remark that 'whom' is italicized and 'what' is not.)
14. To inject a note of self-criticism: I spoke like this myself in 'Moral Integrity', in Peter Winch, *Ethics and Action* (London: Routledge & Kegan Paul, 1972), pp. 171–92.
15. *Culture and Value* (1937), p. 29e.
16. What many people object to under the label of 'relativism' (or alternatively under the label of 'moral imperialism') is very often a product of one or other sort of failure in this task.
17. See especially her wonderful essay: 'The Iliad, Poem of Might'.

Part Five
Religion as the Opium of the People

9

Is Religion the Opium of the People? Marxianism and Religion

Kai Nielsen

Is there a viable materialist conception of religion? This is a less simple question than it appears to be. Plainly, there are materialist conceptions of religion, from Epicurus through Marx and Engels, which explain religion as a function of material needs, and of the material conditions of human life which give rise to these needs. The question is: Are such theories viable or adequate to explain the phenomenon of religious belief? A viable conception of religion is one which doesn't simply explain religion away, but rather explains its origins, its distinctive cultural and historical forms, its persistence in various institutional contexts, its changes and development, its continuing and present existence in the modes of belief and action of individuals. The question of whether there is a viable materialist conception of religion is therefore a question of whether any of the presumptively materialist theories meet these requirements. What would it take for a materialist theory of religion to do so adequately?

Marx W. Wartofsky

INTRODUCTION

I shall first describe in unnuanced terms the canonical core of Marxian social theory, that part of the theory which makes it a distinctive social theory and must remain, though perhaps in some rationally reconstructed form, for Marxianism to continue to be a distinctive social theory. I shall then turn to a characterization of the proper sense of 'ideology' to be utilized in giving a Marxian account of religion as ideology.[1] In doing this I will argue that there is an important distinction to be made between claiming that beliefs (including religious beliefs) are ideological and claiming that they are false or incoherent. Marx, Engels and the other classical Marxists as well presupposed, like Freud, that the cognitive errors of religious beliefs (their falsity or incoherence) had been firmly established by previous thinkers (e.g., Hume and Bayle); they took it as their task not to repeat or update those old arguments, but to reveal religion's ideological functions; to show the role that religion plays in our life and to show that that role is an ideological one.

In sections III and IV, I shall characterize the core of Marx's and Engels' account of religion (principally Engels', for he wrote more extensively than did Marx about such matters); I shall, that is, characterize their materialist conception of religion. I shall show how they conceived of religion's origins, its distinctive historical cultural forms, its changes and how these changes match with, and are functional for, modes of socioeconomic production. I shall then ask whether we have good grounds for believing that that conception, taken as a sociological generalization about religion in class societies, is true, or is at least a plausible candidate for being true. After some initial disambiguation and a locating of the proper scope and claims of the theory, I shall argue that it is a very plausible account indeed. It does not show us what the sole function of religion is – there is no such thing – but it does give us a compelling account of certain key functions of religion. It yields, I argue, a viable materialist conception of religion.

I

What is central to Marxianism is *historical* materialism and the conception that societies are divided into antagonistic classes with ideologies which, standardly, without such an awareness on the part of the agents involved, function to answer to the interests of one or more of the classes in the societies in which the agents live. The master claim of historical materialism is that 'it is in the nature of the human situation, considered in its most general aspects, that there will be a tendency for productive power to grow'.[2] What Joshua Cohen has called *minimalist* historical materialism 'is simply an elaboration of that master claim, it would only be defeated by what defeats the master claim, and so it is the final fall-back position for the defender of historical materialism'.[3] Such a minimalist account is not committed to the claim that all phenomena, not even all phenomena of great cultural significance, can be explained by historical materialism, but only phenomena which (directly or indirectly) are economically significant.

Minimalist historical materialism is also a *restricted* form of historical materialism. By this is meant that 'it restricts itself to explaining those non-economic phenomena which possess economic relevance'.[4] Classical historical materialism, the historical materialism defended by Marx, Engels, Lenin and Trotsky, claimed that all phenomena of great cultural significance, including, of course, all such religious phenomena, were economically relevant phenomena and were explained by historical materialism. This is *unrestricted* historical materialism and it is a stronger claim than the minimalist needs to make. But centrally, historical materialism in any form is an attempt to provide a theory of epochal social change. For *restricted, minimalist* historical materialism this is limited to explaining the rise and fall of whole systems of economic relations such as capitalism, feudalism and relatedly, directly or indirectly, economically important phenomena. For *inclusive, unrestricted* historical materialism, by contrast, there is an attempt to explain the emergence of all major changes in society such as the emergence of Catholicism, Protestantism, pietism, and the like and to explain them as being *required* to unfetter the productive forces at a given epoch. But to claim that Christianity is required for the unfettering of the productive forces at a certain stage of their development, let alone to claim that Protestantism is required for capitalism to arise and be sustained, is to make a very strong claim concerning the predominance of material factors in explaining social evolution. Protestantism, particularly Calvinistic Protestantism, *facilitated* the development of capitalism (was functional for it), but to claim that it was *necessary* for its development is problematic. It is not clear whether Marx was committed to making such a strong claim or that (what is more important) whether contemporary Marxians should make such a strong claim. I am inclined to think not. Be that as it may, the weaker claim about Protestantism's facilitating the unfettering of capitalist productive forces, and thus being functional for capitalism, will suffice for my purposes. That, more generally, the various religions tend to facilitate the development of different productive forces, and that religion is in this way functional for them, is what I am claiming for a Marxian conception of religion.

Class as a conception is equally important as historical materialism for Marxianism. Class, for Marxians, is not a matter of a person's consciousness of her position in society, but (whether the person is conscious of it or not) is a matter of her relationship to the means of production in the society in which she lives. In our society, the principal classes are capitalists and workers. Capitalists own and control the means of production, buy labour-power as a commodity and put that power to work under their direction (whether direct or indirect) typically in their enterprises. Workers sell their labour-power and, as they enter the production process, they are dominated by the capitalists or their managers. Workers, without ownership or control of the means of production, or at least any significant means of production, sell their labour-power in a commodity market for a wage and work, under these contracted conditions, for the owners of the means of production, directly or indirectly, under their direction.

In Western society capitalists constitute the dominant class and workers, constituting a class themselves, are members of a dominated class. It is, however, in the interests of the capitalist class that workers are not aware that they are dominated or even that they constitute a class with interests of their own that are distinct, or partly distinct, from capitalist class interests. Socialist political struggle centrally consists in the struggle for workers to attain consciousness of themselves as a dominated class, to see what their interests are, to recognize that they are importantly antagonistic to that of capitalists, to become aware of their power to break capitalist class domination and for them to proceed to struggle to break that domination and control and so gain a state where they collectively own and control the means of production.

In this class struggle ideology plays an important role. It is capitalist class ideology in our societies which works to keep workers from being aware of their position in the world and of their own interests. (This is not to say that the *production* of ideology is always or even typically deliberate.) In speaking of an ideology Marxians are speaking of a general outlook or belief system about human beings and society, about some sort of world outlook, with an associated set of practices, about how people cannot, so the ideology claims, but live in certain ways, about how, in those small areas where there is any choice in the matter, people should live and about how society should, or even must, be ordered. These outlooks, beliefs and associated practices answer to the interests of a determinate class (or classes) in a particular society (or cluster of related societies) during a certain epoch.

This being so, 'class ideology' is pleonastic. Without classes, on a Marxian conception of ideology, there would be no ideology. Standardly, but not invariably, ideological beliefs are false beliefs and also standardly, but again not invariably, people in the grip of a ideological beliefs are not aware that their beliefs are false. Indeed, they typically think they either are or presuppose deep truths about the human condition. It is for this reason that Marxians speak of ideological illusions and false consciousness. But false consciousness should not be taken as a defining feature of an ideology, but as something that normally goes with having an ideology or thinking or acting ideologically. What is a defining feature of an ideology is that *an ideology answers, or takes itself to be answering, to class interests.*[5]

Religion – all religion – is taken by Marxians to be ideology. Religious beliefs are said by Marxians to be ideological illusions, expressive of the false consciousness of the religious believer in the grip of a religious ideology. That is to say, the religious beliefs of believers are at best false and not infrequently incoherent. But Christians, Hindus, and the like suffering from false consciousness, take them to be deep, mysterious, sometimes ineffable truths about ultimate reality. Moreover, they are taken to be beliefs essential to sustain and to make sense of their lives – lives which, without these religious beliefs, would, the people in the grip of the ideology believe, lack all significance. But this, Marxians contend, is an ideological illusion, which is standardly, but not invariably, used in various ways – some subtle, some not – to further or protect the interests of the dominant class. Thus, in capitalist societies, Christianity typically but not invariably functions to support capitalism, and it does so by giving people a false or incoherent conception of their nature and destiny.

II

I have stated here, crudely and unqualifiedly, and with no attention to nuance, a central part of the canonical core of Marxian social theory, a theory which I think is, in its sophisticated articulations, the most plausible, holistic, social theory available to us. Be that as it may, this is not the place to examine historical materialism or a Marxian conception of class or ideology critically, though I shall remark in passing that I think a much stronger case for Marxianism can be made, and indeed has been made, by analytical Marxians such as G.A. Cohen, Andrew Levine, John Roemer, Richard Miller, Erik Olin Wright, Rodney Peffer, Debra Satz, Joshua Cohen, Philippe van Parijs and David Schweickart, than has usually been acknowledged. But that for another day. I shall assume here what I have argued for elsewhere, namely that some rational reconstruction of Marx's social theory shows it to be a sound, or at least a plausible and attractive, social theory, and see what, given that assumption, should be said for a rather standard Marxian account of religion as ideology in the sense of 'ideology', that I have outlined.[6] Indeed, its treatment of religion *might* be one of the places where Marxian theory stands in need of revision. And, whether this is so or not, there is the sociological fact that not a few theologians have thought of themselves, perhaps confusedly, as being both Marxians and Christians or Jews, and have taken the militant atheism of Marx and Engels to be inessential to their theories and revolutionary practice. Most Marxians believe that that conjunction rests on a mistake, even if in some circumstances it is a humanly and practically useful mistake. That is to say, Marxians could agree that it may be a very good thing indeed that there is a Red Archbishop in Brazil, that there are working-class priests who are Marxist militants and that there are liberation theologians and radical Christians.

Be that as it may, not a few have thought that Marxian explanations and critiques of religion are powerful as explanations of religion and as a critique of religion. Indeed, explanation and critique run in tandem here, for if a Marxian explanation of religion is on the mark, that very kind of explanation is also a critique. Marxian explanation explains religious beliefs as ideological illusions mystifying, for the people hoodwinked by them, their social relations and conception of the world in a way that supports the socioeconomic structure – the relations of production – of their society. Moreover, it supports it in a manner that in reality does not, in most instances, answer to their interests or meet their needs. They (to situate it for a moment in our epoch) are taken in by capitalism in a way that conflicts with their own human flourishing and their leading as good a life as they could live. So explanation and critique run together here. They are *conceptually* distinct, but in this case you cannot do the first without doing the second. If the explanation is on the mark, religion has, in being explained, been *ipso facto* criticized.

However, what is often not noticed is that Marxian explanations and critiques of religion, like Freudian explanations and critiques, are dependent for their soundness on the soundness of secular, non-ideological critiques of religion such as those of Holbach, Hume, Bayle or contemporary atheistic or agnostic critiques such as those of Bertrand Russell, Axel Hägerström, J.L. Mackie, Richard Robinson, Antony Flew, Michael Martin, Wallace Matson, or my own. Marxian accounts assert that religious beliefs, as expressive of false consciousness, are either false or incoherent. But they do very little by way of arguing for that, but, taking it to be obvious, seek rather to show that religious beliefs are ideological beliefs. But that ideological part by itself is not enough for their critique of religion, for ideological beliefs could be true. Most of them are not, but are rather false or incoherent beliefs, expressive of false consciousness, but there is at least conceptual space for ideological beliefs to be true or well warranted. What shows they are false or incoherent is not that they are ideological. But what makes them ideological is rather that they belong to a system of beliefs or an outlook concerning persons and society which answers to, or takes itself as answering to, class interests. Marx's *Capital* is as ideological as Smith's and Ricardo's political economy. They supported capitalism, helped sustain the class interests of capitalists and, while making some important and at least putatively true claims (claims on which Marx built), they made some importantly false claims too. But both their true and false claims were often genuinely scientific claims which, at the very same time, were also ideological claims – they supported capitalist class interests. And their theories as a whole, while being genuinely social scientific theories, were also ideological theories in support of capitalist class interests.

The same can be said of Marx's *Capital*. It is both an ideological theory and a scientific theory. It is deliberately designed to support working-class interests and was plainly also believed by Marx to be true ('objectively true' being pleonastic) and it indeed could be true, or, on some rationally reconstructed account such as G.A. Cohen's or John Roemer's, it is at least a plausible candidate for being a true, or at least an approximately true, theory with its linked practices. Louis Althusser notwithstanding, ideology and science, and ideology and truth, do not need to stand in conflict. They often – indeed, even typically – do, but they need not and perhaps sometimes do not.

What Marx and Engels, and Marxian accounts generally, show, if true, is that religion is ideology and that religious beliefs are ideological. But it is a further step to show that they are false or incoherent and are expressive of false consciousness. That they are false or incoherent is not shown, or, even in any remotely careful way, argued for, by Marx or Engels or by the other major figures in the Marxian tradition. They rather presuppose it and take it as something evident to anyone with a reasonable education and not beguiled by ideology. That such beliefs are false or incoherent, they argue, has been well shown by Enlightenment thinkers such as Holbach, Hobbes, Hume and Bayle. Marxians, even such historicist Marxians as Antonio Gramsci, were children of the Enlightenment, building on and extending in new and striking ways the tradition of the Enlightenment,[7] as did Freud as well (though very differently). Marx and Engels assumed that philosophers such as Holbach and Hobbes had it basically right about the *grounds* for religious belief. A contemporary Marxian, who is more philosophically sophisticated about the logical status of religious beliefs than were the classical Marxists, will shy away from Holbach and Hobbes on such issues and turn instead to Hume and Bayle or, in our time, to J.L. Mackie, Axel Hägerström or Antony Flew (Flew's rather fanatical conservatism notwithstanding). Marx and Engels, in an interesting little narrative in *The Holy Family* about the history of philosophy (including its discussion of religion) from Descartes to Hegel and Feuerbach, argue that Hume and Bayle have shown that religious beliefs are at best false.[8] That critical task, that is, was carried out, they believe, by classical Enlightenment thinkers. Building on that, the distinctively Marxian contribution *vis-à-vis* religion is, by contrast, to show religion's ideological functions: to show how in this domain false consciousness functions ideologically to support particular modes of production.

So it is in this way – a way that is utterly different from, but still complementary to, a Humean, Hägerströmian or Mackian critique – that Marxian accounts of religion become important. If one is justified in setting aside a broadly Humean scepticism about religion, then the Marxian critique of religion would be less interesting, for, even if it shows that religious belief is ideological, that in itself would not show that religious believers have succumbed to false consciousness or (what is something else again) that religious beliefs are false or incoherent. Indeed, their being ideological might diminish their moral attractiveness somewhat, but it would not be impossible to believe that, with some alterations, the ideological dimensions might be excised or in some way neutralized on the one hand, or, even without alteration, justified because the class interests they support should be supported, on the other. However, if a broadly Humean and Baylean scepticism about religion is in place, then the Marxian explanations and critiques of religion gain in interest. If, that is, religious belief – belief that God exists and belief in God – is in error, indeed in unexcisable error, then religious beliefs are at best false; further, if, as Marx and Engels believed, this has been more or less evident for a very long time, then the question naturally arises, why has religious belief been so tenacious? This is also a question that Freud, holding similar beliefs about the cognitive import of religion, addressed, that Feuerbach wrestled with and that Marx and Engels considered. Let us see what Marx and Engels had to say about it.

III

Following Ludwig Feuerbach, Marx and Engels regard 'the Christian God', in Engels' words, as 'a fantastic mirror image of man'.[9] In fact, all religious entities in all the various religions are, they believe, such projections of human attributes and wishes. Where religion developed beyond animism, these human projections were turned into what in the imagination of human beings were thought to be supernatural entities. But such conceptions are incoherent; belief in them is, as Engels put it, nonsensical.[10] That the dominated have these religious beliefs answers to the interests of the ruling class, but these projections of human feelings also answer, though in a deceptive and illusory way, to the interests of the dominated, despised people in class society, people with little hope that their needs could be met, their earthly aspirations satisfied, their lives made decent or, in some instances, even tolerable. If their lives contained even the possibility of becoming tolerable, Engels maintains, religion would not answer to their interests, but since their tangible, genuine needs and interests cannot be met, such an eschatological religion gives them an illusory hope and in that way goes some way towards answering a need in their lives. Moreover for them religion, and a certain kind of religion at that, was factually speaking inevitable. In perhaps his most famous passage on religion, Marx remarks:

> *Religious* distress is at the same time the *expression* of real distress and the *protest* against real distress. Religion is the sigh of the oppressed creature, the heart of a heartless world, just as it is the spirit of a spiritless situation. It is the opium of the people.[11]

Both the remark 'it is the opium of the people' and 'it is the sigh of the oppressed creature, the heart of a heartless world' have been quoted again and again, but while they are compatible, they cut in rather different directions. A religious person could enthusiastically accept that 'religion is the sigh of the oppressed creature, the heart of a heartless world', but not – or at least much less easily – that it is the 'opium of the people'. A Christian, for example, could very well see the condition of human beings in such stark terms, as the remark about the sigh of the oppressed creature gestures at. This in part is what brings us to sickness unto death: to despair of the world as it is, and indeed as, even in the most favourable conditions, it could be, and of our lives in it.

However, as, say, with liberation theology (but not only with it) Christians could see the Christian message, as Moslems see Islam, as one demanding a struggle against those conditions, a call to resistance to conditions of oppression and heartlessness, even while not blinking at the fact, but fully taking it to heart, that this is the way the world is and indeed may always be. But when Marx goes on to say that religion is the opium of the people, he adds something, namely that this sigh of the oppressed, this protest against real distress, takes the form, with one attitude or another, of an acceptance of this dreadful world, an acceptance of one's lot, of one's station and its duties, no matter how harsh. And instead of placing one's faith, as did the Anabaptists, in the coming to be of the Kingdom of God on earth, and struggling to attain it, one places one's faith in another, better world, a 'Spiritual World', beyond the grave, where all the woes of this life will be a thousand times recompensed in a life of bliss in communion with God. What we have to look forward to is not a better earthly condition, but a life, after bodily death, in God's Spiritual Kingdom. This has been thought by people of a secular disposition to be a heavenly swindle and has been crudely called 'pie in the sky by and by'. Life for many people is hell now, in almost every sort of way, and there is no escaping this earthly hell, or even significantly ameliorating it, but, on such a religious conception, by a commitment to Christ, and by living in righteousness, we can be sure that we shall enter the heavenly kingdom of God after our death, and live forever in a state of bliss.

Engels and Marx – most especially Engels – trace how this and related conceptions are worked out in Christianity, though they are not denying that broadly similar things obtain for other religions, particularly for religions that have the status of what Engels calls world religions.[12] But the emphasis is on Christianity, given Engels' emphasis on its ideological role in the Western world: how it facilitated, and continues to facilitate, the rise, stabilization and development of capitalism. But this account is also a narrative about the origin and development of religion. I think it is clear that Engels, a pure child of the Enlightenment, gives us a rationalistic narrative, which, as Wartofsky puts it, is also a materialist conception of the origin and development of religion in general and of Christianity in particular. But it may be none the worse for that.

IV

I will set out some of the core elements and then, in the light of this narrative, and critically reviewing it, say something about the import of Marxian claims about religion as the opium of the people and particularly about Christianity, as an ideological mask which helps sustain capitalist class society as it, albeit in different forms, helped sustain the slave society of Rome and subsequently feudal society, both with their distinctive modes of production.

I would like first to make a disclaimer. I am neither an historian nor a biblical scholar and am too much of a *fachidiot* to know whether Engels' historical narrative, particularly in the light of what has been discovered since his time, is a reasonably accurate account of that period and those developments, or whether instead, it is what anthropologists like to call 'a just so story'. *Perhaps* it is something in between, a reasonable account of the origin and development of Christianity, given what was known in Engels' time, but nevertheless somewhat one-sided and inaccurate in important details. I simply do not know. And perhaps anyway there is no reasonable prospect of telling it like it was.

What I shall assume, and I think not unreasonably, is that it is a plausible narrative, a reasonable just so story (if you will), and then, on safer philosophical ground, see where we can go with it. If, I shall ask, this was the way it was, or something approximating it, what does this tell us about the ideological functions of religion in such a world and about the viability of religion in general and Christianity in particular? Things could have been as Engels portrays them; perhaps they were, and still are. And if they were and are, what should we think about Christianity and about religion more generally?

Before turning to Engels' narrative, there is a further preliminary to which I should attend. The treatment of religion in Marx and Engels and most Marxian writings is not philosophy as we have come to understand it, at least in an Anglo-American and Scandinavian philosophical ambiance. In the *philosophy* of religion we find claims such as 'If God exists, His existence is necessary', 'God is eternal', 'God is the perfect good', 'God is said to be an infinite individual but the very idea of an infinite individual is self-contradictory', '"God created the world out of nothing" is incoherent', 'What is good cannot be identified with what God commands', 'God's existence can be proved', 'God's existence cannot be proved', 'The very idea of taking it that the attempt to prove God's existence is a religiously serious or important matter reveals an incipient atheism'. These and like claims, are the stuff of the philosophy of religion and philosophers, who deal in any way with religion, if they are at all competent, know how to argue for or against them in ways that are clearly recognizable as philosophical.

Marx and Engels do not engage in such arguments. Indeed, I think that it is evident that they would regard concern with such arguments as fatuous. From the narrative they gave in *The Holy Family* about the development of philosophy, we can see that they think that what is to be said here has been well said by philosophers such as Holbach, Locke, Hume, Kant and Bayle, and that there is no need to repeat their work.[13] In this way they believe that results in philosophy or in intellectual history can be established.

What Engels gives us, as we shall see, is a social and psychological description (a heavily interpretive description all the same) and an explanation embedded in a narrative resulting in a critique wedded to that description and explanation. But there is little in the way of argument or conceptual elucidation. Thus, as philosophers in the analytical tradition have come, perhaps in a too *parti-pris* manner, to view philosophy, there is little *philosophy* in their accounts of religion. Their claims are, for the most part, empirical – sociological, broadly economic, historical and psychological – and are establishable (or disestablishable) by empirical investigation and careful reflection on that investigation. Philosophical argument and elucidation, as we have come to understand them, have little place here. Apart from the fact that I cannot argue for or against them in the way I am accustomed to argue for philosophical claims, I do not care in the slightest whether they are philosophical or not.[14] What I am interested in is their plausibility, whether we should accept them and the import of their acceptance or rejection. What is important is whether it is reasonable for us to believe that their central claims, at least on some rational reconstruction, are true.

But to return to Engels' narrative of the origin, development and function of religion. Engels remarks that our conception of the gods first arose through the personification of natural forces.[15] As he put it in *Anti-Dühring*: 'All religion . . . is nothing but the fantastic reflection in men's minds of those external forces which control their daily life, a reflection in which the terrestrial forces assume the form of supernatural forces.'[16] In the most primitive societies, religion so reflected the forces of nature. But, as societies grow more complex, and particularly as a social division of labour becomes embedded in the social fabric of people's lives and classes come into existence, 'social forces begin to be active – forces which confront man as equally alienated and at first equally inexplicable, dominating him with the same apparent natural necessity' as the forces of nature themselves. 'The fantastic figures, which at first only reflected the mysterious forces of nature, at this point acquire social attributes, become representatives of the forces of history.'[17]

The religions of more complex societies – religions which have become more elaborately socialized – quickly took various forms among different peoples, who were differently socialized. In the general cultural area from which Christianity sprang, among the Egyptians, Persians, Jews and Chaldeans, for example, we had what Engels calls 'national religions' with their distinctive ceremonies, with their particular gods with their distinctive chosen people, with rites so distinctive and demanding that 'people of two different religions . . . could not eat or drink together, or hardly speak to each other'.[18] Christianity emerged from this world of exclusively national religions – entering 'into a resolute antithesis to all previous religions', as, in that cultural area at least, 'the first possible world religion'.[19] Christianity, Engels remarks, 'knew no distinctive ceremonies, not even the sacrifices and processions of the classic world. By thus rejecting all national religions and their common ceremonies and addressing itself to all peoples without distinction it becomes the *first possible world religion*'.[20]

However, and that fact (if it is a fact) notwithstanding, just as with the previous national religions, Christianity arose under and reflected certain distinctive socioeconomic conditions. It emerged in the Near East during the ruthless hegemony of the Roman Empire and spread rapidly throughout the whole Roman Empire. At first savagely persecuted by successive Roman emperors reaching its epitome with Nero, in some 300 years it came to be the state religion of the Roman Empire. In short, things so evolved that Christianity eventually brought 'the Roman Empire into subjection and dominated by far the larger part of civilised humanity for 1,800 years'.[21] Why, Engels asks, did the 'popular masses in the Roman Empire' come to prefer 'this nonsense'? And why did 'the ambitious Constantine' finally see 'in the adoption of this religion of nonsense the best means of exalting himself to the position of autocrat of the Roman world'? Engels here seeks to explain the origin and development of Christianity 'from the historical conditions under which it arose and reached its dominating position'.

Engels argues that we can 'get an idea of what Christianity looked like in its early form by reading the so-called Book of Revelation of John'.[22] This book, he claims, can be definitely dated to 68 or 69 AD; it is 'the oldest, and the only book of the New Testament, the authenticity of which cannot be disputed'.[23] And in it, we have Christianity in the simplest form in which it has been preserved. There is only one dominant dogmatic point: 'that the faithful have been saved by the sacrifice of Christ'.[24]

What Engels is principally interested in here is the character of that Christianity, the socioeconomic conditions under which it arose, the people who became its adherents and their life conditions. 'Christianity', Engels asserts, 'was originally a movement of oppressed people: it first appeared as the religion of slaves and emancipated slaves, of poor people deprived of all rights, of peoples subjugated or dispersed by Rome.'[25] It emerged at a time when in the Greco-Roman world, and even more so in Asia Minor, Syria and Egypt, 'an absolutely uncritical mixture of the crassest superstitions of the most varying peoples was indiscriminately accepted and complemented by pious deception and downright charlatanism; a time in which miracles, ecstasies, visions, apparitions, divining, gold-making, cabbala and other secret magic play a primary role. It was in that atmosphere, and, moreover, among a class of people who were more inclined than any other to listen to these supernatural fantasies, that Christianity arose'.[26]

The Book of Revelation – this authentic depiction of early Christianity, the earliest Christianity of which we have any knowledge – consists in a series of apocalyptic visions, which make up almost the whole of the book. Christ – the lamb – appears in the garb of a high priest. Christ is depicted as the son of God, but 'by no means

God or equal to God', though, as an emanation of God, he is said to have existed for all eternity. But, as important as he is, he remains subordinate to God. And, crucially, the Christ of the Revelation 'has been sacrificed for the sins of the world and with whose blood the faithful of all tongues and nations have been redeemed to God'.[27]

What is revolutionary here is that we have a universal religion, a religion applying fully to all the oppressed, exploited and despised elements of society (themselves often very different people) of which there were very many in the Roman Empire. In a 'social Darwinian' struggle for the survival of the fittest among competing religions, the vital and deeply appealing message of Christianity, which enabled it to emerge supreme, was that in Christ, by 'one great voluntary sacrifice of a mediator the sins of all times and all men were atoned for once for all – in respect of the faithful'.[28]

The first Christians were mainly slaves, but not exclusively so; in the towns many freemen lived lives nearly as impoverished as slaves', with no hope of escaping their destitution, while 'in the rural districts of the provinces' they were peasants 'who had fallen more and more into bondage through debt'.[29] These were people who had been utterly crushed by the iron fist of the Roman Empire. But, in addition to their different class status, they were also culturally diverse people, coming from many different societies. It was these peoples who became the first Christians. After the crushing defeat of the slave uprising under Spartacus, the slaves had no hope of earthly (worldly) emancipation. The same was true of the impoverished freemen and peasants. Moreover, their social units (tribes, or unions of kindred tribes) had been destroyed by the Roman military juggernaut and its accompanying system of government. Their social systems, their systems of ownership and ways of life, 'had been smitten down by the levelling iron fist of conquering Rome'. And 'Roman jurisdiction and tax-collecting machinery completely dissolved their traditional inner organisation'.[30] They were plundered and pillaged, treated in all sorts of appalling ways, and, like many people in the Third World today, they were growing steadily more and more destitute: 'Any resistance of isolated small tribes or towns to the gigantic Roman power was hopeless.'[31]

In such people the Christian message of salvation found fertile ground. It provided a heart in a heartless world by promising freedom from bondage and misery in a life beyond, after their earthly death, in God's Spiritual World, in heaven, if only they would live righteously now. (This, remember, was the message that Nietzsche scorned.) Given their material and intellectual resources, it was a message of salvation that made sense to them and that they could take to heart. With no hope of earthly emancipation, misery and destitution was inescapable. So for any hope to exist, it must be a hope for a 'world beyond this world'. Thus, their way out – their only way out – was salvation 'not in this world', but in a 'new world', a 'Spiritual World', the world prophesized by Christianity, in which the faithful would live with God in His heavenly kingdom after their bodily death.

Against the religious conceptions and conceptions of *Weltanschauung* of the Judaic world, which put little stock in such beliefs, the Christian vision magically answered to the desperate aspirations of such people living in such appalling socioeconomic circumstances. Christianity triumphed in the cultural struggle, and belief in life after death, and the desirability of life after death, gradually became 'a recognised article of faith throughout the Roman World'. Christianity, taking 'recompense and punishment in the world beyond seriously', created 'heaven and hell, and a way out was found which would lead the labouring and burdened from the vale of woe to eternal paradise'.[32]

Here we see clearly how, in a particular circumstance, religion can be the opium of the people and, to return to that famous passage from Marx's *Contribution to the Critique of Hegel's Philosophy of Right*, 'the sigh of the oppressed creature, the heart of a heartless world, the spirit of a spiritless situation'. It is evident why people so situated should flock to such an eschatological religion.

Marx next remarks that 'the abolition of religion as the illusory happiness of the people is required for their real happiness'. Traditional criticism of religion limits itself to showing (trying to show) the falsity or incoherence of religious beliefs. But this kind of critique is not sufficient, though it is necessary, because it is through such a critique of religion that people become disillusioned and are made to think and to shape reality as people who have been disillusioned and have 'come to reason'. But we must not only learn, Marx argues, that religious beliefs are illusory, even necessary illusions for people caught in certain life conditions, we must also, from careful economic and social study, establish what Marx called the 'truth of this world'.[33] We need to learn about the conditions which need illusions and how we could have a world that did not need religious illusions or any other kind of illusion, and learn as well how to struggle (a struggle informed by theory) to gain that world. But, of course, in certain circumstances (for example, for slaves during Nero's time), we would also see, if we were at all clear-headed, that any advance was a long way off. It was not something that was at all possible for them.

The early Christianity Engels describes fits well with the mode of production that obtained in the Roman Empire: a mode of production based on slave-labour. But modes of production change. And, with these changed modes of production, Christianity also changes. Indeed, as long as we have class societies, Christianity will change with these changes, in ways that match better and serve better the new modes of production. Thus, the feudal mode of production produced Catholicism with its hierarchies, the capitalist mode of production, Protestantism (most particularly and effectively, Calvinist Protestantism, or in England Anglicanism, resulting from a political compromise fuelled by an economic struggle, that yielded an Anglicanism which was a blend of Puritanism on the one hand, and Catholicism on the other, with the king as in effect a rather constrained pope). In France the violent bourgeois revolution, going hand in hand with the tenets of the Enlightenment, moved, in a way at first favourable to capitalism, to both materialism and social ferment and, with that, to a massive rejection of tradition. While initially liberating, affording the bourgeoisie a free hand unencumbered by feudal constraint, it was also unstable, given that it unleashed the rising proletariat. Principally as a matter of expediency, there was eventually a return to a rather chastised Catholicism, as the ruling classes, recognizing that they 'had come to grief with materialism', came to stress, instead of Enlightenment values, that 'religion must be kept alive for the people', for 'that was the only and the last means to save society from utter ruin'. For a ruling class with little in the way of faith and for some intellectuals with a stake in the status quo, religion came to seem a useful device to keep the working class in line. Sometimes they were not that clear-headed, but, clear-headed or not, they saw the social indispensability of religion, if *their* civilization were to be saved.

Central to Marxism is historical materialism which, as Engels puts it, designates 'that view of the course of history which seeks the ultimate cause and the great moving power of all important historic events in the economic development of society, in the changes in the modes of production and exchange, in the consequent division of society into distinct classes, and in the struggles of these classes against one another'.[35] In accordance with this grand empirical hypothesis (for that is what it is), we have Engels' empirical claim that with the changes of economic development of society, with the changes in the mode of production and exchange, a society will get the form of religion that is most functional for that mode of production. But in doing so, since we are talking about class societies, that religion, to be so functional, will work to keep the dominated classes in line, to accept in one way or another their station and its duties, and to regard this, all things considered, as necessary and proper, or at least inescapable. In that way religion is the opium of the people, and usefully so, for the dominant classes and sometimes, when their situation is very hopeless, even, in a mystifying way, for the dominated classes too, for it gives them a consoling illusion of a heart in a world that is actually heartless.

V

Is this view true or a reasonable approximation of something that is true? If it is true, it is true as a *sociological generalization*, a generalization across all class societies. It is not a claim about what religious belief *must* be for every individual. It is a claim about how religion functions, or, more weakly, tends to function, in class societies. I am now asking whether we should believe that such a claim, so understood, is so.

If a claim is made as strong as the claim that this is the *sole* function, or even the sole social function, of religion, we have very good reason indeed for believing that it is false. Even with a basically Feuerbachian projectionist theory of religion, which in its essentials is Marx's and Engels' as well, we have the Freudian alternative which is also a projectionist theory, only the image we project in believing in God is that of a perfect but also an almighty father, a figure who is projected as a heavenly father but also as both a feared and revered father, and different psychological mechanisms are invoked. If we are making such a strong claim, we need to be given reasons for believing that the Freudian account is false and the Marxian one is true. Actually, I think sometimes – that is, in certain circumstances – one account is true and sometimes the other. And sometimes both are arguably true at the same time. The image we project in our imagination could be that of both a heavenly father and a distorted image of our social relations functioning to lead us to accept this vale of tears. As has often enough been argued, the Freudian accounts and the Marxian accounts are both compatible and complementary, if not pressed dogmatically. Neither is very plausible as yielding the sole account of the psycho-social functions of religion. And Emile Durkheim's account, which tells us that what people worship is really society itself, though ideology leads them to misrecognize the object of their worship, is another rival materialist functional account of religion. But then no theory, neither Durkheim's, nor Freud's nor Marx's, yields the *sole* viable functional account of religion. Moreover, for projectionist accounts of the status of religious belief, Frankfurt School social theorists, such as Erich Fromm, Max Horkheimer and Theodor Adorno, have pointed out that there are still other social psychological functions of religion not covered by the classical Marxian accounts and only inadequately covered by the Freudian and Durkheimian ones, which are humanly speaking very important indeed. We need religion not only to make intolerable social conditions psychologically tolerable, we also need, besides opium – or at least some people need in certain determinate circumstances – religion to make sense of their (our) tangled lives and (if we live long enough) to come to grips with the decline (often a radical decline) of our powers. Whether we are rich or poor (or somewhere in between), whether we are dominated or dominant, we need in some way to come to grips with the inevitability of our own death and with the death of others, particularly with the death of those we love. We know that we must die, but we need, or at least very much want, an account of our death's significance and with that an account of the significance, both singly and together, of our lives. (If our lives have no significance, our deaths have no significance either.) We have, as well, to gain something of such an account, to learn to come to face, and in some way understand and come to grips with, the failures in our lives and face all the heart-breaking face-to-face problems between intimates – between lovers, parents and children, between siblings, between friends and between acquaintances in the workplace.

These problems not infrequently leave us in a tangled mess, sometimes with a feeling that we do not know how to act or try to be, and with the feeling that these problems are intractable and inescapable, that somehow we must learn to live with them. It is not impossible, when confronted with such things, to feel that life makes no sense at all and that even posing these questions is senseless. Many of us experience a deep sense of alienation and feelings of despair. And the alienation in question, as Fromm has argued, is a different kind of alienation from the alienation of which Marxists speak; but it is real for all of that.[36] In the face of this, religion functions to help at least some of us make sense of, or at least face and come to grips with, our tangled lives. This is not just, or perhaps even at all, for religion to be an opiate of an oppressed people or an opiate for anyone.

These existential functions of religion, as I shall call them, would persist in any kind of society, including a classless society. They might be less pressing in societies which are less harsh, less beset by injustice and domination of one class or gender or strata by another. But they would remain all the same. Marx, Engels, Lenin and Trotsky thought that, as societies moved towards classlessness, so religion would wither away. With the coming of a completely classless society, if such a society could ever come into being, we would have an egalitarian society of considerable affluence, enjoying high levels of universal education. In such a circumstance religion would in time completely wither away. They are, however, forgetting what I have called the existential functions of religion. They will remain in any society, even a classless society. These societies are supposed to be truly human societies where social relations, including our personal relations, will generally become clear. We will at last understand the truth about our world and about ourselves and finally have a just society, or *perhaps* even a society 'beyond justice', of equals. In such a world, some of these existential problems, it is reasonable to believe, would become more tractable, perhaps some would even disappear, but death, declining powers and human estrangement (something we see graphically depicted in the fictional world of Edna O'Brien) would remain. The latter might not be as frequent or perhaps as severe. But that estrangement, personal conflict, and the like would disappear in a classless society is, to put it conservatively, very unlikely. So some of the needs related to our existential problems, needs that fuel religion, would remain. The idea that religion would wither away with classlessness is, to put it conservatively, problematic.

Injustice, destitution, lack of control over one's life surely do exacerbate existential problems. But death, failing powers, damaged relations, deep human conflicts will remain in those classless societies. Death and failing powers are plainly not going away and there is no good reason to believe that the other existential problems would wither away in a classless society. They are part of the human condition. Some – particularly interpersonal problems – *might* even be intensified with greater clarity about our lives, our being freer of domination and our having greater leisure and more options. The burden (if such it be) of choice of life-plans in such a circumstance would be greater.

I think, however, that it is unlikely that this, or anything very like it, would obtain. The greater life stress of a class society of limited abundance and opportunity is arguably still more damaging to such relations. But that is an open question and I do not intend to beg it here. The crucial point is that these existential problems of religion, though perhaps in a moderated form, would remain in any society, including any classless society.

Existential problems will remain, but it is not obvious that our responses to them must take a religious form. Unless the use of 'religion' is eccentrically extended, as Feuerbachians, Frommians, Braithwaiteians and Wittgensteinian fideists do, to cover many things that would not standardly be covered by 'religion', there could, in such classless or near-classless societies, as there can be now for some privileged few in the rich capitalist democracies, be, more or less society-wide, a non-religious, broadly secular ethical response to such existential problems.

Still, as a matter of fact, such existential problems, and the responses to them, have traditionally remained firmly in the domain of religion except for a privileged few. Moreover, this has, culturally speaking, been very persistent, and we need to be given very good reasons indeed for believing that this function will wither away or assume a non-religious form. Still, it may not be unreasonable to expect that, as the level of social wealth and security rises, as well as the general educational level of a society (if indeed anything like this ever happens), religion will very likely become *optional* for increasingly large numbers of people in that society, as it has already increasingly become optional for the privileged, educated few in rich capitalist democracies. But that is not to say that it will wither away or even that it should wither away. We need evidence for the first contention and arguments for the second.

VI

I think Marxians can and should accept this. They should say that these existential functions are functions of religion that might very well persist even with the demise of class societies. But they should also respond by saying that recognizing this does nothing to undermine their claims about the ideological function of religion, claims about how it serves as an opiate to reconcile the oppressed to their condition. This is a pervasive fact of life in class societies. It is massively with us now. It is not just a function of religion in early Christianity in the Roman Empire, or for a medieval serf, or for German peasants during Luther's or Munzer's time, or for the English peasantry during the Wars of the Roses, or for a Russian serf or peasant of the nineteenth century, or for the slaves in the American South. It is pervasive in popular religion today. Protestant missionaries of a more or less fundamentalist persuasion carry out this opiating of society with a vengeance in the Third World. Whether they aim at it consciously or not, when they are successful – as they often are – in bringing religion to such destitute people, they also bring them an opiate. Religion there is the opium of the people. The religion they bring so functions for destitute peasants, primitive peoples whose cultures are in the process of being destroyed and the masses of lumpenproletariat crowding into the huge cities of the Third World – São Paulo, Mexico City, Lagos, Lima, Cairo and Manila. It also functions this way for many poor blacks and whites in the American South, as is graphically portrayed by Bertrand Tavernier and Robert Parrish in their documentry film *Mississippi Blues* (1984). Such proselytizing religions offer these impoverished down-and-outs the hope of a heavenly afterlife and it persuades them to be quiescent before the great capitalist powers that savagely exploit them and rule their lives. The religious Right is aggressive in its opposition to liberalism, which it sees, completely unrealistically, as disguised socialism or worse, while it teaches uncritical acceptance of the capitalist order.

Here what might become revolutionary or at least a radically reforming activity on the part of such destitute people is diverted into fantastic religious beliefs, in many ways not unlike the beliefs of the early Christians suffering under the Roman fist or the German peasants in Luther's time suffering under the oppression of the German princes with Luther's blessing. Like cheap schnapps introduced to the workers of northern Germany in Marx's time, such religion works to keep them passive, accepting without question the capitalist status quo. Popular religion (consider tele-evangelists in Canada and the United States) serves a similar function, though perhaps a little less blatantly. People are diverted from thinking critically about their society and from looking for real options for change. Set to roll back the more progressive elements in their society (e.g. feminism and some forms of liberalism), caught up with issues that are both trifling and reactionary – issues that should not even be issues – such as homosexuality in the armed forces in the United States or women members of the clergy, capitalism, and indeed its correctness, is not only accepted, but celebrated in its supposedly 'pure form', though care is taken to agitate against, and to seek to aid in the excising of, any 'socialistic' (social democratic, welfare state) appendages that some liberals add, or try to add, to a 'really genuine capitalism'. So here, as in the Roman Empire, or the Middle Ages, or in Luther's time and again in Marx's, popular religion – the vast mass of religious activity – has, however unwittingly, served the ruling or, if you will, the dominant, classes by supporting, sometimes adroitly, their socioeconomic order.

There have, of course, been exceptions throughout history, as part of the class struggles going on, even in popular religion: the Albigensians in southern France during the Middle Ages, the Levellers in England and the Anabaptists in Germany and Central Europe during Luther's time. But these movements have been comparatively short-lived and have repeatedly been defeated. While Martin Luther was eventually glorified and became the founder of an important branch of Protestantism, his great contemporary Thomas Munzer, was rewarded for leading the peasant rebellion and preaching the Kingdom of God on earth, by being hounded across Central Europe until he was finally cornered, then hanged, drawn and quartered.

Still, it might be responded, that for our time at least, I have been one-sided and partisan: militant atheism once more raises its ugly head. There are, it can be continued, the phenomena of Martin Luther King in the United States, Beyers Naudé and Desmond Tutu in South Africa, the 'Red Archbishop' in Brazil, militant Marxist priests in Italy, Gregory Baum in Canada, Dorothea Sölle in Germany and the whole movement (to speak more generally) of liberation theology. In a more reformist manner, there have been movements in the United Church of Canada and some of the mainline Protestant Churches in the United States to aid refugees, to provide sanctuary for some of those political refugees declared illegal by the state, to struggle for the protection of the rights of gays and lesbians, and the like. And while the Catholic Church is massively, and sometimes dangerously, reactionary on many issues, the Catholic bishops of Canada took a stand for social justice for workers and against nuclear proliferation. In short, while religions display massively and pervasively the ideological functions that Marxists have specified, religion is not always an ideological bulwark for the status quo. Sometimes religion acts as a force for social change. Sometimes, it is even a force for radical social change, involving a commitment to a radical transformation of society, as in liberation theology.

That religion sometimes plays this role should be acknowledged, and Engels' discussion of Thomas Munzer makes it perfectly evident that he, like Marx, recognized that. But they also recognized that this transformative stream is a minor strand of religious thought and practice, which has always been either defeated or gradually absorbed into large religious groups better fitting with the mode of production of the time. Thomas Munzer's movement failed. Gradually, after his assassination, Martin Luther King's movement lost its distinctiveness and thrust for progressive change. Beyers Naudé and Desmond Tutu were effective as aides to the ANC, but as aides to a powerful *secular* political movement. There are transformative elements in the Catholic Church, but they exist in the interstices of a very conservative, and presently, and indeed for a long time, a capitalist sustaining Church hierarchy, as was exemplified by Cardinal Spellman and, somewhat more subtly, is now exemplified by Pope John Paul II. Indeed, it is even possible to believe that, the good intentions of the Catholic progressives and radicals to the contrary notwithstanding, they in effect aid in sustaining the legitimacy and authority of 'The Church' (a generally very conservative Church) by showing that it has room for many mansions – it can be all things to all (or almost all) people. So by ideological lights 'The Church' stands vindicated, yet remains a Church which, as a whole, and particularly where it is secure, defends very reactionary policies (think of Catholicism in Ireland or in Quebec thirty years ago).

The situation is somewhat different with the mainline Protestant Churches. With a membership which increasingly largely comes from the more educated and affluent strata of society, these denominations often have reasonably progressive social policies, though hardly policies that seek to challenge the system. But without such policies, its more educated membership would drift into secularism, with the increasing disenchantment of the world. But, by advocating such policies, it has paid the price of losing much of its working-class and really impoverished (lumpen-proletariat) members to more popular religions which tend to be unapologetically reactionary, in both socioeconomic and theological terms. So, conveniently for the established order, we have one kind of Church for one strata of society and another kind for another.

There is a lot more to be said here, including perhaps qualifications to what I have said above. Some of it would require more detailed and accurate knowledge than I have at my disposal. But it seems to me that my descriptions are close enough to the mark to make the Marxian sociological hypothesis a good one. Religion acts in fact overwhelmingly as the opium of the people. Intentionally or unintentionally – presumably most of the time unintentionally – religion supports the dominant mode of production, which in our society is capitalism, and with that the usually conservative cultural accoutrements that go with and are generally functional for it. Occasionally, of course, religion does not take that path, does not play that role, does not refute that hypothesis; but this is a sociological generalization about *tendencies* and not an attempt to state an irrefutable law sustaining contrary-to-fact conditionals, something that would, at best, have a very small place in most social science in any event.

VII

I want to return to something I merely gestured at earlier. Could one be an *historical* materialist, a communist, a believer in the class struggle and still accept much of the substance of the Marxist critique of religion as ideology, while remaining in a reasonably orthodox sense a Jewish, Christian or Islamic theist? My argument will be that this is at least a logical possibility and *perhaps* a reasonable possibility as well. Recall, as we have seen, that while Marx and Engels were materialists in more or less the same way that Holbach and Hobbes were materialists (what we would now call physicalists), they did not argue for their materialism or develop it, but simply accepted it as something that had been firmly established by these Enlightenment thinkers.[37] And with this, they accepted – I think rightly – as a corollary, atheism and the denial of immortality. Here they were good Feuerbachians. Moreover, with this they also, of course, rejected the Judaeo-Christian-Islamic worldview. But this rejection was not original and was not, in any very extended or careful way, argued for by them. But what they did argue for, and here they were original, was historical materialism, a theory of ideology, the labour theory of value and a theory of classes, class conflict and class struggle.

However, in the present context at least the phrase 'historical materialism' is misleading, for, while it is compatible with materialism understood as physicalism (the thesis that matter – physical realities – alone exists or at least the claim that nothing else has a non-derivative and independent existence), it has at best only a tenuous relationship with materialism (physicalism). It neither affirms nor denies that matter alone exists, or that all reality, or at least all independent reality, is physical. It says, rather, as an account of epochal social change, that the ways the forces (the powers) of production develop are the fundamental determinants of major long-range social change, or at least of socioeconomically important change. It is the claim that, as we have already quoted Engels as saying, 'the great moving power of all important historic events is in the economic development of society', is 'in the change in the modes of production and exchange'. But this is not materialism (physicalism). Indeed, it has very little, if anything, to do with it. It just so happens that Marx and Engels were materialists in both senses. But a dualist (whether religious or not) or a theist (Christian or otherwise) could accept *historical* materialism. A Christian, Jew or Moslem could also be a socialist or communist, believing in both the desirability and immanent feasibility of such a socioeconomic ordering of society. A certain kind of Christian radicalism or egalitarianism might aid her in that. She might be a kind of contemporary Thomas Munzer. But her communism or socialism might be held independently, without being in conflict with her Christian beliefs. Similar things could be said for her belief in classes, class conflict and the importance of class struggle. Not all Christians have been pacifists or politically quiescent by any means, to say nothing of Moslems or Jews. The stumbling block for the theist might perhaps be in the Marxian belief that religion is ideology. She could not, of course, say with Engels that all 'religion is *nothing but* the fantastic reflection in men's minds of those external forces which control their daily life', and she could not accept the claim that God was *merely* a projection of our emotions. She could not accept such a reductionist, projectionist, error-theory conception of God. Such an account is a semantic account of what 'God' means, or 'belief in God' means, that is incompatible with Christian, Jewish or Islamic belief, or at least with theism, and, in articulating their accounts of religion as ideology, Marx and Engels do indeed articulate it in such Feuerbachian terms and they make it perfectly plain – and perhaps in this they are right – that Feuerbach did not only have deep insight, but that they believe that the general structure of his projection theory is correct. (What they object to is his articulating a new humanist religion of man, instead of rejecting the society in which it is necessary to have religious beliefs.) They claim that religious belief-systems and practices generally tend to function to support and sustain the dominant socioeconomic structure of the society. Religious institutions (Catholicism, Calvinism, Judaism) generally function to reconcile people, and most particularly the dominated and oppressed people in the society, to the social order in which they live, no matter how miserable the social order is for them. In this way religion is, or pervasively tends to be, the opium of the people.

These are the core claims of the Marxian theory of religion as ideology and these claims could be true even if the projectionist semantic or ontological claims are false, or the projectionist claims could be true while this account of religion as ideology is false. Freudians and Feuerbachians have a projectionist theory, but not the Marxian account of religion as ideology. And a Christian believer could accept the Marxian theory of religion as ideology while rejecting, as she must, the projectionist theory of religion with its utterly naturalistic account of what it means to speak of God and to believe in God. Marxians, as we have seen, are also projectionists about religious belief. But their projectionism is distinct from their account of the ideological functions of religion. The latter, which is distinctive of a Marxian account of religion, could be accepted without the former. *In fine, a Christian theist (if that is not pleonastic), or indeed any kind of Christian at all, could accept what is distinctive of, and canonical for, Marxianism, without abandoning her Christianity.* She could accept, unqualifiedly, historical materialism, the labour theory of value, the theory of class, class conflict and class struggle, the Marxist conception of praxis and communism. She could not, of course, accept Marx's atheism and materialism (physicalism), but that is not distinctive of Marxianism. Holbach, Hobbes, W.V. Quine, Richard Rorty, Daniel Dennett, J.C.C. Smart, Peter Strawson, Stuart Hampshire and Donald Davidson all accept physicalism, in one form or another, and with that they must, to be consistent, accept atheism. But they could do this – and, indeed, all the above do – and still be utterly distant from Marxianism. They might even, as is the case for Quine, be very conservative and positively hostile to it. And, while atheism and materialism (physicalism) was indeed important for Marx and Engels, and Lenin and Gramsci as well, it was arguably not canonical for their theories, for all the elements listed above as canonical, get along quite well without it, while materialism (physicalism) and atheism, as say in Holbach or Quine, do not require these canonical Marxian doctrines for their support or further rationalization.

A Christian could even consistently accept the opium conception of religious ideology and be either a Christian quietist or a liberation theologian. She could believe, to consider the first alternative, that, given the sinfulness and corruption of humankind, Christians should have nothing to do with politics or the secular ordering of society. That religion makes people pacific or quiescent before Caesar is just as it should be. In that way it is a good thing that religion is an opiate. Render unto Caesar what is Caesar's and unto God what is God's. The important thing is to attain purity of heart, to spread the Word and prepare for, and contentedly and confidently await, the coming of the Kingdom of God. This is a 'Spiritual World' which we will come to after our bodily death. Focus on purity of heart and 'these last things' and forget about politics. Given what we sinful human beings are like, it cannot but be a dirty business anyway. We should turn away from it and strive to develop what some Germans, under Hitler, called an attitude of inner emigration.

This quietist, pietistic response is not the only, or (to put it mildly) the best, Christian response to a Marxian theory of the ideological functions of religion, and it is certainly not compatible with a Marxian theory of class struggle. A better Christian response, accepting class struggle as well as a Marxian account of the ideological functions of religion, is that of liberation theology. Such a Christian could, and I believe should, say that Christianity almost invariably functions as such an opiating ideology. But, as we have seen, Marxianism does not say that religion always functions this way, let alone that it *must* do so. Such a radical Christian could say that Marxian theory does us a very considerable service in pointing out that this is the pervasive role that religion has played in history and that it continues very powerfully and effectively to play this role today. Our task, such a radical Christian could remark, as Christians, aware of this ideological function, is to align ourselves with atheists, or anyone else with a similar political awareness and human commitment, to struggle to bring an end to class society and the exploitation of one human being by another and to create a socialist

society of equals to bring about, if you want to use religious terminology, the Kingdom of God on earth, where exploitation and injustice would be at an end and where human beings would finally
form a genuine community. It would be a community where they
would at long last stand together as equals in caring relations. Jesus'
identification with the poor and downtrodden, and his injunction
for us to love one another, gives us a religious rationale for so acting and for so being.[38]

Thus, I think, that there are Christians, and not Christians in any
sham sense either, as in (for example) the Braithwaite–Hare conception of what it is to be a Christian, who could consistently be
Marxians or Marxists, if to be a Marxian or Marxist is to hold most
of the things that I have claimed to be distinctive of, and canonical
for, Marxianism or Marxism.[39]

VIII

Many Marxists or Marxians will be uneasy about my argument in
the previous section. Are there any good reasons why they should
be? Should we, if what I have called the canonical portions of Marxianism are approximately true, be militant Marxian atheists?

Most Marxians, in addition to seeing Marxianism as a emancipatory social theory, have also seen it as a *world-view*. Moreover, they
have attached considerable importance to its being a coherent and
rationally sustainable world-view. As Wilfrid Sellars and Richard
Rorty take philosophers to be doing, and legitimately so, Marxians
also want to see how things hold together in the broadest and most
inclusive sense of that term. They want to establish, in doing this,
that talk of a spiritual or supernatural world is nonsense, or at least
a mistake, and, as Marx put it grandly, to establish 'the truth of this
world'. Some of them were what we now call historicists (Gramsci
most clearly), but none of them, not even Otto Neurath, were rela-
tivists, sceptics or what some now call postmodernists, who think
that there is no truth of this world, or of any world, to be established. They might, if they could have studied Quine and Davidson,
and could have read Putnam or Rorty, have come to be convinced
that there is and can be no one uniquely true description of the
world. But that would not lead them to relativism or scepticism or
to a Mannheimist sociology of knowledge-orientation anymore than
Quine, Davidson, Putnam and Rorty are so inclined or so entrapped

(so conceptually imprisoned). It is one thing to say that there is no uniquely true description of the world and it is another thing again to say that there are no true accounts of what goes on in the world that can be warranted. Science, including social science, and careful common-sense description – aware of ideological snares – will give us knowledge, much of which is cumulative, and an increasingly more adequate grip on the world (including the social world). While remaining, as were Marx and Engels, resolutely anti-metaphysical, Marxians thought, and contemporary ones continue to think, that we can gain an increasingly more adequate thoroughly naturalistic world outlook.[40] But this excluded religion as a source of truth and required us both to regard it as a cluster of human projections and to treat it as a mystifying ideology, though, some thought it, in certain circumstances (as with Munzer) a useful instrument (mythical as it is) to use in achieving emancipation. But, more typically, as we have seen, it functions as an instrument for conservatism: an instrument for sustaining the hegemony of the ruling classes, impeding the coming into existence of a genuinely democratic society, in which we would live in a world of equals.

However, could we not reject the Marxian naturalistic worldview while still accepting what I have called the canonical parts of Marxianism, that is, the emancipatory social science or critical theory perspective, that arguably really turns the machinery, if anything does, on the theoretical side of the struggle for socialism and a classless exploitation-free society?[41] The answer is yes: a Christian, a Jew or a Moslem could consistently reject such a naturalistic worldview while wholeheartedly accepting the canonical parts of Marxianism. Would it not, however, be a *reasonable* thing – or perhaps even the most reasonable thing – to stick with the naturalism *and* the canonical parts of Marxianism? That, I believe, depends on your estimate of the intellectual strength of naturalism. If, on the one hand, you think, as Marx and Engels evidently did, that a materialistic or naturalistic anti-metaphysics on the Holbach–Hobbes–Hume–Bayle continuum has plainly and unassailably, or even with a considerable degree of plausibility, established a naturalistic view of the world, then you will conclude that building anything on the mere fact that canonical Marxianism and some forms of Christianity are not logically incompatible is not a reasonable thing to do.[42] If, on the other hand, you think that naturalism is a mistaken, problematic or at least a rationally unmotivated world-view, indeed perhaps even itself an unwitting metaphysics, revealing more about our

Weltgeist than anything else, then you will not (or at least should not) think that that is so. You may be more sympathetic to a Christian-Marxian possibility.

IX

The reason that this is the way that things stand in Marxian discussions of such issues, and that there is little argument for naturalism in Marxianism, is that Marxians, like Santayana, who politically speaking was very conservative, take it as given that physicalism and atheism are true. I think this is so too, but I realize that a good number of knowledgeable people do not, so I have in my writing on religion, my Marxianism notwithstanding, *argued* for naturalism. If one does not, one just sidesteps argument and discussion with theists or Wittgensteinian fideists. That, for good or for ill, is the situation in 'the philosophy of religion game'. I wish the *philosophy* of religion game would wither away.[43] It seems to me to pose no intellectually challenging problems, but that notwithstanding, like Gramsci and Durkheim, I think religion is a very important cultural phenomenon indeed. Religion is not just superstition or a series of intellectual blunders or cognitive mistakes. I agree with Marx Wartofsky's remarks, quoted above, that an adequate materialist conception of religion could not so treat religion. But, like Wartofsky, I wish we would look at religion in good Durkheimian fashion as *no more than an important cultural phenomenon* and orient ourselves, and orient our understanding of the world and our struggles in the world, accordingly. But, alas, we cannot start there, if we wish to engage in the deliberations about religion current in our society. As long as there are thoughtful and informed Christians, Jews and Moslems in our midst, we cannot, if we wish to carry on a discussion of religion which includes them too, *simply assume naturalism*. So we must, in our attempt to gain some reasonable consensus about the truth about our world, engage in the whole discussion again (mopping up after Hume, as I call it) and write about religion as J.L. Mackie, Antony Flew, Wallace Matson, Michael Martin, Ronald Hepburn and I have, hoping that one day we will be able to progress the discussion on to the purely cultural territory on which Feuerbach, Marxians, Freudians and Durkheimians have placed it: to come to ask, *not* whether its doctrines are true, or reasonably to be believed to be true or rationally to be accepted solely on faith, but instead to consider questions concerning religion solely as questions about what role religion plays, should play, can come not to play and should come not to play, in society and in the lives of human beings. Can human beings – not just a few relatively privileged individuals in a sea of religious people but whole cultures of human beings – live without religion? And, if they can, should they? These are some of the questions that we should be asking: these are questions that should be on our intellectual agenda. Looking at things this way, among other things, provides common ground for discussion between physicalists–materialists–naturalists, on the one hand, and, Jews, Christians and Moslems, on the other. Here we have something that, from our position now in cultural history, no thoughtful and informed person should think she has a good answer to.

Many Marxians – most notably Marx, Engels, Lenin and Trotsky – thought they had good answers to these questions. Human beings, they believed, could, and indeed will, attain a classless society, and, when they do, they will no longer need religion. They will also not need religion when they are self-consciously travelling on the road to a classless society, as many will be, near the end of the bourgeois era with late capitalism. When, that is, they are close to it, and self-consciously struggling for it, they also will not, in such a circumstance, need religion and indeed should not have it, for it generally stands in the way of their emancipation (including their resolutely acting) and of their flourishing. Religious beliefs, they believe, are at best false and generally have harmful effects. In this they are at one with Hume, though Hume understandably was more circumspect about this than were the classical Marxists. Thus, when the circumstances are right, religion can, and indeed should, gradually disappear from the cultural life of human beings, except as a cultural memory: an artefact, though a very important record of how human beings in the trying circumstances of class societies, came to grips with their lives. And religion, they believed, will so gradually disappear with the stable achievement of socialism and then communism. Even if some form of liberation theology is coherent, truth being a not inconsiderable value too, religion is not something to be believed in and it should only be regarded as desirable as a *tactical* measure in certain circumstances: circumstances in which it would be useful in the progressive movement of society.

The atheism of Marxists is not the wistful atheism of Santayana or the resigned atheism of Freud or the ironical atheism of Hume, but is, like Holbach's, a militant atheism. (Indeed, with Lenin it takes an extreme form of militancy.) Marxians want a true view of the world and our place in it (if such can be had) to be available to as many people as possible and for it to become a part of their lives; and they want, as well, people, themselves included, to be able to live without illusions and opiates, and that means, they believe, *doing without religion*. This would come to a liberation of human-kind from both the illusion of religion and the conditions that make that illusion necessary.

X

That Marxian vision of things is more problematic for us now, standing where we are in history, than it was for the classical Marxists, for at least two reasons. We can no longer reasonably share the optimism of Marx, Engels and Lenin that a classless society is plainly achievable. We seem as far from it as ever, perhaps even farther. The Soviet Thermidor was a bad thing, but when what replaced it was not a demystified democratic socialism, or at least social democracy, but the violent, lawless and corrupt mess we have now, for a time at least, a great hope went out of the world.[44] It can come to seem to us, looking at what was once the Soviet Union and was once Yugoslavia, a hopeless ideal, as unworldly as Christian ideals. To take socialism and then communism as being something to be taken to be reasonably on the agenda can come to seem like a bad joke, something out of line with the world we know or can reasonably expect to come into being. I hope that that scepticism is an overreaction to our recent history. But it may very well run deeper than that as common wisdom has it now. Perhaps socialism and a Marxian vision of the world are dead. That is a reason, a reason that Marx did not have, to rethink questions about the import of religion as a cultural phenomenon, the truth of atheism (if indeed it is true) to the contrary notwithstanding. Perhaps it is both an opiate and a saving *myth. Perhaps*, but only perhaps, if we are naturalists, we should have either the wistful atheism of a Santayana or the resigned atheism of a Freud and *not* the militant atheism of a Marx.

The second reason for greater pessimism than Marx and Engels and the other classical Marxists had is the neglect by classical Marxists of what I have called the existential problems of religion (our tangled lives, the inevitability of death, failing powers, and the like). These problems are not going to go away in any kind of society, no matter how classless and enlightened it may be. Even if religion functions ideologically in the manner characterized by Marxists, it also, and even looked at just as a cultural phenomenon, functions as a set of beliefs and practices which provide, if not an answer, at least a response to and a stance to be taken towards, these existential problems. Is there a secular alternative that is as adequate or even more adequate than Jewish, Christian, Islamic or other religious responses? Some of us can, as Hume and Freud did, face our death, our pain, and the destruction and madness, cultural and otherwise, all around us, stoically and with a measured stance, not availing ourselves of the consolations of religion. Indeed some of us *could not*, given our beliefs about what is and can be the case, so avail ourselves of the consolations of religion even if we wanted to. But should we, and can we, reasonably expect this to be the response of more than a very few resolute and clear-headed intellectuals? Should we want it generally to be the response of human beings to religion – particularly human beings in conditions of reasonable security and abundance?

Both Hume and Freud thought such an atheistic option was a live one for only a very few. Perhaps they were too pessimistic and elitist. But perhaps not. And perhaps even Freud had his substitutes for religion. Some, of course, would say that the same obtains for Marx. Still, if we can, assuming we have had the good fortune to be soberly educated, should we learn, as did Hume, Freud, Marx, Lenin, Gramsci and a host of others, to face these existential problems without the benefit of religion? The standard answer is that we should because truth, though surely not the only good thing in the world, is one of the very important good things. But we should also not forget Nietzsche's and Foucault's reminders of the tricks we play on ourselves here.[45] But that notwithstanding, to overcome self-deception, other deception, cultural deception and to come to see things, as close as we can come to see them, rightly is something of not inconsiderable value. If the cumulative arguments and ways of viewing things of the Holbachian–Hobbesian–Humean–Feuerbachian–Marxian continuum are on the mark, or at least near to it, then, given the very great value that truth has for us, we should be led away from a religious response to these existential problems.

However, we should not forget that truth – though a very great good – is one good among others and it might, in this context, be outweighed by other considerations. A Kierkegaardian might respond to the taking of such an atheist stance by saying that only self-deception, or at least a not reflecting long enough and hard enough or responding non-evasively enough to such existential problems, can lead us to think that we can overcome despair and utter hopelessness without a commitment to Christ. To do so, we must indeed crucify our intellects, believe in what is utterly absurd; but without it, if we are cursed with being reflective and non-evasive about ourselves, we will find our lives utterly meaningless.

However, such a claim, at least if taken straightforwardly, is false and, taken unstraightforwardly, question-begging. People in many cultural situations have made sense of their lives without such a religious leap and it is, moreover, hardly conducive to self-respect to believe, or try to believe, what we also believe to be absurd or, what comes to much the same thing, to crucify our intellects. If faith really requires that, perhaps we can make sense of our lives, face death and the madness around us, without that Kierkegaardian blind leap of faith.

Human beings rather more generally (or so we like to think), and not just philosophers and other intellectuals, wish to see life as a whole and to see how things hold together as a whole, so that they can come to have something of a coherent view of the world they live in. And with this, they wish to make sense of their lives. They often also have some hopes (perhaps unrealistic ones) of making this world a little more human: a better world with less injustice, more trust, caring and flourishing. Moreover, if these hopes are serious, they also want to know what must be done for that to be in some measure achieved – if indeed it can be achieved or even approximated.

An Enlightenment view of the world, say the view resulting from a coherent amalgamation and rational reconstruction of the core conceptions, arguments and narratives of Enlightenment thinkers – for example, the Holbach–Hobbes–Hume–Feuerbach–Marx continuum – provide something of that. Perhaps the greatest weakness in such naturalism has been in grappling with what I have called the existential problems of life. Its attitude here has often been too rationalistic, but here some progress is being made. Antonio Gramsci, Richard Robinson, Erich Fromm, Max Horkheimer and Theodor Adorno, in different ways, have shown how those existential problems can be treated from a thoroughly naturalistic, but still a thoroughly non-scientistic and non-rationalistic perspective.

XI

Let me see, with that in mind, if I can pull together some of the strands of my discussion and produce something that bears some resemblance to a conclusion. Marx and Marxians see religion as a collection of at best false beliefs and, as well, of beliefs that are essentially ideological. Religious beliefs and practices function most typically as a support for the dominant class structure. That is their typical ideological function. They very often do that by consoling and mystifying the downtrodden with a belief in a glorious afterlife in God's kingdom. There can be no doubt that religion functions in this way, but, little noticed by Marxians, it also has what I have called existential functions. It helps us to make sense of our lives and to face our deaths, various human trials and even the tragedies and horrors that may be our lot: the various ills that Simone de Beauvoir has described so starkly and so powerfully. It helps us to face things such as the loss of our powers, or disability (such as a decline into senility or the pain of cancer) or our death, and of those we love. And it helps us come to grips with seeing all our hopes for a more humane world defeated.

Marxianism as a militant atheism, with a firm belief in the desirability of the withering away of religion when the situation warrants, must, to yield a fully plausible materialist conception of religion, supply secular substitutes for the religious ways of meeting those existential problems. It has traditionally had little to say here, but, I think, consistently with its naturalistic and historical materialist framework (with its related materialist conception of religion), it can make a good response. Let me broach this first by a little social description, followed by a couple of possible scenarios for the future and then a comment on them.

First, the social description. The advent of socialism, and after that of communism, and the achievement of a classless society would have to bring with it high levels of material abundance for all, with security, leisure and educational opportunities for all human beings to develop their capacities, to pursue their interests and to have the means to live decently together. It would also be the coming to be of a democratic society of equals, where people together would control and order their own lives. In such a world there would also be justice and conditions where people could live with dignity. But these things have not been achieved anywhere. Instead, considered globally, we live in a horrible world – a world which seems to be getting steadily worse. Multitudes of people live in conditions which in some key respects are not so different from those of slaves, impoverished freemen and peasants in the Roman Empire or the peasants in Germany during Luther's and Munzer's time. People die of malnutrition at the rate of 50,000 a day and many who manage not to starve are so malnourished in childhood that for the rest of what in all likelihood will be their rather short lives, they are incapable of functioning normally. More generally, multitudes of people live desperate, marginalized lives in utter poverty and without any reasonable expectation or even hope that their lot will substantially change for the better. In such circumstances, just as Marxians expect, religions flourish in fantastic forms and plainly, and understandably, function as opiates, as an *ersatz* heart in a heartless world. The existential problems add an even greater overload to the problems that weigh them down. They are not only impoverished, but their personal relations with their intimates are corrupted as well. It is the world of *Shortcuts* together with general poverty. In the face of such conditions, the capitalist world might be progressing inexorably to what looks like a state of utter inhumanity for vast numbers of people. In such circumstances, neither Marxians nor anyone else, if they are at all reasonable, will expect religion to disappear. The conditions that make it necessary remain firmly in place.

Suppose, however, after a bit, one of two things happen. Suppose, first, that social democracy gains a new lease on life with neoliberal and libertarian market romanticism disappearing, so that we can finally get capitalism with a human face (something similar to what obtains in Scandinavia) and suppose further, on this first scenario, this gradually becomes global. Globally, that is, we gradually come to have security, reasonable material well-being, reasonably high levels of education and leisure and some reasonable measure of equality. There, if such a situation ever comes about, we can reasonably expect religion to wither away, as it in fact has in Scandinavia, a few Bergmanesque frettings aside. The existential functions of religion in such circumstances will be replaced by secular ones, the practice probably preceding the theory. We will have Weberian disenchantment with the world without despair or *angst* being pervasive in our societies.

Suppose, alternatively, no such humanizing of capitalism is possible; social democratic ways to affluence and equality do not work. We might in such a circumstance stay mired, for a not inconsiderable time, in the same nightmarish world. If that obtains, then there will be plenty of ideological work for religion to do and it will flourish in the doing of it. It will remain an opiate and its existential functions will not be replaced by secular existential functions. But suppose, to go to our second scenario, in the face of the collapse of such social democratic hopes, a new militancy emerges among the proletariat and the lumpenproletariat (the great mass of poorly off or relatively poorly off or destitute people, if you do not like Marxian categories). Suppose, in addition, that among the poorly off, currently the majority of society, there exists an often reasonably well-educated workforce (including here professional workers). But their lives, let us further suppose, like the lives of the unemployed (functionally unemployable), become very vulnerable and their material conditions, including their workplace conditions and job security, steadily worsen. Suppose further that these are conditions that obtain, among other places, endemically in the advanced industrial societies (the great capitalist democracies). Eventually, in such a circumstance, let us further, and not implausibly, assume, becoming militant, many of these workers, together with the unemployed, so act as to topple capitalism and begin the construction of, and eventually set in place, a socialist socioeconomic order (perhaps now some form of market socialism). In doing this they also bring about a democratically ordered, roughly egalitarian society, of abundance and security. Again we can reasonably expect, as in the social democratic scenario, religion to wither away. The memory of religion's ideological support for capitalism will be in the awareness of the people making the revolution. Moreover, given the changed material conditions, and given the Marxian world-view that would go with such a socialism, religion's existential functions would, or so at least it is reasonable to expect, be gradually replaced by purely secular ones. Given its actuality and the interests it answers to, it is not unreasonable to expect of that world, with that world-view, that secular existential functions would replace the religious ones rather more readily than in the social democratic scenario.

Here are two ways to a world without belief in God or any other religious conceptions. If they are unfeasible, it is not because of the thought that religion in such societies (if they should ever come to be) would not be given up without life being adversely affected. If they are unfeasible, it is rather because we think that it is very unlikely that either of these socioeconomic orders will ever come into being, let alone be sustained, on anything like a world-wide scale. It is easy to believe that this conception is as hopelessly utopian, or at least nearly so, as pie in the sky. Without speculating on the likelihoods here, what I think we can and should say is this: given the truth of naturalism, there are describable circumstances, and *perhaps* feasible circumstances (circumstances which would be good to have in any case), where it would be possible (if the circumstances obtaining are possible) to have a godless world where it would, as well, be a good place to live. (Suppose Iceland, with its fish stocks still in place, were the world.) It surely would be a much better world than anything we have now.

In the world we have now, it is, of course, *unthinkable* that religion would disappear, or even that it would disappear as an opiate keeping only its existential functions. Is it a good thing that people are religious in such situations (that is, in our real-life situations)? The answer is both yes and no. Yes, in that it gives something of a heart in a heartless world; no, in the sense that it diminishes, with its opiating and obfuscating effects, the ability of such exploited and degraded people to struggle against the conditions of their existence or to see clearly their condition and the possibilities for its alteration. The obfuscating and opiating effects of religion – social effects of religion which are both pervasive and persistent – stand in the way of their seeing the possibility of, the desirability of, and the necessity for, struggle to make it the case that the conditions where religion is a need no longer obtain. However, the crucial point here is that it is pointless to ask if it is good or bad for them to have religious beliefs when they cannot but have them in their actual circumstances. Munzer plausibly claimed that struggle against such conditions, for the very down and out, can only take form in the garb – the vocabulary and the conceptualizations – of religion; hence his stress on the Kingdom of God on earth. In circumstances of poverty, ignorance, hopelessness, relentless, exacting domination – conditions where life is intolerable – we cannot but have religion and religion, at least in the first instance, as an obfuscating opiate.

In life situations that are not so severe, but are still bad, as is the situation for most middle strata people in Canada and the United States now, we get things in between, such as the mushiness and mindless blandness of much popular religion in such countries, but mindless and mushy as it is, it still continues to play both an obfuscating and opiating function in such societies. (I do not speak of the Religious Right, which, though mindless and opiating, is not in all instances bland and, in all ways, mushy.) Here Gramsci's stress on Marxism as a world-view taking on, though in an utterly natural-istic spirit, many of the cultural functions of religion is important. Perhaps such a world-view, if Marxian intellectuals could socialize the masses into accepting this 'secularized religion', might come effectively to replace religion. But again, we should not fail to take to heart the fact that nothing like this has happened. Moreover, given our historical experience, the idea of 'The Party' replacing 'The Church' does not resonate with us.

These Gramscian considerations aside, where security levels of work, wealth and education are considerable and democratic insti-tutions are in place and stable, it is plausible to expect, where this persists for some time, that we will get, and valuably so, a move to a greater secularization of society and a diminution of religion. And where in such a circumstance religion persists for some, we can also reasonably expect it to lose more and more of its doctrinal substance and for it, for the individuals involved, to become an optional matter. Given the truth of naturalism, that, in such circumstances, is a good thing. There is no more need for opiates or for crucifying or even an obfuscating of the intellect. And the existential functions of re-ligion, even without Gramsci's 'secularized religion', can be met in purely secular ways. Sometimes it is cloaked in a traditionally re-ligious garb, but, where it is, it has come to have a *secular substance*. (Think here of the Braithwaite–Hare stuff or of Wittgensteinian fideism.) To be in such a situation, Marx took to be a very great good for human beings. And the things human beings would have in such a situation would also be good – indeed great goods – and over both of these matters Marx was right.

XII

Finally, I want, as a kind of coda to my conclusion, to return to the passage from Marx Wartofsky, which I cited at the beginning.[46] Wartofsky pertinently asks, 'Is there a viable materialist conception of religion?' I take it that Wartofsky means 'materialist' in both the historical materialist and the physicalist sense. And, as we have seen, while these conceptions are conceptions that fit well together – they have a kind of *Weltanschauung*ish affinity – still, not being logically or conceptually linked, they are not mutually entailing. It is, that is, very natural without being logically required for someone who is an historical materialist also to be a physicalist. For an historical materialist, they occupy the same cultural space.

I have argued further that we can reasonably be both physicalists and historical materialists. Though independent, the case for both, particularly when historical materialism is given a minimalist reading and the physicalism is of a non-reductive sort, is very strong. It is not just that they conventionally go together, though they do that. Moreover, if we are consistent physicalists, we shall also be atheists. That many who are physicalists (i.e. materialists) do not so label themselves – say they are atheists – reveals much about the evasive fastidiousness, even the finickiness, of many intellectuals with their characteristic fear of being thought to be anything that might be taken to be obvious or vulgar.[47] If, moreover, we are non-reductive physicalists (roughly *à la* Davidson, Rorty or Strawson) and we are atheists of a broadly Humean sort (Humean as updated, *vis-à-vis* religion, by a consistent amalgam of J.L. Mackie, Antony Flew and Bernard Williams) and we are as well minimalist historical materialists, then, if we turn to an account of religion's ideological functions similar to that of Engels, we will have a viable materialist conception of religion, or at least have a good candidate for such a viable conception, if these accounts taken together are plausible candidates for being true.[48] But these things taken independently are good candidates for being true. Moreover, these things hang together in a plausible way, contributing to our reflective and rational desire to see, if we can, how things hold together: to get a coherent overall view of our situation.

Assuming – plausibly, I think – some non-reductive physicalism (the exact form for my purposes is unimportant) and assuming as well a broadly Humean atheism, I have set out, and argued for, a Marxian account of religion, an account that is essentially that of Engels. I have also argued that it is plausible to believe that the story it tells, particularly if supplemented, as I have argued it can be, by a materialist account of the existential functions of religion, is a good approximation to the truth. Moreover, it seems to me to be true also that we have no alternative materialist account which is more plausible, though it plainly is an account which builds on Feuerbach's impressive materialist account and that, in some ways, Feuerbach's account should be seen, though subject to Marx's and Engels' strictures, as filling in their accounts.[49] A Marxian account, or a Marxian–Feuerbachian account, explains religion, without explaining it away, as a function of our needs. It specifies some of these needs and, meeting what in effect are Wartofsky's criteria of adequacy for a viable materialist conception of religion, it explains religion's 'origins, its distinctive and historical forms, its persistence in various institutional contexts, its changes and development, its continuing and present existence in the modes of belief and action of individuals'.[50] It could, of course, be both more nuanced and filled in much more fully than Engels does, or than even Engels and Feuerbach taken together do, and it is likely to be mistaken in some of its details. But this nuancing, filling in and minor correcting is something that can be done while using that very materialist conception of religion. Here we have, as is often the case in science as well, a bootstrapping operation.

Viewing philosophy, as Wilfrid Sellars and Richard Rorty do, as an attempt to see how things hang together in the broadest sense of that term and applying this conception of philosophy here, with a physicalism of a non-reductive, non-metaphysical variety (*à la* Rorty and, in effect, Davidson), with a broadly Humean atheism and with a Marxian conception of the ideological functions of religion, we have (taking them together, and particularly if supplemented by a Durkheimian conception of the function of religion (an equally naturalistic conception of the function of religion)), a very plausible account of how things in some areas central to our lives hang together and we have, as well, a very plausible candidate for a viable materialist (naturalist) conception of religion.

Suppose it is responded that no viable *materialist* conception of religion is possible, for to be a materialist one, it must explain religious beliefs as being at best false, and this is to explain religious phenomena away, rather than to explain the phenomena. But, as Wartofsky well insists himself, an account that explains religion away cannot be an adequate account of religion. However, it is question-begging to claim that a conception of religion which takes key religious beliefs, such as God exists and providentially cares for humankind, to be false or incoherent, must, by making that very claim, be explaining the *phenomena* of religion away. An account which explains how religion arises, how it is sustained, what deep human needs and interests it answers to, how it is crucial under certain material conditions to give meaning to the lives of human beings and to supply, or partially supply, the social cement of society (the bonding between human beings), certainly does not explain the phenomena of religion away, but explains it, and that is exactly what a Marxian account does.[51]

Notes

1. Andrew Levine, 'What is a Marxist Today?' in R.X. Ware and Kai Nielsen, eds., *Marxism Analyzed* (Calgary: Alberta: The University of Calgary Press, 1989), pp. 29–58. Kai Nielsen 'Analytical Marxism: A Form of Critical Theory', *Erkenntnis*, vol. 39 (1993), pp. 1–21; 'Elster's Marxism', *Philosophical Papers*, vol. XX, no. 2 (1992), pp. 83–106; *Marxism and the Moral Point of View* (Boulder, Co.: The Westview Press, 1989). Joe McCarney, *The Real World of Ideology* (Brighton: Harvester Press, 1980).

2. G.A. Cohen, *Karl Marx's Theory of History: A Defense* (Princeton, NJ: Princeton University Press, 1978), p. 158.

3. Joshua Cohen, 'Minimalist Historical Materialism', in Rodger Beehler et al., eds., *On the Track of Reason: Essays in Honor of Kai Nielsen* (Boulder, Co.: The Westview Press, 1992), p. 161. See also G.A. Cohen, *History, Labour, and Freedom* (Oxford: Clarendon Press, 1988), pp. 3–108.

4. Cohen, *Karl Marx's Theory of History*, p. 173.

5. Nielsen, *Marxism and the Moral Point of View*, pp. 98–116; and 'Some Marxist and Non-Marxist Conceptions of Ideology', *Rethinking Marxism*, vol. 2, no. 4 (Winter 1989), pp. 146–74.

6. Nielsen, 'Analytical Marxism: A Form of Critical Theory', pp. 1–21; 'Afterword: Remarks on the Roots of Progress', in *Analyzing Marxism*, pp. 497–539; 'Elster's Marxism'; 'On Taking Historical Materialism Seriously', *Dialogue*, vol. 22, no. 2 (June 1983); and 'Historical Materialism, Ideology and Ethics', *Studies in Soviet Thought*, vol. 29 (January 1985), pp. 47–64.

7. Gramsci might seem out of step here with the Marxist tradition, for he argued for a 'secular Marxist religion'. However, like Braithwaite and Fromm, he uses 'religion' in an extended sense to connote a world-view, a *Weltanschauung*, with affective practices and commitments, whether naturalistic or not. Antonio Gramsci, *Quademi del Carcere*, ed., V. Gerrantana (Turin: Einaudi, 1975), pp. 2185–6. See also Nielsen, 'Reconceptualizing Civil Society for Now: Some Somewhat Gramscian Turnings', *Arena Journal*, new series, no. 2 (1993/4), pp. 159–74; and 'Marx and the Enlightenment Project', *Critical Review*, vol. 2, no. 4 (Fall 1988), pp. 59–75.

8. See the selection from *The Holy Family*, in Karl Marx and Friedrich Engels, *On Religion* (Moscow: Foreign Languages Publishing House, 1957). This is a useful collection of their writings on religion from Marx's doctoral dissertation (1841) to Engels' late writings on the history of early Christianity (1894–5). The selection from *The Holy Family* is from Chapter VI of *The Holy Family*.

9. Marx and Engels, *On Religion*, p. 290.

10. Ibid., p. 194. Engels does not say what he means by calling them 'nonsensical'. He could simply have meant that they were plainly absurd. There is no reason to attribute to him the strict logical positivist sense of 'nonsensical' as 'being without sense'.

11. Karl Marx, *Contribution to the Critique of Hegel's Philosophy of Right* (1844), p. 42.

12. Marx and Engels, *On Religion*, pp. 193–203.
13. Ibid., pp. 59–68, 289–96.
14. The 'demarcation problem' arises here. From at least Kant to Husserl, to Wittgenstein and to ordinary language philosophy, there has been a concern to demarcate philosophy from other activities and to isolate for it something purely conceptual. Even with a Quinian rejection of that very enterprise, a rejection, that is, of any attempt at a demarcation that would isolate something pure and distinctive for philosophy to be 'uncontaminated by the empirical', the actual *practice* of analytic philosophy (Quine's included) is as if such a demarcation has been made and sustained. Given that practice, what Marx and Engels are doing in discussing religion is, for the most part, not philosophy. In reacting to that, we can go in one of two ways. We can simply say 'So what!' and get on with our business, or we can argue that we should reject such essentialism over and in philosophy and claim instead that concern with demarcation is just that. Whichever way we go, I think it is important to keep hold of the fact that it is truth that we are seeking in discussing the issues Marx and Engels raise. Concerning demarcation, see both the introduction and the contribution by John Passmore in Jocelyne Couture and Kai Nielsen, eds., *Métaphilosophie: Reconstructing Philosophy?: New Essays on Metaphilosophy* (Calgary, Alberta: The University of Calgary Press, 1993), pp. 1–55, 107–25.
15. Marx and Engels, *On Religion*, p. 225.
16. Engels, *Anti-Dühring* (1878), p. 146.
17. Marx and Engels, *On Religion*, p. 147. I think it is quite mistaken to assume, as Engels does, that religion was at first simply a personification of the forces of nature and that only later did religion become involved with the personification of social forces. From what we know about primitive religions both the personification of natural and social forces are involved in the religion of primitive societies. But that Engels is mistaken here, if he is mistaken, has no effect on the general viability of his account of religion as ideology.
18. Ibid., p. 202.
19. Ibid., p. 201–2.
20. Ibid., p. 202.
21. Ibid., p. 194. Engels is plainly, as almost everyone was during that time, Eurocentric here. It is not the Western world, where Christianity reigned, which constitutes 'by far the larger part of civilised humanity'. There were many other great centres of civilization as well.
22. Ibid., p. 197.
23. Ibid., p. 207.
24. Ibid., p. 206.
25. Engels, 'On the History of Early Christianity' (1894–5), p. 313.
26. Ibid., p. 323.
27. Ibid., p. 325.
28. Ibid., p. 325. 'Social Darwinism' is put in scare quotes because it is unclear whether 'social Darwinism' makes much sense. See Morton White, *Social Thought in America: The Revolt against Formalism* (Boston:

Beacon Press, 1957), pp. 6–162, 206–22; and Richard Hofstadter, *Social Darwinism in American Thought* (Boston: Beacon Press, revised edition, 1955). It is very doubtful that socio-biology has made any difference to these analyses and appraisals of the viablity of Social Darwinism.

29.   Ibid., p. 331.
30.   Ibid.
31.   Ibid., p. 332.
32.   Ibid.
33.   Marx, *Critique of Hegel's Philosophy of Right*, p. 42.
34.   Marx and Engels 'On Religion', p. 310.
35.   Ibid., p. 296.
36.   Erich Fromm, *Marx's Conception of Man* (New York: Frederick Ungar Publishing Co., 1961), pp. 24–57. See also his *Psychoanalysis and Religion* (London: Victor Gollancz, 1951) and his *The Dogma of Christ and Other Essays on Religion, Psychology and Culture* (London: Victor Gollancz, 1963).
37.   They, however, no more than Hume, are mechanistic materialists. In that, their materialism differed from that of Holbach. But very few physicalists nowadays are also mechanists.
38.   However, as Engels makes clear in his critique of Feuerbach, it is a mistake to put 'literary phrases in place of scientific knowledge, the liberation of mankind by means of "love" in place of the emancipation of the *proletariat* through the economic transformation of production'. Marx and Engels, *On Religion*, p. 224.
39.   One of the things that I think should be dropped from the canonical core of Marxianism is the labour theory of value. Historically speaking, of course, it has been a central part of Marxism, but it also has been an albatross around its neck and many Marxists with impeccable credentials (e.g., G.A. Cohen, Andrew Levine and John Roemer) have dropped it.
40.   Marx and Engels, *On Religion*, pp. 58–68, 289–96.
41.   Gramsci would be one Marxist who would not accept that. While being a materialist in both the senses we have discussed, he also thought that Marxism needed to articulate a total world-view that could and would be diffused throughout whole societies. He agreed with Croce that *the great problem of the modern age* – perhaps here reflecting too much the particular situation of Italy of their time – *was to learn to live without religion, that is without traditional confessional religion*. Croce thought the central political task was to establish an utterly *secular* 'religion of liberty', what we would now call a secular humanism. Gramsci dismissed that as 'an atheism for aristocrats' and argued that we need a unified and culturally pervasive *proletarian atheism*. Societies, such as Italy, needed a coherent, unitary, society-wide diffused conception of life and of human nature. He called this a 'lay philosophy' (something some now call a 'public philosophy') and, as it gripped a whole culture, it would generate an ethic, a way of life, a civil and individual form of conduct. This 'lay philosophy' was, in his terms, to come to function as a 'secularized religion' and

it would be a functional replacement of traditional religion. It was, as he put it, to be an 'absolute secularization and earthiness of thought, an absolute humanism of history'. He thought that 'Marxism was the only religious faith that is adequate to the contemporary world and can produce a real hegemony' (Gramsci, *Quademi del Carcere*, pp. 1854–64). It is not only, on his conception, that Marxism is a scientific theory, a political strategy, an understanding of history, a philosophy, it is also a new secularized religion which would make in an integrated way this world-view and practical ethic into a distinctive and total culture pattern. So to speak of religion and faith is a similar extension of the use of 'religion' as we find it in Feuerbach, Fromm, Braithwaite and Wittgensteinian fideists. But it is very plain that for Gramsci this religion was a Marxian atheistic *Weltanschauung*. His concern is with the dynamics by which it would become an integrated part of modern culture and come to be hegemonic in society. Indeed, it would provide a deep and holistic transformation of society. When we attend to the content of what he is saying the phrase 'secularized religion' ceases to be misleading. The key question for us to ask now, standing where we stand, is to ask of his conception the question that Rawlsian social democratic liberals ask of communitarians. Given the *de facto* intractability of pluralism in the societies of the capitalist democracies, is such an integrated total *Weltanschauung* achievable and sustainable without a morally unacceptable use of force? Indeed, is it even stably achievable with the use of such force? Our historical experience in recent decades should incline us to think not. See the references in note 7 and see W. Adamson, 'Gramsci and the Politics of Civil Society', *Praxis International*, vol. 7 nos. 3–4 (1987–8), pp. 327–8. See also his *Hegemony and Revolution: Antonio Gramsci's Political and Cultural Theory* (Berkeley, The University of California Press, 1980).

42.   Relying, it could be further replied to the Christian, on such purely logical possibilities and setting aside what makes a good claim to be a more plausible conception of things (here naturalism) because it is not *conclusively* established is just the quest for certainty all over again.

43.   Where I discussed such traditional philosophical matters most traditionally and extensively was in my *Reason and Practice* (New York: Harper & Row, 1971), pp. 135–257.

44.   G.A. Cohen, 'The Future of Disillusion', in Jim Hopkins and Anthony Savile, eds., *Psychoanalysis, Mind and Art: Perspectives on Richard Wollheim* (Oxford: Basil Blackwell, 1992), pp. 142–60.

45.   Barry Allen, *Truth in Philosophy* (Cambridge, Mass.: Harvard University Press, 1993).

46.   Marx W. Wartofsky, '*Homo Homini Deus Est*: Feuerbach's Religious Materialism', in Leroy S. Rouner, ed., *Meaning, Truth, and God* (Notre Dame, Ind.: University of Notre Dame Press, 1982), pp. 154–5.

47.   For example, see Barry Allen, 'Atheism, Relativism, Enlightenment and Truth', *Studies in Religion*, vol. 23, no. 2 (1994). For a forthright expression of atheism by a philosopher whose methodology is very

similar to Allen's, see Richard Rorty, 'Religion as Conversation-Stopper', *Common Knowledge*, vol. 3, no. 1 (Spring 1944), pp. 1–6. See my reply to Allen in the same issue of *Studies in Religion*.

48. J.L. Mackie, *The Miracle of Theism* (Oxford: Clarendon Press, 1982); and Antony Flew, 'The Burden of Proof', in Leroy S. Rouner, ed., *Knowing Religiously* (Notre Dame, Ind.: University of Notre Dame Press, 1985), pp. 103–15; and Bernard Williams, 'Review of *The Miracle of Theism*', *Times Literary Supplement* (11 March 1983). See also my *Philosophy and Atheism* (Buffalo, NY: Prometheus Books, 1985), pp. 211–31.

49. See here Wartofsky, '*Homo Homini Deus Est*'; and his *Feuerbach* (London: Cambridge University Press, 1977).

50. Wartofsky, '*Homo Homini Deus Est*', p. 154.

51. I would like to thank Jocelyne Couture for her assistance in preparing this paper. She is not, of course, in anyway responsible for its contents.

10

Is Religion the Opium of the People? A Reply to Kai Nielsen

David McLellan

Kai Nielsen's stimulating paper has an intellectual scope and confidence which I envy but cannot share. My main difficulty is that Nielsen seems to me to be constantly oscillating between an ontological and a functional approach to religion – between the nononsense, rationalist, materialist Enlightenment approach that religion is clearly false and the empirical, sociological, functional investigation of the social role of religion. In this he is, of course, a true disciple of Marx who assumes the former and does the latter, as section III of Nielsen's paper admirably demonstrates. The trouble is that certain innocuous parts of Marx's theory are made, through Nielsen's underlying but unargued-for presuppositions, to mean more than they say. Who could quarrel with the view that Marx's theory 'gives us a compelling account of certain key functions of religion' (p. 178)? But what about the other key functions? And if ideology and truth do not need to stand in conflict (p. 181f), why should the ideological nature of religious beliefs diminish their moral attractiveness – any more than the ideological (according to Nielsen) nature of *Capital* diminishes *its* moral attractiveness?

Let me elaborate a little on what I conceive to be Nielsen's deep ambiguity by considering two areas; what he says about ideology and his account of Engels, whom he clearly takes as an exemplar of what a Marxian theory of religion looks like. As far as ideology is concerned, Nielsen is reading back into Marx the views of Engels and Lenin. Marx never operated with a true/false dichotomy where ideology was concerned. The notion of 'false consciousness' was first introduced by Bernstein and then taken up by Engels: it is foreign to Marx. On the other hand, for Marx ideology had a pejorative connotation: he would never have agreed that his own work

224

was ideological. What made ideas ideological for him was that they concealed the real nature of social and economic relationships and thus served to justify the unequal distribution of social and economic resources in society. It followed that not all ideas were ideological, but only those that served to conceal social contradictions. Hence, while all classes, including the working class, could produce ideology, it was only ideology in so far as it served to further the interest of the ruling class. And since society and its class structure were constantly changing, the same ideas could begin or cease to be ideological. Lenin was the great exponent of 'socialist ideology' which for Marx would have been a contradiction in terms. By following Lenin, Nielsen can give the impression that ideology is a neutral term whose application to religion has no necessarily pejorative connotations. But common (and Marx's) usage means that that connotation does, almost unconsciously, affect our view of religion once we go along with its being so described as ideological.

As far as Engels is concerned, Nielsen is in real difficulties. Marx wrote little about religion, but most of his scattered metaphorical remarks are rich with possibility. Of all the classical Marxist theorists, Engels (with the exception of Gramsci who is, in my opinion, by far the best) wrote most about religion – but it is largely a farrago of nonsense. Nielsen should not be so modest about his inability to tell whether Engels' historical narrative is reasonably accurate and still less should he assume its plausibility. Engels was indeed a 'pure child of the Enlightenment' (p. 184) – and it shows. Engels' scattered remarks on primitive religion do not easily fit it to a coherent perspective. On examination, they seem to be informed more by the rather undeveloped state of cultural anthropology at the time than by any recognizably Marxist orientation. For Engels was prone, in the spirit of late nineteenth-century positivism, to oversimple generalizations. This involved the application of the Darwinian model of evolution to the study of primitive society and the consequent attribution to primitive peoples of both 'childish' ignorance and also a penchant for speculating about the world in the manner of a nineteenth-century rationalist. As far as his comments on early Christianity are concerned, it is surprising that Engels devoted so much space to analysing Christian doctrines and their intellectual sources and so relatively little to any recognizably materialist account of their origin and growth. Repeatedly, Engels fails to subject early Christianity to any serious class analysis. For his view that Christianity recruited 'from the lowest strata of the people, as becomes a revolutionary movement'[1] contrasts with the view of Christianity as having universal appeal in face of the levelling power of Rome. Indeed, he says that 'in all classes there was necessarily a number of people who, despairing of material salvation, sought in its stead a spiritual salvation, a consolation in their consciousness to save them from utter despair'.[2] And when he continues that the majority of those pining for consolation were necessarily slaves, it is not clear whether this is a quantitative necessity simply because most people were slaves. In any case, recent analysis suggests that the description 'religion of slaves' is highly misleading, as is Engels' opinion that most revolts in Antiquity were slave-based. Talking of early Jewish recruitment, a topic neglected by Engels, Gerd Theissen writes that its origin was 'not so much the lowest class of all as a marginal middle class which reacted with peculiar sensitivity to the upward and downward trends within society which were beginning to make themselves felt'.[3] And as far as the social composition of Christianity in the Graeco-Roman world goes, Robert Grant marshals a lot of evidence to show that the Christian movement should be regarded 'not as a proletarian mass movement but as a relatively small cluster of more or less intense groups, largely middle class in origin'.[4] And Engels' views on Christianity and the rise of the bourgeoisie, although more nuanced, are far less impressive than Weber's.

All this is rather harsh on Engels. But his attitude is partly explicable in terms of the appalling pietism of his upbringing. And his conceptual tools and intellectual milieu go a long way to explaining why Engels, who could be so good an historian, is so weak when it comes to dealing with religion. In the three periods to which he devotes serious attention – primitive religion, early Christianity and the Reformation – Engels relies uncritically on a single authority. For primitive religion he relies on Tylor, for early Christianity on Bauer and for the reformation on Zimmermann. Tylor was a positivist and a rationalist, Bauer a conservative idealist and Zimmermann was a radical Young Hegelian. And Engels makes only the most meagre efforts to combine their views with any sort of Marxism. For the kind of Marxism he elaborated simply did not have the conceptual wherewithal to come to terms with his authorities.

As far as the functional side of Engels' (and Marx's) account goes, it is in principle unexceptionable. It is difficult to contest the claim that a good deal of religion a good deal of the time tends to fit in with the prevailing political, social and economic mores of society and thus be in some sense conservative and thus even just about describable as opium. The same rather banal claim could presumably also be made of philosophy or art or literature. The claim only becomes interesting when religion is said 'almost invariably' (p. 204) to have an opiate function. But then the claim is also highly contestable. The sliding definitions and the huge areas of time and space covered by these sorts of grand generalizations make them very difficult to handle. But at least large swathes of contemporary Islam might occasion cause for further thought. And I only wish that the New Christian Right *were* sunk in an opium-induced dream instead of being only too aggressively active. Even on the Left, while it is true to say that religion as a force for social change has either been defeated or absorbed (p. 200f) – to reappear, of course, later – precisely the same can be said of Marxism which has its own history of suppression, compromise and takeover. An additional trouble is that the concept of religion itself is notoriously slippery. And Nielsen's does indeed slip. The concepts of religion employed by Feuerbach, Fromm, Braithwaithe and Wittgensteinian fideists are declared 'eccentric' (p. 197). Yet on p. 200 we learn that Feuerbach articulated a new humanist *religion* of man. Both Max Horkheimer and Walter Benjamin are counted among the naturalists, despite the theme in the writings of the former of religion as the location of opposition to the contemporary world and the latter's penchant for theological themes such as messianism and redemption, which he was loath to mediate with the secular.[5]

The ambiguity running through Nielsen's paper can also be seen in the relations of dialectical materialism to historical materialism. Nielsen thinks that historical materialism fits well with what he calls physicalism. But Marx was no physicalist. It is no accident that the word 'matter' does not occur in his works – though those of Engels are replete with it. The one exception in Marx is *The Holy Family* – but such philosophical interpretations of the world were put behind him for ever in the *Theses on Feuerbach*. This is because Marx remained in some sense a disciple of Hegel – of whom curiously there is no mention in Nielsen's account. This is important because a dialectical Marxism which takes its debt to Hegel seriously is capable of a more fruitful approach. The only approaches open to 'physicalist' Marxism are either negation or exclusion, saying of religion either 'it is false' or 'it has nothing to do with me'. And we can see that this is borne out by a glance at the classical Marxist thinkers. Although Marx said little about religion, most of what he *did* say – connected with the subject of alienation, for example – has provided much food for Christian thought. Engels, on the other hand, is rather more sparse when it comes to material for dialogue – except in his early period, which is, of course, precisely the time when he was busy secularizing his Young Hegelian views. Kautsky and the Second International's Marxists had no time for Hegel and – correspondingly, so I am arguing – no interest in the content of religion. Lenin's view of religion as 'medieval mildew' or 'one of the most odious things on earth' and of the idea of God as a concept of 'inexpressible foulness' go hand in hand with the simplistic *Materialism and Empirio-Criticism*: Lenin's views are much more muted after his serious study of Hegel in the war years. Stalin reinforced, in philosophy at least, the worst aspects of Leninism and had as little time for religion as he did for Hegel – except as an added support for Russian patriotism during Hitler's war. Certain sections of the Frankfurt School, Gramsci, the later Sartre, have all conserved something of the legacy of Hegel and thus talk, in some respects, the same language as Christianity. It is significant that one of the factors leading to a loss of interest in Marxist-Christian dialogue in France was the growing popularity of the anti-humanist, anti-Hegelian, anti-religious Marxism of structuralist inspiration *à la* Althusser. After so much muddying of the waters by such as Roger Garaudy when it was difficult to spot the difference between progressive Communists and left-wing Catholics, many a party member must have breathed a very heavy sigh of relief when at last their arose an intellectual leader whose version of Marxist doctrine was of a rigour and rigidity that precluded any sort of conversation with wayward Christians, existentialists, and the like.

Running through Nielsen's paper is a belief in secularization which again indicates a confidence more at home in the nineteenth century than in the twentieth, with Nielsen as a contemporary (though more sympathetic) version of Leslie Stephen. Once again, the question of the definition of religion arises. For example, in the rich Durkheimian tradition of thinking about religion such conceptions of secularization make no sense. Or again, in the apophatic version of Christianity, religious symbols and images disappear in the Kingdom of God.[6] That role will disappear when we know as we are known: no temple in the New Jerusalem.[7] In any case the contemporary world is, for better or (often, I fear) for worse absolutely awash with religion of which the richest country in the world, the

United States, is as good an example as the poorest. Historically, for quite understandable reasons, those on the Left have failed to leave some space for religion in their approach to society and politics. But religion in some shape or form has been a deep and enduring aspect of human activity – and there is every reason to think that this will continue to be so for at least the near future. Benign neglect or outright rejection by the Left will mean that the immense power of religion can be captured by the ideologies of the Right. Consider here the dangerous role of the so-called 'moral majority' in America and the way in which, almost by default, a whole string of repressive social measures, let alone aggressive nuclear stances, appear to many to have behind them the weight of the whole Judaeo-Christian tradition.

At a deeper level, however, what we need is a bit of faith. And, as Kolakowski remarks, 'to spread faith, faith is needed and not an intellectual assertion of the social utility of faith'.[8] I agree with Charles Taylor in the moving conclusion to his *Sources of the Self*: a stripped-down secularism with its abandonment of any religious dimensions or radical hope in history involves a self-mutilation which lobotomizes the most radical aspirations of humanity.[9] In a world increasingly colonized by the corrosive and meretricious imperative of instrumental reason we should not abandon too readily what spiritual resources of resistance that we still have left.

Thus the answer to the question whether religion is the opium of the people is yes, sometimes, like television or Marxism or art. But the comparison of religion to opium is neither very precise nor original to Marx. This famous metaphor was anticipated by Bruno Bauer in his book *Die gute Sache der Freiheit*, where he talks of how religion 'in the opium-like stupefaction of its destructive urge, speaks of a future life where all shall be made new'[10] and again in *Der Christliche Staat* of the 'opium-like influence'[11] of theology on mankind. Indeed, references to religion as opium are commonplace among the Young Hegelians, who may well have taken it from Hegel's description of Indian religion.[12] To what extent this comparison is valid should be left to sociologists of religion and not mixed up with questions as to the falsity of religious belief – which, in any case, in Nielsen's paper we are asked to accept as 'given'. Better, here at least to follow Marx: the truth, that is, reality and power, of thinking is proved in practice and the dispute over the reality or non-reality of thinking divorced from practice is a purely scholastic question.[13]

Notes

1. F. Engels, 'On the History of Early Christianity', in K. Marx and F. Engels, *On Religion* (Moscow: Foreign Languages Publishing House, 1971), p. 330.
2. Engels, 'On the History of Early Christianity', p. 201.
3. G. Theissen, *The First Followers of Jesus: A Sociological Analysis of the Earliest Christianity* (New York: 1978), p. 46.
4. R. Grant, *Early Christianity and Society* (London: 1978), p. 11. See also pp. 79ff.
5. For Horkheimer, see his *Critical Theory* (New York: 1972), pp. 129ff. And on Benjamin, see the discussion in M. Lowy, *On Changing the World: Essays in Political Philosophy from Karl Marx to Walter Benjamin* (New Jersey, 1993), chs 12–14.
6. See the sharp consequences drawn from this view about the impracticability of Christianity in a non-Marxist society by Denys Turner in his *Marxism and Christianity* (Oxford: 1983).
7. Book of Revelation, 21: 22.
8. L. Kolakowski, *Modernity on Endless Trial* (Chicago: 1990), p. 9.
9. See C. Taylor, *Sources of the Self: The Making of Modern Identity* (Cambridge: 1989), p. 520.
10. B. Bauer, *Die gute Sache der Freiheit* (1842), p. 213.
11. B. Bauer, 'Der Christlicher Staat', in *Hallischer Jahrbucher* (1841), p. 538.
12. Cf. E. Benz, 'Hegels Religionsphilosophie und die Linkshegelianer', *Zeitschrift für Religions und Geistesgeshichte* (1955).
13. K. Marx, *Selected Writings*, ed. D. McLellan (Oxford: 1977), p. 156.

Part Six
Is Immortality an Illusion?

11

Dislocating the Soul

D.Z. Phillips

> There might also be a language in whose use the 'soul' of the words played no part. In which, for example, we have no objection to replacing one word by another arbitrary one of our own invention.
>
> We speak of understanding a sentence in the sense in which it can be replaced by another which says the same; but also in the sense in which it cannot be replaced by another. (Any more than one musical theme can be replaced by another.)
>
> In the one case the thought in the sentence is something common to different sentences; in the other, something that is expressed only by those words in those positions. (Understanding a poem.)
>
> (Wittgenstein, PI, I: 530–1)

In philosophy of religion we are often offered analyses which pay no attention to, and hence fail to capture, the 'soul' in the words of religious beliefs. When this happens we have a dislocation of language, including a dislocation of language concerning the soul. This dislocation is fed from many sources, not all of them philosophical. It is fed by the character of certain desires that go deep in us. A philosopher may want to heal these dislocations. Given their character, more than the intelligence of the audience will need to be addressed. Contact will have to be made with their souls as well.

I

What do I mean by a dislocation of language? Not all dislocations are of the same kind. A comparison of some philosophical and non-philosophical examples will bring this out.

It would be mistaken to think that a dislocation of language occurs every time expectations are not fulfilled; for example, when intentions or promises are not kept. She had every intention of coming to see me, but had a telephone call to say that her mother was ill, so she did not come. Or: she promised on impulse, but, on reflection, decided it was unwise to keep it. Thwarted intentions, broken promises, foolish promises – when these happen there is no dislocation of language. They are part of the lives and discourse we share with each other, in which intending and promising have their sense. When intentions and promises are not kept, there are familiar stories to tell. In the early hours of the morning at a party, one friend says to another, 'Let's go home.' The other replies, 'Yes, let's.' Neither moves. Perhaps they do want to go home, but are physically incapable of doing so. Perhaps they are not expressing a serious intention, but posturing verbally in a glass of Dark. No dislocation of language here, only the invoking of a familiar scene.

In Beckett's *Waiting for Godot*, one character says to another, 'Let's go.' The other replies, 'Yes, let's.' Neither moves. Here people *have* wanted to speak of a dislocation of language. Why? I think because the characters, unlike the women and the party-goers in our previous examples, would not think they owed us reasons for their immobility. If someone asked them, 'Why aren't you going? You said you intended to,' they'd reply, 'What's that got to do with anything?' For Beckett's tramps certain words have been dislocated from their familiar contexts. They no longer carry their normal implications. Some critics have said that Beckett is showing us the meaninglessness of language. Others have called this a vulgar reading, and they are surely right. The trouble with the tramps' words is not that they are meaningless, but that they have the meaning they do. The trouble is in what intending and promising have become for them.

One day, apropos of nothing in particular, apart from a desire to relieve boredom, one tramp says to another, 'Shall we try some repentance?' The other asks, 'About what?' The first replies, 'Oh, we wouldn't have to go into details.' Repentance is cut off from its religious contexts. Within and outside the Church, confession may become confused. It may seem like a mechanical cleansing. A sick soul may seem like a sick stomach, and sins may be thought to be washed away like dirt. But, it might be argued, unworthy participations in sacraments are like thwarted, broken or foolish intentions and promises. They are part of the practices we share with each other. Yet, this does not capture the condition of the tramps. They are losing hold or have lost hold of what it is to participate worthily or unworthily in a sacrament. They are not refusing to apply a concept, as Oscar Wilde did when he said, ' "Blasphemy" is a word I never use.' For them, where repentance is concerned, a dislocation of language has occurred. Their confusion has taken on a life of its own.

Yet, even including the tramps, we are still considering familiar scenes. But, now, consider much stranger examples. A person says 'I'm off', but does not move. No contexts such as those we have mentioned are present to help us understand the situation. The same person says, 'The house is on fire' quite passively, with no reactions at all. At other times, the following words come out of the person's mouth, 'I am in agony, are you?', again, without any facial expression or reaction of any kind. Such a person would be a complete enigma to us. We would not know how to take the words; they wouldn't mean anything. Perhaps we could say that they are mentioned, but not used.

What if we were asked to imagine this as a pervasive phenomenon? We'd probably think of zombies. And if we were asked to imagine human beings, wouldn't we imagine them with fixed stares, no plasticity in the faces, with words coming out of their mouths: 'I'm off', 'I'm in agony', 'The house is on fire'. For all the difference it makes *any* words could come out of their mouths. We would not talk to these creatures, because they have nothing to say.

I have said that these are strange examples, but we can note even stranger facts about them. For example, they are quite compatible with the way in which many philosophers speak of the soul. It will be said that we fail to appreciate the possibility of the soul because we concentrate on the body. The well-formed sentences that come out of the mouths are indirect communications from the thinking part of a person. This is the soul speaking. We understand the sentences. It is only a contingent fact that the behaviour normally accompanying these words is missing. But this reminds us of Beckett: 'Repent of what?' – 'Oh, we wouldn't have to go into details.' But without the details, the words are bereft of sense. In the philosophical example, there are no details, no surroundings, no play by Beckett, in which the words can mean anything. No amount of uttering of the words will yield sense devoid of practice, and by 'practice' we mean the familiar features of the relationships and everyday lives we share with each other, features which include the various facial expressions we recognize, the gestures we make, the bodily postures we adopt, our laughter and our tears, and so on. That is why Wittgenstein says that the best picture of the human soul is the human body.

Wittgenstein's insight cannot be accommodated by saying that the soul, by some kind of causal operation, brings about our behavioural practices. If this relation obtained, the words of the soul should have a meaning quite independent of the practices they cause. After all, the words coming out of the mouths must be indirect communications since the words, of course, are physical sounds. The view we are considering implies that, prior to practice, the soul could simply communicate with itself in thought-language. But no alleged mental operation can confer meaning on words. The soul, so conceived, cannot baptize signs with sense. We are tempted to think that the meanings are already *in* the thoughts. But *what* meaning? Once we ask that question, we need a distinction between getting the meaning right and thinking we have got it right. To have that distinction we need something independent of any silent thought or inner ostensive definition by the soul. As determinants of meaning, the so-called inner operations are redundant, they are idle wheels. The required independence is given in our practice. Wittgenstein discusses the needed corrective in our thinking as follows:

> 'Everything is already there in . . .' How does it come about that this arrow →→→——→ *points*? Doesn't it seem to carry in it something besides itself? —— 'No, not the dead line on paper; only the psychological thing, the meaning, can do that.' —— That is both true and false. The arrow points only in the application that a living being makes of it.
>
> This pointing is *not* a hocus-pocus which can be performed only by the soul.
>
> (PI, I: 454)

This philosophical picture of the soul dislocates words from practice and tries, in vain, to infuse them with sense. Among the words it dislocates is the word 'soul' itself, cutting it off from human life. Philosophers feel that we should not mix what should, in their view, be kept apart: soul and body, mental and physical, spirit and matter. Commenting on this reaction, Wittgenstein says:

> It seems paradoxical to us that we should have such a medley, mixing physical states and states of consciousness up together in a *single* report: 'He suffered great torments and tossed about restlessly'. It is quite usual; so why do we find it paradoxical? Because

we want to say that the sentence deals with both tangibles and intangibles at once. —— But does it worry you if I say: 'These three struts give the building stability'? Are three and stability tangible? —— Look at the sentence as an instrument, and at its sense as its employment.

(PI, I: 421)

Think of tragic breaks in the medley: the severe dislocation in a child where there is no coordination between its words and its facial expressions. When the child smiles, the words 'I hate you' come out of its mouth. It is an eerie and terrifying phenomenon. The parents would feel cut off from the child. This does not mean that the child is not an object of pity and compassion, but it is our normality which determines the terribleness of the child's condition.

So if the words, 'I'm off', 'I am in agony', 'The house is burning', 'So glad to see you' come from the mouths of the robot-like beings we have imagined, we would not take ourselves to be addressed by them at all, least of all by their souls.

II

If the notion of an inner substance called 'the soul' is the philosophical chimera we have suggested it is, whatever is meant by the immortality of the soul cannot be the continued existence of such a substance.

Where does this leave us? With the task of healing the dislocation of language concerning the soul; healing it, that is, where such a dislocation has occurred. But this is no easy task since, as we have said, it is fed from many sources. Let us look at some of the philosophical sources. Immediately after the passage in which Wittgenstein urges us to look at the sense of a sentence as its employment, he asks:

What am I believing in when I believe that men have souls? What am I believing in, when I believe that this substance has two carbon rings? In both cases there is a picture in the foreground, but the sense lies far in the background; that is, the application of the picture is not easy to survey.

(PI, I: 422)

Why should this be so? In the case of some pictures they suggest immediately the application they actually have. Other pictures tend to mislead us when we philosophize since they suggest to us an application which is not the one the picture actually has in our lives. The difficulty, for us, is created by the picture itself. Consider Wittgenstein's treatment of the following example:

> 'While I was speaking to him I did not know what was going on in his head.' In saying this, one is not thinking of brain-processes, but of thought-processes. The picture should be taken seriously. We should really like to see into his head. And yet we only mean what elsewhere we should mean by saying: we should like to know what he is thinking. I want to say: we have this vivid picture – and that use, apparently contradicting the picture, which expresses the psychical.
>
> (PI, I: 427)

This passage is important for our purposes. First, we have a vivid picture which may mislead us: 'While I was speaking to him I did not know what was going on in his head.' We may be clear that we are not seeking brain-processes, but then think that inside the head analogous processes are going on which could be found there: thought-processes, something essentially psychical. To demystify this suggestion, Wittgenstein says that, elsewhere, the sentence 'I wonder what he is thinking' will do just as well. Countless examples of 'I think . . .' could be given to stop us looking in the wrong direction for the psychical essence of 'thinking'.

But that is not the puzzle I want to discuss. If 'I wonder what he is thinking' will do just as well as 'While I was talking to him I did not know what was going on in his head', why doesn't Wittgenstein advocate dropping the second sentence in favour of the first so that we shouldn't be misled any more? One answer is to say that there is nothing wrong with the picture. It is we who are confused about its use. But this is not the whole story. The two sentences cannot be equated in *all* circumstances. To avoid certain confusions similarities between the two sentences may be emphasized. Wittgenstein says that *elsewhere*, in *different* circumstances, 'I wonder what he is thinking' might do just as well. But in the circumstances under consideration that is not the case. 'While I was talking to him I did not know what was going on in his head' makes its own contribution to what we want to say when we find other people enigmatic, puzzling or even sinister. This is what Wittgenstein means when he says, 'The picture should be taken seriously. We should really like to see into his head.' The picture says what it says and cannot be replaced without loss. But our misunderstandings of the picture hide its seriousness from us. Confronted by a person of peculiar maliciousness I may say, 'I'll never know what goes on in his head. It must be very dark in there.'

Consider now another picture, an opposite, in which a close affinity with another is expressed:

And how about such an expression as 'In my heart I understood when you said that', pointing to one's heart. Does one, perhaps, not *mean* this gesture? Of course one means it. Or is one conscious of using a mere figure? Indeed not – it is not a figure that we choose, not a simile, yet it is a figurative expression.

(PI, II, p. 178)

Again, the picture may mislead us. We may start wondering what sort of process goes on in the heart. To demystify the picture, to avoid *that* misunderstanding, we may say that, elsewhere, all that is said is, 'I felt a close affinity to you when you said that.' But for the reasons we have already mentioned, that does not mean we can dispense with the expression, 'In my heart I understood when you said that.' The latter expression is itself a contribution to what we want to say, sometimes, when we do feel an affinity with what another person has said.

Consider a related example. Comparing certain discussions with Drury and Moore, Wittgenstein said: 'I can't speak to Moore's soul.' What is said makes a contribution to the distance we may feel when discussing with someone, but it could not be replaced, without loss, by, for example, 'I could not make contact with him' or 'I could not get close to him'.

In all three cases we have mentioned, the pictures tempt us to go off in the wrong direction: 'If the picture of thought in the head can force itself upon us, then why not much more that of thought in the soul?' (PI, II, p. 178). In all three expressions, 'While he was talking I did not know what was going on his head', 'In my heart I understood when you said that', 'I can't speak to Moore's soul', we have expressions which cannot be replaced without loss. The same is true when we speak of saving or damning our immortal souls. The trouble is that the language so often offered by philosophy of religion to discuss the soul is one which pays little attention to the 'soul' in expressions concerning the soul. We are offered talk of immaterial substances, disembodied spirits, and so on. Here, too, the religious pictures have misled us. The resultant analyses are a dislocation of the religious expressions.

III

> Religion teaches us that the soul can exist when the body has disintegrated. Now do I understand this teaching? – Of course I understand it – I can imagine plenty of things in connexion with it. And haven't pictures of these things been painted? And why should such a picture be only an imperfect rendering of the spoken doctrine? Why should it not do the *same* service as the words? And it is the service which is the point.
>
> (PI, II, p. 178)

In this context, too, religious pictures may lead us astray. They may suggest applications they do not have. The picture of the soul leaving the body may create images akin to a butterfly leaving the chrysalis. This dislocates the religious picture. We have already noted the confusions which come from thinking of the soul as an immaterial 'something' inside the body. We noted the dislocation of body and soul which results.

When someone dies, we may say, 'She's gone'. That is not captured by 'Her life is over'. But if we ask, 'Where has she gone to?' expecting the kind of answer we would get to the question, 'Where is her body?' we have been led astray. The replies, 'In heaven' or 'With her Lord' are not answers to *that* kind of question. An artist might paint a picture which shows her soul leaving the body. The picture might tell us something about her completed life or about the destiny of her soul, but the picture is not meant to be a diagram. We could say of such a picture, with suitable substitutions, what Wittgenstein said of Michelangelo's *Creation of Adam*:

> If we ever saw this, we certainly wouldn't think this [the soul]. The picture has to be used in an entirely different way if we are to call [that figure the soul], and so on. You could imagine that religion was taught by means of these pictures.
>
> (LRB, p. 63)

Wittgenstein imagines someone saying:

> 'Of course, we can only express ourselves by means of pictures.'
> This is rather queer . . . I could show Moore the pictures of a
> tropical plant. If I showed him the picture of [the soul leaving the
> body] and said: 'Of course, I can't show you the real thing, only
> the picture'. . . . The absurdity is, I've never taught him the tech-
> nique of using this picture.
>
> *(LRB,* p. 63)

If you show me her photograph, I may tell you that she is dead
and that she is buried in Llangyfelach Cemetery. But to look for
that comparison with the picture of the soul leaving the body is
entirely misplaced. The picture is not that kind of picture, nor does
it attempt to approximate to it. The picture may tell you something
about the eternal destiny of a person's soul.

So whatever is meant by the immortality of the soul, it has to do
with the eternal destiny of a human being as a whole. But, having
said this, the picture of the soul leaving the body may still mislead
us in different ways. We may have given up thinking of immaterial
substances, but now think that new tensions are created by what
we know of material substances: 'If it is the soul of a human being
which may attain immortality, how is that consistent with our knowledge that a body is decomposing in such-and-such a cemetery or
has been cremated?' Wittgenstein recognizes one form the conversation may take:

> Suppose I say that the body will rot, and another says, 'No. Par-
> ticles will rejoin in a thousand years, and there will be a Resur-
> rection of you.'
> If some said: 'Wittgenstein, do you believe in this?' I'd say:
> 'No.' 'Do you contradict the man?' I'd say: 'No'.
>
> *(LRB,* p. 53)

Wittgenstein is saying that there is a huge intellectual distance
between himself and the person who talks in this way. To say he contradicted him, or believed the opposite, would give the impression
that he was playing the same game and advancing a rival hypothesis
within it: 'Particles will rejoin in a thousand years' – 'Particles will
not rejoin in a thousand years.' Wittgenstein is saying that he cannot do anything with these words; they mean nothing to him.

Imagine how the discussion may continue. 'I do not think particles will reassemble.' 'What do you think happens then?' 'I have to
confess that I do not know, but it is fascinating how it comes about.
After all, it must happen somehow.' Someone else may say: 'No,
particles do not reassemble. A soul-stuff survives.' Yet again: 'Particles reassemble and a replica-body is miraculously created.' Another view: 'I think we are looking in the wrong direction. We
should concentrate on near-death experiences to get clues on the
nature of the after-life.' All these alleged hypotheses are examples
of what I mean by analyses which ignore the 'soul' in the words of
expressions concerning the soul.

Other writers who reject such analyses are, nevertheless, under
their influence. As a result, unlike Wittgenstein, they think the religious expressions should be either reformed or abolished. They,
too, miss the 'soul' in the expressions. An example of misguided
reformers is John Robinson, the late Bishop of Woolwich, in his
book *Honest to God*. He argued that, in our scientific age, we can no
longer say that God is on high. For him, 'height' belongs to mathematics and calculation. If God is on high, we should be able to ask,
'How high?' Looking at the state of philosophy of religion in his
day, O.K. Bouwsma asked whether 'High is our God above all
gods' is to be construed as 'High is the Empire State Building above
all other buildings in New York', and replied, 'I'm afraid so.' What
has happened is that Robinson, influenced by a language in which
the 'soul' of the words does not matter, advocates reforming a language in which the 'soul' of the words does matter.

We have an example of a misguided abolitionist in E.B. Tylor's
vulgar reading of a ritual among the Seminoles of Florida. When a
mother was dying in childbirth her baby would be held over her
mouth to receive her parting breath. The mother gives her soul for
her child. Tylor calls this an example of unequivocal significance.
According to him it illustrates a superstitious belief in the soul. He
said that Seminoles believed the soul to be a little white cloud,
imbued with special powers, which came out of the mother's mouth
and went into the child's, so giving the child the power the mother
had. Tylor's crassness shows that he is the confused one. For him,
in order for there to be a soul, it *would* have to be something like
a little white cloud. Recall Wittgenstein's remark that Frazer is more
savage than the savages. But Wittgenstein did not think Frazer's
lack was merely a lack of intelligence. The pointlessness of the ritual
for Tylor, too, points to the lack of a certain point in his life. This

might be put by saying that certain possibilities of meaning are closed for Frazer and Tylor. They do not misunderstand the logic of the language, if by that is meant misunderstanding the grammar of possibilities they recognize. No, the language does not get off the ground for them.

It seems to me that certain language concerning the immortality of the soul escapes many philosophers, too. The Seminole mother gave her soul to her child. To believe in the immortality of the soul is to want to give one's soul to God. This has a special significance at death, since it is here, it is said, that the mortal puts on immortality, and the corruptible puts on incorruption. The mother was able to say farewell to life in giving it to her child. The believer says farewell to life in giving it to God. Of course, there are important differences. The mother does something for her child. The child is dependent on the mother, but God is not dependent on the believer. To want to do something for God at death is to want to die in God; to give one's life to God.

How different this is from those discussions of immortality which make it sound like a dispute about whether human beings can or cannot exist below a certain temperature. There may be disagreement: 'Yes they can exist' – 'No they can't.' It seems that what we can say about immortality of the soul depends on such findings. Either '*p*' is or is not the case. Here we have a radical dislocation of religious expressions concerning the soul. But what right have I to say this? Are there not many ways in which people think of the immortality of the soul?

IV

So far, we have been concentrating on dislocations of language which come about in two ways: first, where misleading accounts are given of expressions concerning the soul; second, where accounts of the soul betray the fact that the philosophers lack any sense of the 'soul' in the expressions they are dealing with.

It is important to remember that the religious character of belief in the immortality of the soul is not captured by simply giving a truth-value to the proposition. The soul is immortal. Immortality of the soul is said to be something we have to strive for. Belief in this context is said to be a virtue, while failure to believe, failure to strive, is said to be a sin. Many things stand in the way of such striving, as we saw in the dislocation of religious language which occurred with Beckett's tramps. Wittgenstein noted that religious expressions call for an appropriate level of devotion. For example, a belief such as predestination, which at one level seems to be destructive of morality, may be a profound belief in the life of someone like Saint Paul. May not the same be true of belief in the immortality of the soul? The picture of the soul leaving the body may be taken up into people's lives in very different ways.

If we are dependent on our fortunes in this world alone, it may seem as plain as day that there is no correlation between morality and worldly prosperity. Why should we be asked to make such sacrifices? They may seem pointless until someone tells us that there is more life to come after death, when virtue is to be rewarded and vice punished. The picture of the soul leaving the body will then be understood as the soul going to receive its desserts in these terms.

These reactions do establish a relation between my whole life and immortality of the soul, but, surely, it is a problematic one. Simone Weil says that many religious families tell their children not to lie because God is watching them. They make God a policeman in the sky. The obedience induced would not be a virtue since the conformity to morality is simply a means to self-interest. On such a view, if God were to reward vice and punish virtue, the believer would switch his options. The conception of religion involved cheapens morality, and the apologetic appeals made on such a basis are themselves morally despicable. Here is one reaction to such appeals:

> Is the reason for not worshipping the devil instead of God that God is stronger than the devil? God will get you in the end, the devil will not be able to save you from his fury, and then you will be *for* it. 'Think of your future, boy, and don't throw away your chances'. What a creeping and vile sort of thing religion must be.
>
> The difference between the power of God and the power of the devil: it is difficult to understand at all clearly what this difference is (otherwise there might be no idolatry); and yet people with any religion at all will have a lively idea of it, generally. The power of God is a *different* power from the power of the devil. But if you said that God is *more* powerful than the devil – then I should not understand you, because I should not know what sort of measure you used.
>
> If you tried to explain by comparing the different physical

causes, as you might if you said that one explosion was more powerful than another – meaning it had more far reaching effects – then I think you would have sidetracked things well and properly. (When Satan said that dominion over this world had been left to him, Jesus did not contradict him.)

I should think that any natural theology which rested on a quantitative comparison between the power of God and the power of physical agents or operations – or: a quantitative comparison between the physical effects of God's power and the physical effects of anything else – would be a pretty unholy sort of thing.[1]

If this is how the picture of the soul leaving the human body enters human life, there is no sense of saying farewell to life. On the contrary, this life's lowest motives and desires seem to determine the conception of immortality involved.

But the picture of the soul leaving the body may enter life in a different way, namely, as a direct result of a perception of tension and contradictions within morality itself. Morality asks the impossible of us. There is a gap between what we ought to be and what we are. We feel that an opportunity is needed to put this right. Our own imperfections seem to call for an extension of life after death. In this way, reflection on morality leads to belief in immortality.

In this reaction too, it seems to me, there is a failure to say farewell to life. There is the feeling that it is intolerable that I should end like this with all my flaws and imperfections, in the tangle of circumstances over which, for the most part, I have no control. My improvement, it seems, *must* be part of the final story.

The strength of this reaction is that is emphasizes a connection between belief in immortality and ethical considerations, but the connection is still problematic. It is hard to see how it addresses the limitations of moral endeavour. Would not any further endeavour after death, were it to qualify as such, be equally imperfect. Wittgenstein expresses the point as follows:

> Not only is there no guarantee of the temporal immortality of the human soul, that is to say of its eternal survival after death, but, in any case, the assumption completely fails to accomplish the purpose for which it has always been intended. Or is some riddle solved by my surviving for ever? Is not this eternal life as much of a riddle as our present life.

(*Tractatus*, 6.4312)

Wittgenstein suggests that understanding the picture of the soul leaving this life as the hope of a temporal eternity, 'completely fails to accomplish the purpose for which [the picture] has always been intended'. The hope of immortality is offered, not, as this view suggests, as a hope of overcoming one's flaws and imperfections, but as a hope offered despite one's flaws and imperfections.

The picture of the soul leaving the body may be thought of as a temporal eternity which constitutes a hope, not for *my* improvement, but for the improvement of *others*. It is the improvement of others which must be part of the final story. Those who have enjoyed even modest affluence may find it intolerable that so many should have lived their lives in abject poverty and deprivation. No attempt to correlate such affluence and poverty to personal merit makes any moral sense. So matters must be put right in the end if talk of God's love and justice is to mean anything at all. Even if one can say farewell to one's own life, is it not intolerable to say that others should say the same when their lives have been so wretched?

This reaction to the liberation of the soul from this life is a powerful one. Its power comes from two sources. First, there is the weighty consideration that religion must address the conditions in which people live their lives. If believers think of themselves as children of God, vehicles of grace, that belief is empty if it does not have implications for the way we have towards our fellow human beings. Nothing I go on to say is meant to deny that.[2]

Yet the outcome of our endeavours on earth is contingent; there is no guarantee. The world may not smile on us. There is then a certain kind of religion which, as Simone Weil says, invents a God who does. This is the second source of the power of the reaction. It recognizes the belief that if in this life only we have hope we are the most miserable. But what it then offers is a compensatory extension of it; a temporal immortality. For Simone Weil, this hope is an illusion: 'The thought of death calls for a counterweight, and this counterweight – apart from grace – cannot be anything but a lie' (*Gravity and Grace*, p. 16).

On the last two views we have considered, the earthly imperfections of myself or others, together with the circumstances which limit us in various ways, are thought to be intolerable. Temporal eternity offers compensation. Immortality, on the other hand, offers a hope in God which transcends these limitations.

The most fundamental barrier to a belief in the immortality of the soul is the desire for self-preservation. Some of the reactions we have considered can be seen as manifestations of it. The picture of the soul leaving this world then becomes a function of this desire. It was for this reason that T.S. Eliot said that Tennyson's *In Memoriam* was moved more by love of man than a desire for God.[3] For Simone Weil, saying farewell to life, dying to the desire for compensation, is a condition for passing over into religious truth:

> The principal claim which we think we have on the universe is that our personality should continue. This claim implies all the others. The instinct of self-preservation makes us feel this continuation to be a necessity, and we believe that a necessity is a right. We are like the beggar who said to Talleyrand: 'Sir, I must live', and to whom Talleyrand replied, 'I do not see the necessity for that'. Our personality is entirely dependent on external circumstances which have unlimited power to crush it. But we would rather die than admit this. From our point of view the equilibrium of the world is a combination of circumstances so ordered that our personality remains intact and seems to belong to us. All the circumstances of the past which have wounded our personality appear to us to be disturbances of balance which should infallibly be made up for one day or another by phenomena having a contrary effect. We live on the expectation of these compensations. The near approach of death is horrible chiefly because it forces the knowledge upon us that these compensations will never come.
> (*Gravity and Grace*, p. 151)

But this knowledge does not force itself on those philosophers who see in the picture of the soul leaving this life, the hope of a temporal eternity. I heard a philosopher invoke Jesus' promise to the thief on the cross, 'Today thou shalt be with me in paradise', as support for this view. And although all detailed knowledge of what the promise came to was denied, from all that was said Jesus' words were treated as a transcendentalized version of 'See you later'. In another discussion I heard a philosopher claim that getting to heaven is no different, in principle, from getting to Bloomington, Indiana. We simply do not know the details of how we get there, that is all. A former teacher of mine, as surprised as I was, said, 'Well, there are some rather important differences.' Challenged to produce *one*, he replied, 'You've got to be dead.' In the previous discussion I mentioned, the philosopher said explicitly that belief in immortality meets a desire we all have, the desire to survive death. That desire cannot be fulfilled unless the minimal condition of our *being there* is met. Speaking of this conception of temporal eternity, Simone Weil says: 'Belief in immortality is harmful because it is not in our power to conceive of the soul as really incorporeal. So this belief is in fact a belief in the prolongation of life and it robs death of its purpose' (*Gravity and Grace*, p. 33).

V

We have considered four examples of beliefs in temporal eternity. First, the looking for a recompense after death for pursuing a virtuous life. Second, the desire for temporal eternity born of the conviction that it is intolerable that my imperfections and drawbacks should not be rectified. Third, temporal eternity is seen as the means by which people whose lives are wretched are compensated for what they have suffered. Fourth, temporal eternity is seen as a belief born of the instinct for self-preservation. This instinct goes deep in us. The thought that we should cease to exist is intolerable to us. The promise of a temporal eternity allays this fear. But in allaying it, according to Simone Weil, we are robbed of what death can teach us. According to Wittgenstein, temporal eternity fails to fulfil the purpose for which belief in immortality had always been intended.

In the four cases we have considered, no farewell is said to life. It is various concerns within that life that determine the nature of immortality. It could be said that in these cases, the mortal determines the nature of eternity. That is why Simone Weil speaks of this belief as belief in the prolongation of life, and why Wittgenstein calls it a belief in a temporal eternity.

In the religious belief in immortality I am concerned to elucidate, the mortal does not determine the immortal. Rather, it is the eternal which gives sense to the temporal. Death is no respecter of persons. For a religious person, it can show that life is given and taken away; that we are not the centre of the universe. The religious expression of this fact is to say that we are in God's hands. Our relations with the natural world and with other human beings are to be mediated via a notion of grace. They are gifts of grace and have to be responded to accordingly. Since birth and death are special mediations of grace, the coming of death is the culmination of a life of sacrificial spirituality.

Yet, one must not give a romantic account of this religious pilgrimage. Much stands in the way of it, as everyone knows. The self rebels against God, as it does against fellow human beings. Wittgenstein said on one occasion that one source of a belief in immortality is the conviction that not even death can erase a moral obligation. But what of our obligations to God, before whom, as Kierkegaard said, we always feel remorse? When Wittgenstein was asked whether he believed in hell, he replied, 'Certainly, there is no seriousness without it.' I believe he meant that we have it in us to damn our souls. He even said that he could make sense of a picture in which he stood, with some queer kind of body, before the Judgement Seat. The whole life is to be answerable to God.

At death, it is tempting to see it as an easy way out; to turn one's back on one's life with all its imperfections. But that is not what Christianity asks of us. It offers a hope that the believer, with all his weakness, becomes more than he or she could ever be by their own efforts. That is what happens at death if it is offered to God. How is this offering made? It is not that death is sought by most. They would say, at most times, as Jesus did in Gethsemane, 'If it be possible, let this cup pass from me.' But, on the Cross, Jesus commits his spirit into God's hands. The death of the believer is placed in God's hands. Notice the nature of the promise: that where God is, there will we be also. God is a spiritual reality. We become more than ourselves at death when we become part of that spiritual reality.

Speaking of the slaying of the priest-king at Nemi, Wittgenstein said that if we put the phrase 'the majesty of death' alongside the rite, we see that they come to the same thing. To die in God is to be able to see one's death as part of the majesty of God's will. Saying farewell to life is not a negative act. It is part of what is meant by giving glory to God. It is in this way that the believer becomes more than he or she is; it is in this way that the mortal puts on immortality, and the corruptible puts on incorruption.

It would be a mistake to think of this offering as abstract or impersonal. Unless making the sacrifice is mediated through the details of one's life, it is not what Christianity calls for. Sometimes, at death, a believer may be conscious of these religious reflections. They may be uttered in a prayer, or in sentiments communicated to close acquaintances. But such explicit reflections need not be necessary for a life or death to be offered to the majesty of God's will, or to be seen as an expression of it. This is important given that children die, often in appalling or horrific conditions, and that any expression of faith in a person may be crushed by the world's afflictions. What then is left is what those lives show; the spirit they exemplify. It is that which enables us to say that light perpetual shines on them. (Another expression in which the 'soul' of the words matters.)

VI

Many philosophers will say that I have reached my conclusions under the pressure of certain philosophical arguments which have led me to forsake what they take to be traditional Christian beliefs. Nothing could be further from the truth. What I am trying to elucidate I have *always* found in Christianity. When I read certain writers such as Kierkegaard, Wittgenstein, Simone Weil, Thomas Merton and Rush Rhees, they gave me perspicuous representations, in a philosophical context, of what I had already known in a religious context.

When many philosophers of religion speak of traditional religious beliefs, what they are really referring to is the traditional philosophical accounts they give of them. Their confidence that they are capturing, in their accounts, what it means to believe in God, or in the immortality of the soul, I believe, is misplaced. It is true, however, that a believer whose life exemplifies the beliefs I have been talking about, may nevertheless give a confused philosophical account of them. As we have seen, religious pictures may suggest applications which are other than those they actually have. The confused applications ignore the 'soul' in religious expressions. This is sometimes appreciated by non-believing philosophers with whom, as a result, I feel a greater affinity than with certain philosophical apologists for religion.

But, as we have seen, some of my disagreements are not of this kind. Rather, I encounter very different ways in which the picture of the soul leaving this life enters the lives of human beings. We are offered analyses which ignore the 'soul' in expressions concerning the soul. We have seen how the very notion of the soul may be dislocated from human life. When the immortality of the soul is discussed, the dislocation takes a different direction: the mortal determines the immortal, and the temporal determines the eternal. These philosophers assume that the interest in immortality *must* be an interest in temporal eternity. They ask, with Antony Flew, 'For what are three-score years and ten compared with all eternity?', not understanding Kierkegaard's rejoinder to such questions, 'Eternity, on the other hand, never counts.'

The atheistic critic is correct in seeing in belief in temporal eternity an inability to say farewell to life. What the critic does not see is a mode of saying farewell to life in which the mortal puts on immortality, and the corruptible puts on incorruption. To appreciate this possibility, whether it is personally appropriated or not, is to see the importance of the 'soul' in the words of religious belief. Such appreciation is not simply a matter of the intelligence.

Long ago, in Plato's *Phaedo*, Socrates said that to know more about death is to know more about ourselves as persons. For where immortality is concerned, where our treasures are, there will our beliefs be also.[4]

Notes

1. Rush Rhees, 'Natural Theology', *Without Answers* (London: Routledge, 1969), p. 113.
2. For a discussion of some of these implications see 'Scripture, Speech and Sin', in *Religione, Parola, Scrittura* (Religion, Spoken and Written Word) ed. M.M. Olivetti, *Archivio di Filosofia* (Padova: Cedam, 1992).
3. For a further discussion, see my 'Emptying Heaven', in *From Fantasy to Faith* (London: Macmillan, 1991).
4. This paper was required as a late replacement in the conference. In the meantime it appeared in *Religious Studies*. I am grateful for permission to reprint it here.

12

Immortality without Metaphysics: A Reply to D.Z. Phillips

John Hyman

The purpose of 'Dislocating the Soul' is to compare explanations of the nature of the soul and doctrines about the soul which can be found in philosophy of religion with what Professor Phillips calls 'the "soul" in the words of religious beliefs' (p. 233). The paper falls into two parts. In the first part, sections I and II, Phillips argues that philosophers who have tried to formulate religious beliefs about the soul in precise and explicit terms have tended to misrepresent them, by unwittingly misinterpreting the words in which they are expressed. And they have misinterpreted these words because they have failed to consider how they are used in their natural habitat – the lives of religious men and women. Phillips describes this failure as 'a dislocation of language' (p. 233). In the second part of the paper, sections III–VI, Phillips tries to provide what philosophy has in the past failed to provide – a plausible discursive exposition of religious beliefs about the soul, and in particular of the belief that the soul is immortal, which is sensitive to the natural habitat of the words used to express these beliefs, and which avoids the confusions he detects in philosophical treatments of the subject. In short, he attempts to sketch a picture of immortality without metaphysics. I have some reservations about both parts of the paper. I shall consider them in turn.

In section I, Phillips introduces the idea of a dislocation of language with some examples:

A person says 'I'm off', but does not move. No contexts . . . are present, to help us understand the situation. The same person says, 'The house is on fire' quite passively, with no reactions at all. At other times, the following words come out of the person's mouth, 'I am in agony, are you?', again, without any facial expression or reactions of any kind.

(p. 235)

'Such a person', Phillips says, 'would be a complete enigma to us. We would not know how to take the words; they wouldn't mean anything.' In fact, Phillips himself seems uncertain what to say about these utterances, for although he suggests in the passage quoted that 'we would not know how to take the words; they wouldn't mean anything', his comment on an analogous case is that 'The trouble with the tramps' words [in a passage from *Waiting for Godot*] is not that they are meaningless, but that they have the meaning they do' (p. 234). Perhaps the point is that what the speaker's words mean is perfectly clear; but it seems uncertain whether he meant anything by uttering them. For example, the person who said 'I'm off' said something whose meaning is obvious, but the context and his behaviour make it reasonable to doubt whether he was announcing an intention to leave, or wanted anybody to believe that he was going.

Phillips is interested in these vacuous utterances because he believes that a view about the nature of the soul held by many philosophers implies that our normal use of words is as pointless as they – the vacuous utterances – are. 'This philosophical picture of the soul', he says, 'dislocates words from practice and tries, in vain, to infuse them with sense' (p. 236).

The philosophical picture of the soul Phillips has in mind is the Cartesian doctrine that a soul is an immaterial thinking substance which interacts with a living body. He says that, according to the philosophical picture, the soul is 'an inner substance' (p. 237) and 'the thinking part of a person' (p. 235); that 'by some kind of causal operation, [it] brings about our behavioural practices' (p. 235); and that philosophers who find this picture of the soul plausible 'feel that we should not mix ... soul and body, mental and physical, spirit and matter' (p. 236).

I agree with Phillips that this picture of the soul is demonstrably incoherent; I agree that it implies both that we learn language by associating words with thoughts, ideas or sensations, and that understanding a language, or words within a language, is a matter of having certain mental experiences; and I agree that Wittgenstein showed – in the so-called private language arguments – that it is therefore susceptible to *reductio ad absurdum*.

However, precisely because I agree with Phillips on these important points, I do not find his analogy between the use of words by soul–body composites, and by the man who said he was off, but wasn't, entirely satisfactory. For what makes the man who said he was off difficult to figure out is his failure to act in a way which makes it plausible that he intends to leave or wants us to believe that he does, and, I suppose, the lack of any reason to believe that he was speaking ironically; whereas the insuperable difficulty with supposing that we learn language by associating words with ideas is – as Phillips implies (p. 236) – that this procedure alone cannot possibly endow a sign with meaning, since it cannot provide us with an independent standard which can be used to distinguish between the correct and incorrect use of the sign.

Phillips begins section II by drawing the following conclusion:

> If the notion of an inner substance called 'the soul' is the philosophical chimera we have suggested it is, whatever is meant by the immortality of the soul cannot be the continued existence of such a substance.
>
> (p. 237)

I have to say that I find this inference unconvincing, because I see no reason why it should be impossible to espouse, seriously and sincerely, doctrines that are demonstrably incoherent. In fact, since almost every philosopher has managed it at some time or another, it *must* be possible. The trick, presumably, is to avoid explicit contradictions; but while it may sometimes take a philosopher's ingenuity to do this, when challenged or cross-examined, a like-minded community with a reassuring intellectual elite seems, to me, quite likely to make it as easy as falling off a log. If the immortality of the soul *is* a contradictory doctrine, it does not follow that one cannot believe in it.

One important source of support for incoherent beliefs is the use of figurative language. It's a familiar fact that analogies can explain; but sometimes the explanations are bogus. There is a nice example which crops up from time to time in the philosophical literature: an explanation of wireless. It begins with an explanation of wire. Wire is like a dog that is so long that when you pull its tail in Boston it barks in New York. And now for wireless. Wireless is just the same, but without the dog. Figurative language, like analogies, has its authentic and its bogus uses; and its principal bogus use is to make us imagine that we understand something. That is why Aristotle, who argued famously that metaphor is the main part of excellence in diction, also insisted, in the *Posterior Analytics*, that one should never attempt to define by means of metaphor.

I think Professor Phillips would agree that a figurative use of language can be confusing, because the picture it suggests may mislead us (p. 238). And in section II, he takes a decisive step in his argument, arguing that expressions of religious beliefs about the soul are themselves typically figurative uses of language, which philosophers have misunderstood, because of the influence of the pictures they suggest. Thus, he quotes, apparently with approval, Wittgenstein's comparison of the belief that men have souls and the belief that a substance has two carbon rings (p. 237); and then examines a number of figurative psychological idioms, such as 'In my heart I understood when you said that', which Wittgenstein explicitly calls a 'figurative expression' (p. 239).

So, the conclusions Phillips reaches in the first part of his paper are as follows:

1. expressions of religious beliefs about the soul are typically figurative uses of language;
2. the pictures these suggest have led many philosophers to mis-interpret them;
3. these misinterpretations are demonstrably incoherent;
4. in order to correct them, we need to examine the role that words which are used to express religious beliefs play in the lives of believers.

He adds, quite rightly, that figurative expressions may be indispen-sable, because it may be impossible to replace them, without loss, with non-figurative expressions. As we have seen, Phillips also argues that the fact that some philosophical doctrines about the soul are incoherent is sufficient to establish that they are misinter-pretations of the religious beliefs of philosophically innocent men and women. However, the main conclusions I have listed, and the view that they encapsulate of the relationship between philosophers and (philosophically innocent) believers, could be correct even if I am right in thinking that this argument is fallacious. In the course of criticizing the remainder of Phillips' paper, I shall argue in favour of a different view of the relationship between philosophers and believers – the (traditional) view that philosophers construct precise formulations of ill-defined beliefs, and try to establish whether they are coherent and plausible.

In the remainder of his paper, Phillips does two things. First, he examines and rejects four motives for hoping that the traditional doctrine of immortality, as this is generally understood by philosophers, is true; and second he expounds and defends his own interpretation of the belief that the soul is immortal.

The four motives I mentioned are, first, the desire that virtue should be rewarded and vice punished (p. 244f); second, the desire for an opportunity to overcome our own moral imperfections (p. 245); third, the desire that some compensation should exist for the unjust distribution of wealth and happiness (p. 246); and finally, the desire for self-preservation (p. 246f). Phillips argues that these motives are all culpable to some degree. The first cheapens morality (p. 244f); the second, he implies, is a form of pride (p. 245f); he treats the third and fourth more gently, but argues that all four signal an unwillingness to 'say farewell to life' (p. 248ff), and as such are dishonest and inconsistent with religious truth (p. 248f). I do not share these judgements, but I shall pass on to the last part of Phillips' paper, and return to this matter later.

Phillips' own interpretation, if I have understood it correctly, is that the belief that the soul is immortal cannot be true or false because it is, in the final analysis, an *attitude* towards death. He says:

> To believe in the immortality of the soul is to want to give one's soul to God. . . . The believer says farewell to life in giving it to God. . . . To want to do something for God at death is to want to die in God; to give one's life to God.
>
> (p. 243)

> To die in God is to be able to see one's death as part of the majesty of God's will. Saying farewell to life is not a negative act. It is part of what is meant by giving glory to God. It is in this way that the believer becomes more than he or she is; it is in this way that the mortal puts on immortality, and the corruptible puts on incorruption.
>
> (p. 249)

I think it would be perverse to deny that the attitude Phillips describes can be an admirable one. It has some affinity with the attitude which the fifteenth-century treatises on the art of dying well were meant to foster – an attitude which will enable a Christian to overcome the temptations that can assail him or her as death approaches. And not only is it an attitude which commands respect; it is also, I imagine, one that a Christian believer is likely to aspire to. Moreover, Phillips may have succeeded in showing that it can be expressed figuratively by saying that the soul is immortal. Be that as it may, he still seems to me to fall short of proving that, outside the philosophy of religion, this is 'what is meant by the immortality of the soul' (p. 231). I suspect, on the contrary, that this is what is meant by the immortality of the soul only *within* a philosophy of religion, albeit an unorthodox one.

How can we resolve this disagreement? I think we need to return to a sentence I quoted earlier, the sentence which is the crux of Phillip's argument:

> If the notion of an inner substance called 'the soul' is the philosophical chimera we have suggested it is, whatever is meant by the immortality of the soul cannot be the continued existence of such a substance.

> (p. 237)

I have already said why I find this unconvincing: I see no reason why either philosophically sophisticated or philosophically innocent men and women should be incapable of having incoherent beliefs. Now I want to look briefly at its source. This, of course, is Wittgenstein's later philosophy, and in particular, his thoughts about the relationship between language and what I have called its natural habitat.

In the years following 1929, Wittgenstein came to regard language as a part of the complex web of human action and interaction in the world, and so his interest shifted from the 'geometry' of language to its place in human life. Speech and writing don't occur in a vacuum. They are used in human activities which take place and have significance only in the context of human forms of life and culture. Wittgenstein came to believe that the question of what an expression in a language means can only be answered by considering it in its context, and by asking how it is used. He once made the following remark:

If I had to say what is the main mistake made by philosophers of the present generation . . . I would say that it is that when language is looked at, what is looked at is a form of words and not the use made of the form of words.[1]

When Wittgenstein writes about religious belief he therefore tries to explain how concepts such as sin, redemption, judgement, grace and atonement might have or come to have an indispensable place in an individual's or a community's way of life. For example, he talks at length about the belief that there will be a last judgement. His intention in this case is to show that 'in religious discourse we use such expressions as: "I believe that so and so will happen," and use them differently to the way in which we use them in science.'[2]

In Wittgenstein's view, believing in a Last Judgement does not mean thinking it highly probable that a certain kind of event will occur sometime in the future:

Here believing obviously plays much more this role: suppose we said that a certain picture might play the role of constantly admonishing me, or I always think of it. Here there would be an enormous difference between those people for whom the picture is constantly in the foreground, and others who just didn't use it at all.[3]

This example is not atypical: Wittgenstein seems to equate having religious beliefs with using religious concepts and having the attitudes that their use implies. He says this most explicitly as follows: 'It strikes me that a religious belief could only be something like a passionate commitment to a system of reference.'[4] And when he talks about coming to believe in God, he writes:

Life can educate one to a belief in God. And *experiences* too are what bring this about; but I don't mean visions and other forms of sense experience which show us 'the existence of this being', but, e.g., sufferings of various sorts. These neither show us God in the way a sense-impression shows us an object, nor do they give rise to *conjectures* about him. Experiences, thoughts, – life can force this concept [sc. the concept of God] on us.[5]

Now it is one of the fundamental themes of Wittgenstein's later philosophy that the concepts we use cannot be justified by reference to reality. We are inclined to think that our concepts, or the concepts of science perhaps, are correct, that they conform to the nature of the things we use them to describe. For example, we are inclined to think that our language excludes saying that colours have a pitch or that musical notes are coloured because red *cannot* be a semitone higher than blue and a musical note *cannot* be visibly orange.

Wittgenstein argues that our network of concepts, which he calls 'grammar', extending the use of that word for good reasons, cannot either conflict with the facts or accord with the facts. For what one says conflicts with the facts if it is false and accords with the facts if it is true. But the concepts we use determine what it makes sense to say, not what is true or false. Grammar is therefore *arbitrary* – not in the sense of being unimportant, capricious, discretionary, dispensable or readily alterable, but in the sense that it is not accountable to any reality.[6] A unit of measurement, for example, is not correct or incorrect as a statement of length is. Although, of course, certain rules or systems of rules may be useful, convenient and easy to take in and apply, while other may be cumbersome and difficult.

So, if Wittgenstein is right, what someone believes who believes in God, the Last Judgement or the immortality of the soul, and what someone has chosen who has chosen or felt compelled to conceive of his life, and the lives of others, in religious terms, is not *true* or *false*; and his beliefs are not *reasonable* or *unreasonable*, if that means that they can or cannot be justified:

> I would say, they are certainly not reasonable, that's obvious. 'Unreasonable' implies, with everyone, rebuke. I want to say: they don't treat this as a matter of reasonability. Anyone who reads the Epistles will find it said: not only that it is not reasonable, but that it is folly. Not only is it not reasonable, but it doesn't pretend to be.[7]

The people Wittgenstein regards as *un*reasonable are apologists for, or against, religion who make the assumption – Wittgenstein calls it 'ludicrous' – that religious beliefs can be corroborated, or refuted, by treating them as though they were hypotheses, and mustering evidence for or against them. But unless religion is confused in this way with something quite different, it is not *un*reasonable. 'Why shouldn't one form of life culminate in an utterance of belief in a Last Judgement?' Wittgenstein asks rhetorically.[8]

I find this account of religious belief unconvincing. I think Wittgenstein is right to remind us that the belief that God exists or that there will be a Last Judgement is very unlike a hypothesis in history or in science. But I see no reason to accept that coming to believe that God exists is *nothing but* coming to feel 'a passionate commitment to a system of reference' – i.e. coming to feel committed to leading a life in which questions will be asked, obligations will be acknowledged, decisions taken and actions performed, which can only be explained or understood by the use of religious concepts. For surely, if a convert makes that commitment, perhaps because he feels compelled to, his belief that God exists will typically be part of his *reason* for doing so. Nothing in Wittgenstein's later philosophy of language, and in particular no part of his doctrine about the relation between language and forms of life, implies that a form of life cannot involve historical or metaphysical beliefs (such as that Jesus rose from the dead or that the soul is immortal) as well as concepts and attitudes: all of them – beliefs, concepts and attitudes – in a mutually supporting relation. Nor does it imply that the beliefs which form part of the core of a form of life cannot be incoherent.

Again, I think we can agree with Wittgenstein that there are many different kinds of existential proposition. Norman Malcolm mentions the following examples, 'There exists an infinite number of prime numbers'; 'A low pressure area exists over the Great Lakes'; 'There still exists some possibility that he will survive.' And I think we can also agree that belief in God's existence is *not* the same sort of existential belief as a belief in the existence of Australia. (Kierkegaard was drawing attention to this sort of difference when he wrote: 'God does not exist; He is eternal.')

But one good way of seeing the differences between these propositions is to consider the different ways in which they are proved or supported. And since evidence and argument are not the exclusive property of science, Wittgenstein cannot be right to insist that if we try to prove or support the proposition that God exists, we are treating religion as if it were science, and are therefore already trapped in confusion. It would, I think, be a mistake to maintain that because Anselm and Aquinas sought to prove the existence of God, they were peddling a variety of pseudo-science, a superstition which has nothing to do with religious faith.[9] And it is surely implausible to maintain, as Wittgenstein does, that when we consider God's existence 'what is here at issue is not the existence of something [dass es sich hier um eine Existenz nicht handelt]'.[10] The disanalogy between 'God exists' and existential propositions in science or history or geography does nothing to support this proposition; and neither does the doctrine that God cannot begin or cease to exist. If Democritus believed that atoms cannot begin or cease to exist, it does not follow that he did not believe that an atom is *'eine Existenz'* – an entity, or something which exists.

I think that Christians have traditionally believed a number of rather ill-defined metaphysical propositions about the soul, resurrection, personal survival and immortality; and that the Thomist and Cartesian theories of the soul contain precise formulations of some of these propositions. This is not to say that the Thomist and Cartesians theories tell us *exactly* what Christians have traditionally believed: a precise formulation cannot exactly capture something imprecise, precisely because of its precision. However, it can help us to settle whether the belief is paradoxical or implicitly contradictory. As Wittgenstein put it: 'If we wish to draw boundaries in the use of a word, in order to clear up philosophical paradoxes, then alongside the actual picture of the use (in which as it were the colours flow into one another without sharp boundaries) we may put another picture which is in certain ways like the first but is built up of colours with clear boundaries between them.'[11]

Suppose I'm right. Suppose this is a better account of the relationship between philosophers and (philosophically innocent) believers. There still remains an important question that has not been settled; for although Phillips argues that 'if the notion of an inner substance called "the soul" is the philosophical chimera we have suggested it is, whatever is meant by the immortality of the soul cannot be the continued existence of such a substance' (p. 237), at other times he seems more concerned to show that his own interpretation of the belief in immortality echoes a theme already present in some Christian (and not so Christian) literature (p. 230), and that it is *preferable* to a metaphysically contaminated alternative. So the final question I want to consider is whether the attitude which Phillips describes in the quotations above (p. 240f), and which, he argues, finds apt expression in 'certain language concerning the immortality of the soul' (p. 243) *is* preferable.

Phillips offers two reasons for supposing that the attitude he commends is preferable. First, that the metaphysically contaminated belief is incoherent; and second, that it is motivated by the four

supposedly culpable desires I mentioned earlier: the desire that
virtue should be rewarded and vice punished; the desire for moral
perfection; the desire for distributive justice; and the desire for self-
preservation.

I find neither reason convincing. The first is unconvincing for
two reasons: first, because Phillips does not prove that the traditional Christian belief in the immortality of the soul *cannot* be formulated precisely without bringing an implicit contradiction to light,
and he ignores the substantial efforts of Thomist philosophers to
expound an interpretation of the doctrine which is consistent with
Aristotle's identification of soul and form; and second, because even
if we suppose that no coherent formulation of the traditional belief
is possible, and that it is an essential part of traditional Christianity,
it does not follow that the kind of Christianity Phillips advocates is
preferable to traditional Christianity. Plainly, 'incoherent' does not
mean 'worthless'. The Stoic doctrine of preferred indifferents may
be an incoherent doctrine; and the doctrine that forms are material
certainly is. However, it would be a gross mistake to infer that
Stoicism was a worthless philosophy. Incoherence is a defect in a
system of religious beliefs, because if one can *see* that a doctrine is
incoherent, that is a compelling reason to disbelieve it.[12] But professional philosophers, who have a special interest in coherence and
consistency, are prone to exaggerate their importance. So I doubt
whether the first reason has much force by itself.

The second reason does not impress me either, for three reasons.
First, because these motives are more immediately connected with
the belief in personal survival than with the belief in the immortality
of the soul; second, because Phillips does not show that the metaphysically contaminated belief in personal survival must be motivated by one of these four desires, or even that it is likely to be, but
only that it can satisfy them; and third, because I am not persuaded
that all of them are culpable. I would agree that there is something
perverse and hyperbolical about the second; but the first and third
are laudable, and the last is inevitable, something that nature has
not left to our choice.

No doubt the traditional beliefs in personal survival and the
immortality of the soul, like many religious beliefs, have their corrupt as well as their innocent forms; but the attitude to death Phillips
finds appealing also has a corrupt version – the morbid egoism of
some overenthusiastic martyrs, such as Ignatius of Antioch. Moreover, its diametrical opposite ('Rage, rage against the dying of the

light') can be just as admirable and at least as sympathetic. So, on the final question of which sort of belief in immortality is preferable, I decline to judge.

Notes

1. L. Wittgenstein, *Lectures and Conversations on Aesthetics, Psychology and Religious Belief*, ed. C. Barrett (Oxford: Basil Blackwell, 1978), p. 2.
2. Ibid., p. 57.
3. Ibid., p. 56.
4. *Culture and Value*, ed. G.H. von Wright, trans. P. Winch (Oxford: Basil Blackwell, 1980), p. 64.
5. Ibid., p. 86.
6. *Philosophical Grammar*, ed. Rush Rhees, trans. Anthony Kenny (Oxford: Basil Blackwell, 1974), p. 184.
7. *Lectures and Conversations*, p. 58.
8. Ibid.
9. See *Culture and Value*, p. 72.
10. Ibid., p. 82. As Peter Winch, the translator, pointed out to me in conversation, 'what is here at issue is not an entity' would probably be a better translation.
11. *Philosophical Grammar*, p. 76.
12. There is, of course, a strand in Christian philosophy which denies this. Indeed, Tertullian sometimes held that the absurdity of a doctrine is a *reason* for believing it: 'certum est quia impossibile'. *De carn Chr.* 5; cf. *c. Marc.* 2, 16. See also S. Kierkegaard, *Concluding Unscientific Postcript*, trans. D.F. Swenson and W. Lowrie (Princeton, NJ: Princeton University Press, 1941), p. 189.

Part Seven
Voices in Discussion

13

Voices in Discussion

D.Z. Phillips

A: However we explain it, something happened in the seventeenth century which means that we can never look at religion in the same way again. The challenge of secularism is not going to go away, but is it necessary to view animism as an infantile mode of thought? I don't want to embrace any absolutist position on this matter. The trouble is that science and a religious metaphysic both seek outright victory. We must look for a narrative which will do justice to these competing temptations. What does 'resolution' mean in this context? This kind of issue faced the great Romantic writers, and it may be useful to look back to them for guidance. We must show that we have a use for animism in our culture.

B: I think we agree that animism is neither a scientific hypothesis nor a metaphysical thesis; neither false, nor unintelligible. But when you try to show we still need animism in our culture, that makes the claim seem like a hypothesis.

Similar tensions arise when we ask whether animism is metaphorical or literal. If we choose the former, it is said to be of no significance. If we choose the latter, it is said to be confused.

It would be a help if we didn't run together different uses of animism as *A* tends to do. For example, there are important differences between Christianity, Native American religion and Schopenhauer's philosophy. If we say, as *A* does, that animism is the attribution of souls to plants and animals, this will lead to a misunderstanding of Native American religion, if we think that this entails, as *A* does, that they possess consciousness in the way that human beings do.

Again, Schopenhauer was influenced by Buddhism and argued against the dichotomy between spirits and matter, since he thought it led to idealism or materialism, or to a simplistic distinction between the literal and the metaphorical.

C: I do not think you can simply retain a romantic view of animism, one that emphasizes its spiritual elements. Animism is surely a mixed phenomenon. It certainly offered explanations, and these clashed with more advanced medicine. It certainly contained examples of horrible treatments of human beings, treatments that I undoubtedly would want to combat.

D: I do not suggest for one moment that we should ignore explanatory aspects of animism. But there is a danger in making explanatory concerns fundamental. It can lead to the kind of desire we find in cognitive science, that ordinary ways of talking about our intentions and wishes – what it calls 'folk psychology' – will disappear. What is not noticed is that even when we do want explanations, that is in connection with other things.

A: I agree that explanations only come in when they are relevant to the practices in question.

E: This desire for accommodation is too hurried. Materialism is given a bad name because too narrow a view of it is advanced – as if everything could be reduced to neuropsychology, or something of that sort. Materialism doesn't have to be that of Holbach or Hobbes. Think of what we find in Davidson, Rorty or Strawson.

   Given these nuanced accounts of materialism, why should it share the stage with animism or metaphysics? Can't materialism be rich enough to account for intentions and values?

G: But if we take away scientism from materialism, what's left? What is it to be contrasted with?

E: Well, absolute idealism and dualism, for a start.

B: To go back to the charge of Romanticism; I didn't romanticize animism. On the contrary, I deliberately included examples where terrible deeds occur in the ritual – where the terrible seems to be celebrated.

F: It is particularly hard for us to see how people could wonder at the terrible in life, and not view it as a perversion, or as something the people would like to avoid.

C: I still don't see why I have to confer dignity on these practices – something comparable to what I may find in Rilke. Why must I retain this?

D: Of course, we may regard many practices in other cultures as horrible. We may want to stop them. What is important is not to make that an embattled position. We must pay attention to the spirit of the ritual. How do the agents see what they are doing? How do the people who are the victims conceive of what's happening? – That is important. But when we see it, our revulsion may be greater. Of course, we have to start from our culture, but we don't have to end there.

C: You can with values.

G: Surely, *A*'s initial problem is this: he feels that we cannot simply help ourselves to animism, as it were. Given the fragmentary character of our culture, the task is to find an honourable use for the forms of words connected with animism. My difficulty with what *A* says is this: by the time he gives up all the metaphysical assumptions connected with animism that he mentioned at the outset, does the animism which he is left with at the end come to the same thing?

A: Wittgenstein says that trying to make sense is like 'coming up to someone'. That is the issue when we confront what I have been calling 'animistic thought'. I would ask the warring parties in our culture whether their proposals were freedom-enhancing, rather than assume that the answer must come from within or without the camps. But in attempting to balance the imperatives there is obviously risk involved.

H: Animism and, indeed, religion as such has been said to be the product of wishful thinking. *C* doesn't think this will take us very far, and that it does not help us to understand Feuerbach, whatever we may say of Freud. He's probably right in this latter claim, but I was deliberately confining myself to the phenomenon of wishful thinking. I don't mention theories of projection, and wouldn't be claiming to account for all types of projection.

You might say, in relation to wishful thinking, that religion is an education of our wishes. But it would be wrong to deny lower forms of faith, since they are forms religion may take. And in them, wishful thinking does play a prominent part. It would be wrong to deny, as some philosophers have done, that there is this phenomenon and that it has far-reaching effects.

But suppose we turn away from wishful thinking to the kind of projection which interests *C* – the grids which we are supposed to project on experience to make it intelligible; an intelligibility said to be mediated by sign and symbol. The grids are said to be frameworks which cannot be said to be true or false. Questions of truth and falsity are said to arise within these frameworks.

Does any of this make sense? Because we contrast grid theories with talk of wishful thinking, we may conclude, too hastily, that it does.

It is true that our concepts show us what it means for an object to exist or not, but this should not lead to talk of grids being imposed on reality, as though we had no direct contact with reality. This duality of reality and grid presupposes that we should talk and think in this way. Grids reduce what we have to indirect acquaintance, especially when we start talking of the limits of human perception, which is obscure talk; or of the limits of our conceptual powers, which is even more obscure.

This doesn't mean that it's never useful to talk of grids. It's useful to do so when we speak of models or metaphors and where we want to bring out certain aspects of a situation. X may be seen as Y, without forgetting that it is X. Models are not true or false, but we can ask whether they do justice to the phenomenon. Here you do have a duality between the model and the objective state of affairs.

Now, can religious language be seen as such a model? Certainly, many religious utterances are neither models nor metaphysical; for example, saying that God is the Creator of the Universe. Again, if life is looked on as a gift, certain ways of acting will be involved, such as bearing the burdens of life courageously. Is this projecting a grid? We are trying to make sense of life, but we can't ask, 'Is this way of talking justified?' If it doesn't fit my life (I don't live up to it), I say the shortcoming is in myself, not in this way of talking. This holds of many religious utterances.

C: I confined myself to the notion of projection as an explanatory theory. I wanted to emphasize how varied projection theories are. To see what they come to we must pay attention to their wider philosophical and theological contexts. Concentrating on wishful thinking is not a fruitful strategy in doing so. To bring this out, I distinguished between 'beam' and 'grid' theories of projection. In the former, the projection is of some psychic phenomenon. The cinema is a model employed in this context or, earlier, the magic lantern. What is projected is said to be an illusion, a product of transference, and so on. Some theories in this context are complex and technical, such as Jung's with its reference to archetypes, whereas others, such as Bertrand Russell's, which concentrate on wishful thinking, are so crude that they hardly merit the description 'theory' at all.

What 'grid theories' do is to argue that our interpretations of reality are 'schema-bound'. But for the projection in 'beam theory', the screen would be blank, whereas 'grids' are the sources of the possibilities open to us. In this context, all experience is projected.

But what happens when we begin to compare grids? We can say that scientific grids give us prediction and control. But what is the religious grid for? The scientific categories are needed for survival, whereas, according to Feuerbach, what lurks behind the religious grid is the human ego. On the other hand, someone may say that since all grids are partial and inadequate, religion marks the unknowable which lies beyond them. But Feuerbach argued that this hope is simply the longing to transcend the necessary limitations of human life. Was he a reductionist in saying this? Not if this means that he was a village atheist like Freud and Bertrand Russell. Feuerbach was steeped in Scripture, the Church Fathers and the work of Luther. Karl Barth respected him for that. Feuerbach came to his conclusions because he thought this is what he found there.

F: I accept what you say about the need to distinguish between the different uses of 'projection', but I still think that *H*'s critique of the distinction between grids and reality needs to be answered.

E: The analogy with maps is no good, since we have something independent of the maps by which to judge them. It is not so with the so-called grids. I think the notion is a non-starter.

C: There are many grid theories. A lot will depend on which one you pick. But you may be right in saying that we have a number of projections floundering around for a theory.

E: I think the trouble is deeper, as *H* said. To speak of the grids as different interpretations of reality implies a reality with an undifferentiated content to which they refer.

C: I do not see that. Kant's categories, such as cause, carry no such implication.

E: But what are we to make of the role of the noumenal in his thought?

I: This only shows that we have to ask at what point projection comes in. The essential distinction seems to be this: if we have beam theory, the projection is thought of as something we should be able to get over. Whereas the talk of grids seems to refer to something necessary. So perhaps the distinction between contingency and necessary is more illuminating than that between beams and grids.

A: Rather than stress 'the will to live' as Feuerbach does, why don't we ask which perspectives enhance sexual love and charity?

I: But how are the perspectives to be understood? Believers may pray, but they still make contingency plans.

E: Why not say that thinking they compete is simply stupid and incoherent?

J: I agree with the distinctions made between Freud and Feuerbach, but isn't even the latter obviously culturally limited? In saying that life is a gift, surely, the important thing to emphasize is that it is a gift from God.

F: But I think the phrase needs to be taken as a whole, 'gift-from-God', because it is important to distinguish between the sense of 'gift' in human gifts and divine gifts. Consider: 'The day thou gavest, Lord, has ended.'

H: One difference is that you have no special right to a miracle. No right to escape a car accident. That would be blasphemy. You have a right to ask, but no right to receive. To see what is meant by 'life as a gift' we must not consider it in the abstract, but in the cultural context in which the words have their meaning.

K: I agree it is important to emphasize that the gift is from God, but the fact that it is a gift is also important. A gift, whether from a loved one or not, would impose limits, for a certain kind of person, on what one could do with it.

I: Freud may not have had any kind of ear for religion. When he was asked how he accounted for the 'oceanic feeling', he said he didn't have this feeling. Freud took the challenge seriously, because the feeling was said to be familiar to ordinary believers, and not the conviction of a few intellectuals. Freud wants to consider not only ordinary beliefs, but intellectual defences of them as well. For example, he knew of the use which Kant gave to religion as the foundation of morality. But what if morality can be explained in such a way that religion is not needed. Kant and Freud both recognized that the self is divided, but Freud thought he could give a more satisfactory account of it than Kant's distinction between reason and desire. But Freud's notion of the censor depends on his view of infantile sexuality up to five years of age. Morality cannot be reduced to this kind of mechanism. *K* would agree. In his reference to Rycroft, he argues that moral ideals of love, gratitude and forgiveness can't be understood psychologically. There is more to spirituality. But didn't Freud try to do this? Wouldn't this be an attempt to find the basis for religion in morality?

K: I want to suggest that despite Freud's dream of a scientific psychology, this theoretical framework, purged of its metaphysical presuppositions, yields a perspective which can be found in Proust and Dostoyevsky.

As in the case of culture, Freud's account of morality is negative. It is no more than enlightened self-interest internalized. Morality is a bitter pill for the id. A cultured person sees through morality, but accepts it for realistic, pragmatic reasons. But this motivation is absent in the case of religion. To keep it is to remain infantile. Religion may help to balance infantile fears, but the way it does so is a cover-up and a lie. This is not an individualistic matter. Religion is mass neurosis. People give adherence to religion out of fear and the need for compensation. The problem is that while Freud is not devoid of psychological insight in these matters, he is devoid of religious insight.

Rycroft rejects the God of metaphysics and the God of illusion. God is not a hypothesis or a human being magnified. God is not an object. Belief in Him is an affirmation of love stripped of compensatory elements. The belief is not forced. There is no psychological explanation of religion. Rather, the religious and the psychological are interrelated in a credible way. Religion offers a wholeness, but not as a consolation.

Patients in therapy want to be rid of their persistent distress, but through therapy find that this very desire is a source of much of their trouble. They have to stay with their trouble, and, in this way, their inner divisions are healed. There is some parallel, then, between seeing how it is possible to serve God, and seeing how it is possible to live a more useful life. Rycroft tries to depict this, but it is a pale reflection of spirituality. Are religion and psychoanalysis incompatible? No. There is psychological insight in Freud's discoveries, but there are insights which are only possible in religion.

L: Whatever of these effects connected with religious beliefs, what if you find out that something said to be rooted in the divine simply is not true?

K: I do not think matters can be short-cut in that way. Nothing makes you good except goodness.

I: I find saying that very odd.

K: Well, the same upbringing may have the opposite effect.

D: The fact that it can be explained does not mean that it is not praiseworthy.

F: Does a psychological explanation have to be reductive?

K: What he sees in goodness. What is the psychological explanation of his being this way? Wouldn't an answer detract from his moral integrity?

A: What we need is not an explanation, but a narrative.

K: I agree.

H: So do I. We only ask for a psychological explanation when something calls for that explanation.

E: Kant was looking for reasons independent of natural forces. But if I see the reasoning, taking it to heart, why can't that be a realistic account? Kant can't accept this because he wants a formal analysis. But Gibbard, Rawls and others have given an account of reason which is practical.

I: That is the trouble with Freud's analysis. You do not find the kind of explanations you find in Nagel or McDowell, explanations informed by wider conceptions of the self and practical judgement. So there is an essential gap in Freud's account, a gap which marks a conceptual and moral inadequacy.

G: These references to wider contexts make it important to recognize that the historical story is also a moral story. We can ask whether we have moral resources available for the notion of the self. When Charles Taylor wrestles with this question he already has a theistic conception of the self. He wants to argue that the culture's move away from this conception was an epistemic loss and that a return is an epistemic gain. He argues that secular conceptions have their roots in theism, and cannot provide the underpinning morality needs. Theism may not be true, but it does provide such an underpinning. We need a conception of grace; something between deism (no grace) and hyper-Augustinianism. We need a Thomistic conception of grace, and Taylor finds it illustrated in Dostoyevsky.

The trouble with this emphasis on contextualization is that it seems to make God dependent on it. But we can't move outside all contexts. Furthermore, a claim to be inspired by a moral vision does not lead to subjectivism.

But there are more serious objections. Do you need an impersonal logos, a kind of Hegelian analysis, to account for personal change, the kind Kierkegaard talks of? The trouble is that he treats Kierkegaard's pseudonyms as though they were expressing his views. There is too much appeal to a Hegelian 'we' in Taylor's analysis. Taylor wants to present himself as simply part of the homogeneity, whereas he is proclaiming his personal perspective. The roles are confused. He says that philosophy can only describe, whereas it takes the artist to bring us into contact with sources of moral energy. But if you are doing what Taylor does, you are attempting to do the job he assigns to the artist.

Taylor's meta-ethics is not a preparation for a moral perspective. It is itself the celebration of a personal perspective. But, then, if there is a place for the views of Rawls or Singer, perhaps there is a place for a particular defence of a theistic perspective.

D: I want to address questions to *G* rather than Taylor. If you are going to call religion a 'social construct', you might as well call natural science one as well. Chemistry is a social phenomenon. It has a long history, and its present state is the result of a long development. This is emphasized by sociologists of science, but they are not always careful to say that we can't conclude from the fact that a scientific consensus is reached in a certain way that this is what is meant by saying that what is discovered is true. What we need is to take a look at the accounts given in philosophy of truth and falsity. For example, the kind of misleading accounts we find in Rorty.

Now compare the scientific case with that in which Huckleberry Finn is said to discover something. It is tempting to say that the scientific case is different because there we make contact with the real world. I don't want to deny that such contact is made, but it is easy to miss the fact that this takes place in a network of activities which has a history, and which could have developed differently.

Similarly, we must look at our dealings with religious concepts to see what 'confronting reality' means in this context. This is brought out brilliantly by Thomas Mann in *Joseph and His Brothers* in his account of how Jacob's conception of God develops. You can't separate this from his understanding of himself and his world. The same is true of Huck. What is he to do about Jim, the runaway slave? You might say that he discovers that you can't pray a lie. He had a religious background, but might still say that he came to see what 'God' means for the first time.

Faced with a certain conception of religion as a series of sanctions, Rush Rhees said he hoped he would have enough decency to say, 'Go ahead and blast.' In his remarks, Rhees is speaking in his own voice, and yet his purpose is not to convince us of that point of view. Rather, he wanted to present a way of thinking about it. The difficulty is to present a religious or moral point of view while doing justice to the opposition.

Huck doesn't want to go to heaven if Jim is not there. Tertullian please copy.

I repeat: it is difficult to do justice to opposing views. These other views do not prevent you from having a view of your own.

In 1929, Wittgenstein said that his aim was a temple, a cool place, where he could discuss the passions without meddling with them. You might say that this is the spirit throughout his *Philosophical Investigations*. It is difficult to say which is his own voice because he has been tempted to speak in all the ways he considers. He shows how these cases interact; how one can give rise to another by way of reaction; rather than developing one view you are meant to accept. In this respect, there is a similarity with Plato's early dialogues. The greatness of Plato is not found in any theory he propounded, but in his insight into what discussion can be.

I agree with G that Taylor doesn't appreciate these points, but I don't think G does either. He simply says that if there is a place for Singer and Rawls, there is a place for a religious perspective. Taylor and G do not find a way, it seems to me, of doing justice to the opposition, a situation which may find Mother Theresa on one side and John Stuart Mill on the other.

C: I do not think that D's comments address the reasons why people have talked in the way they have in the social sciences. Take the issue of gender in America. Gender is up for grabs. You can't speak in that way about chemical elements. *D* concentrates on analogies, whereas he ought to concentrate on the disanalogies.

D: I am not denying the disanalogies.

C: It certainly sounded that way to me.

D: No. The problem comes precisely in the way those differences are characterized. It is misleading to say that in science we are in contact with reality, whereas in religion we are not.

F: That's right. Take *C*'s talk of gender being up for grabs. That is deeply misleading. It looks as if, simplistically, we can make things what we want them to be. But in the dispute on gender, one group may say something to which another group reacts, maybe in an unexpected way, the first group may then react to this, and so on. The outcome, therefore, could not be described as 'up for grabs'.

E: But why concentrate on such a simplistic reaction? Why not concentrate on the nuanced accounts of social change given by writers such as Dewey, Rawls or Nussbaum? In these accounts we can appreciate why there are superior accounts of social change which show theism to be untenable.

K: We must be careful not to assume that science had to go in the way it did. Take the dispute between Priestly and Lavoisier over the significance of certain experiments. It was settled in a certain direction, and the issue is closed. But it could have gone the other way. If we say the way it went was 'superior' we must not forget the scientific contexts in which these developments took place.

There may be competing conceptions of divine power. We need to see what the different possibilities amount to. The person's own appropriation comes in at a different point.

G: Taylor does not want to appeal to a meta-ethic. He looks at competing accounts to theism given by Nietzsche and Freud and finds them inadequate. But there is nothing in principle in his procedure against doing justice to the opposition. I am saying that he does not show the superiority of theism.

E: Taylor has promised another book in which he will do this.

I: But Taylor does argue that the secular perspectives are parasitic on a theistic perspective. If he were successful, he claims that would be a good reason to accept the theistic account. But this does not follow. All that is established is the place of the religious ideas in cultural history. If you say that the secular needs to be under-written by the religious we seem to be back to the notion of a meta-ethic. We are back, in fact, to Socrates' question in the *Euthyphro*: the issue is whether the good is good because God wills it, or whether God wills it because it is good.

G: Taylor is not saying, simply, that religion underwrites secular perspectives. He has *ad hominem* arguments against these perspectives, but he also has analytical arguments. He is arguing that they trade implicitly on theistic assumptions. I do not think Taylor succeeds in making that case.

I: That is why I say that it has not been shown that science is underwritten by religion.

E: When we look at prominent secular perspectives, we may have a text and sub-text in what we want to say about them. The text has two senses in Marxism. First, there is an Enlightenment sense in which the fundamental reality is a physical reality, on which all other realities are dependent. Those holding such a view are athe-istic. You cannot be a materialist without being an atheist. Second, Marx is an historical materialist. That is important. What is said in this context is parasitic on earlier Enlightenment thought. Marx and his followers said superficial things about the existence of God and the problem of evil. Hume had deeper arguments. Those arguments have been rationally reconstructed in our time by Flew, Mackie and Nielsen. Marx and his followers had a sociological hope which they thought was liberating. *J* has said that some of these secular think-ers are banal in what they say, but this banality may be important. Religion may lead people to accept their lot; to accept my station and its duties. I am speaking of mass religion. It is not a claim about individual believers, as, of course, there will be exceptions. Gener-ally speaking, religion has kept people down. The harm done in this context has been extensive.

This is not religion's sole function. It is also a way of coping with life's existential crises – death, failure, weaknesses in oneself, and so on. It also facilitates social bonding in certain societies.

Given all these functions, can we say that secular, materialist explanations can explain religion away? Given that the explanations are sufficiently nuanced, the answer must be 'Yes'. But in what sense? One needn't give credence to any conspiratorial theories concerning religion. One needs to make a non-eclectic combination of different accounts – Marx, Feuerbach, Weber, Durkheim, Lévi-Strauss, Geertz. What is excluded from such accounts are explanations such as Jung's, which I think are rubbish, and explanations such as Evans-Pritchard's of Nuer religion where he elucidates their sense of the sacred. Materialist accounts deny that religion can be a source of truth. There is no religious knowledge or justified religious knowledge. If you want to show that philosophically, go to Hume, Nietzsche and Nielsen. Let me ask a question where I am not sure of the answer: could you accept Marx's and Engels' perspective without their critique of religion? I suspect one could not.

Heaven is an opiate for the oppressed and dispossessed. And if one turns on one's radio in Mississippi or Georgia, who could deny that the kind of religion one hears fits this picture exactly? One thinks of the activities of the Roman Catholic Church in the Third World, and the activities of the New Right in America. So far, I have been referring to what I have been calling the text of Marxism.

We come now to what I call the sub-text. If we define canonical Marxism as its leading concepts, the core would have to do with some form of historical materialism, the labour theory of value, classes and class conflict. Why couldn't a certain kind of behaviourist accept this, but without accepting the metaphysics of historical materialism? In short, can he believe Marxism and Christianity?

Having said this, I want to get back from the sub-text to the text. Marxists are atheists. I am an atheist. It is a world-view. If you settle for the truncated view of the sub-text, something is lost. You can have shallow atheism or shallow belief, so you need a good reason for saying that atheism must be shallow.

What is more, the Marxist world-view says that religion will wither away. What would that be like? Imagine the world becoming like a prosperous Scandinavian country, with security, a high level of education and material wealth, democracy and socialism. In such a context, religion could wither away. There are secular alternatives for wonder. I don't know whether any of this will happen. Is it probable it will happen? No. But would it be good if it happened? All told, I'd say, 'Yes.'

In conclusion, let me say that truth is not the only great value, but it is one. Religions are at least false. Religions, for the most part, does an awful lot of harm. They are the source of that harm. As I have said, they could wither away.

J: I have three questions. The first concerns the relation of the origin of a belief to its truth value. The use of the word 'opium' is related to this. Marx has a cascade of metaphors. 'Opium' is only one of them. He also calls religion 'the heart of a heartless world'. Also, opium is meant as a medicine, an aspirin. It is not a pejorative use in Marx's context.

Second, dialectical materialism is a metaphysics found in Engels, a metaphysics about what happens in the world. But Marx is not a physicalist or a dialectical materialist. That is vital, since it concerns what is introduced into Marxism by Engels and Lenin. If you take these elements out, the attitude to religion must be very different.

Third, I agree that Marxism and Christianity are incompatible, but for different reasons from E. His reasons have to do with the Enlightenment view. For me, they are different world-views. Marxism's claims with respect to the other are imperialistic.

There are two other things I want to say. The first concerns the withering away of religion. Religion gives us an image of what is not there. At the end of time, there is no religion. There is no temple in the New Jerusalem. If religion shows us what we lack, it gives us a different way of looking at society. No society can be recommended as the New Jerusalem.

Second, the ills of the world are often attributed to religion. That goes back to Lucretius. But this is true of any human activity – politics, for example. But would we say we'd be better off without politics? At the heart of Christianity, we have the Easter Passion and the early death. Would we be better without that? Of course not.

C: I think there are two kinds of atheism. Hume in the *Dialogues* is mystified by the order in the world. Philo says that it makes sense to suppose that something like an intelligence is responsible for it, but not in a deistic way.

Marxists have a tin ear for religion. E tries to rectify this by introducing references to existential needs. But what is it to experience religion or to experience art? You can't give a causal account of this or explain it in terms of its origins. People suffer and die, and they find comfort in religious symbols. If we say that this helps to meet their needs, why call that an explanation? Why not say it is a description? Why shouldn't people have ways of articulating their needs when they are defeated by life? Why should I say that the world will be better off without that? I can't imagine a human society without suffering, guilt and death. Would it be a human life at all without these features?

E: I did not say that we do not need a way of articulating the crises of human life you mention. Gramsci was well aware of this. He wanted to see the emergence of an atheistic morality which would answer these needs. But theological or religious ways of answering them would wither away. I have no deep commitment to the term 'explanation' in this context. We could speak of interpretive descriptions.

G: You have argued that since it is true that religion has the effect of an opiate, we should not be religious. But surely that is parasitic on the issue of whether religious beliefs are false or incoherent.

E: I agree.

L: But didn't you say that not all religious experiences are incoherent – those of worker-priests for example?

E: I am not committed to saying that what I say has no exceptions. I am speaking about mass religion. It is sufficient to show that what you refer to is not a pervasive phenomenon.

L: But, surely, you claim to have logical arguments which show that these experiences can't occur. But people have them. So, why not argue against them?

E: We intellectuals do argue about the truth or falsity of such experiences, or about their coherence. But I may think that, in certain circumstances, this is useless. The people can't help believing. Their needs are too deep, and they find the beliefs psychologically satisfying. I say, 'But for the grace of God, there go I.'

J: But, then, why not say more about these effects, compare them, see what they amount to? Compared with this, arguing about truth and falsity may seem to be a barren exercise. But, then, I'm a social scientist, not a philosopher.

F: I don't think you should apologize. If issues of truth and falsity are divorced from the matters you refer to – I wouldn't call them 'effects' – what you have is not an advance to reflection, but a retreat to a distorted form of it – more 'blackboard thinking'.

J: I retract my apology!

D: When *E* says that religion supports the status quo, I suppose
he is referring, in the main, to Churches, centres of established power.
The emphasis on the distinctive character of religion is not so much
the issue in this context. Rather, a study in the sociology of power
seems more appropriate.

E: Yes, I do talk about Churches. I think the sociology of power
would miss the particular kind of power religion has.

H: Isn't it odd to ask, *in vacuo*, whether religion is a good theory,
or whether it is a language game?

E: I agree that religious language games are enmeshed with other
things. Marx and Engels had a tin ear for religion, but the questions
can be asked on the basis of religious practices and from other
perspectives.

J: Engels didn't have a tin ear for religion, but Marx did. He was
brought up in a pietistic background.
    But in view of *E*'s remarks I want to say that you don't have to
prescind faith to ask questions. I hope I am a decent Catholic, but
I experience the strongest resistance to what some of my fellow
Catholics say. On the other hand, if you think of accounts of large
epochs, Marxism is the best account around.
    It is misleading if that account concentrates exclusively on indi-
vidualistic features of human life – suffering and death – because
the form of life is so evidently a communal life. Religion is a fundamental part of a communal project.

M: Isn't it as unjust to relate institutions to religion as it is to relate
totalitarianism to Marxism?

E: Again, I emphasize that I am talking about religion as a mass
movement. In this context, exceptions are unimportant.

I: Social escapism, so far from being ignored by theologians, has
been taken up by them. So can't the Marxist critique be adapted to
theological purposes?

E: I mentioned this possibility in what I called my 'sub-text', but
think, in fact, that it will go another way. I regard liberation theologians as my comrades, and the needs they address are real needs.
On the other hand, I find their metaphysics incoherent.

N: I am a Marxist and a non-believer, but I don't see a strong connection between what you say and the world in which we live. After the *Theses on Feuerbach* Marx becomes committed to explanations in materialist terms. But we must look to actual practices. What is important is not the truth of a proposition considered in abstraction, but its place in a living practice. The appeal to Gramsci is not of much use in our pluralistic world.

E: Our world is not Gramsci's world. It would be better if it did not think about religion. Let it think about something else. But Marx holds to the truth of his dialectical materialism.

J: Taking bits out of historical materialism is intellectually problematic. We can't reduce Marx to a superior social scientist, like Durkheim or Weber. *D* was right in emphasizing the importance of doing justice to a point of view. Don't take liberties with it, and see all you can in powerful alternatives.

Marx had a Victorian conception of human nature, which is incompatible with a certain kind of religious belief. We don't do justice to Marx by imagining him to be less prickly and divisive than he in fact was.

O: One of the most problematic religious notions in face of logical objections is belief in the immortality of the soul. I'm glad to see that *F* agrees that this notion is incoherent. But I do not think that the Cartesian chimera of an immaterial substance can be treated with other dislocations of language, such as those found in Beckett's plays.

F: I was not running them together. I was saying that, in some ways, the Cartesian soul is stranger because it is supposed to reflect normality, rather than any kind of conceptual decline or literary dislocation. There are all sorts of connections between my examples: pick them up and travel with them as far as they'll take you, but I wasn't saying that they are all of the same kind.

O: You do seem to be saying that if a belief is incoherent, it cannot be sincerely and seriously espoused. I don't see any contradiction here.

F: Your objection comes from a misunderstanding of my emphasis. I am not saying that because X is incoherent, people can't have sincerely and seriously enjoined X. Of course not: if their espousal were not sincere and serious I shouldn't think it worth combatting.

The same is true of the temptation to such a view in myself. But if a view is incoherent, then it follows that it cannot mean what its espousers want it to mean. If the immortality of the soul means anything, it cannot be what Cartesian dualism tries to mean by it.

O: Of course, if a belief is incoherent it can't be true or false. You seem to try to avoid these difficulties by speaking of an 'attitude' instead of a belief. It is then said that the attitude, and the concepts it manifests, cannot be compared to reality. Belief in God becomes a commitment to lead a certain way of life.

F: What does this mean? Do I equate having a belief that there is a tree in a garden with using physical object concepts and having the attitudes they imply? Concepts in their natural habitat show us what beliefs in this context, true or false, amount to.

You say that you find all this unconvincing because people wouldn't use religious concepts unless they believed that God exists. But what is the context for this belief? This is thought trying to catch its own tail. Malcolm and others sometimes deny that God exists only because those with whom they are discussing think of 'existence' solely in relation to what can come to be or pass away. Obviously, God cannot be thought of in this way, hence Kierkegaard's remark, 'God does not exist. He is eternal.' But people do speak of the existence of God, and its grammar has to be investigated.

O: If you eschew the Thomist or Cartesian conception of the soul, is the alternative you offer preferable to the metaphysical doctrines which strive to capture traditional belief?

F: Don't confuse traditional belief with traditionally dominant philosophical theories concerning it. The latter, I argue, distorts the former.

O: You reject the traditional belief on the grounds that it is motivationally culpable. It destroys morality, fails to say farewell to life, desires compensation, and wants to promote survival after death.

F: No, I was doing something different. I wasn't analysing traditional belief at all, or considering confused analyses. Rather, I was noting different ways in which the picture of the soul leaving the body may enter into people's lives. I link the examples under a single description – the desire for a temporal eternity. I did this because you find those applications in contemporary philosophy of religion where, for the most part, 'the other world' and 'immortality' seem to be versions of this world writ large. Ironically, my claim would be that these apologists for the supernatural are, in fact, wedded to the natural world. Back to Feuerbach maybe.

O: Even if one agrees that the examples you give are confused, the vital question is how one continues from there. Of course, you offer suggestions and I find some of them penetrating. What I cannot see is that they reflect what ordinary believers believe. Rather, they seem to me to be the creation of a minority within contemporary philosophy of religion.

F: Although that accusation is not new – I have heard it often enough from *E* – I find it deeply depressing, since it is itself an indication of a distance between our contemporary philosophical audience and expressions where the soul in the words matter. I am arguing for a philosophical sensibility regarding these expressions which would transcend the distinction between belief and unbelief, a sensibility which I find in *E*'s spontaneous interjections about what is irreligious. Missing the soul in the words vulgarizes, not only acceptance of religion, but its rejection as well. If I thought these expressions were my creation, I would give them up tomorrow.

O: I do not say that religious beliefs are incoherent, only that that is my reaction to the accounts I have encountered so far.

F: Perhaps that is because you think that a belief that 'something survives' is a minimal requirement of a belief in immortality. The promise of immortality is to be where God is, so everything will depend on what that means. To talk of 'the persistence of something' reminds me of those discussions in pubs where one says to another, 'Can't all be chance. Must be something behind it all.' Or the pop song that tells us that 'Someone in the great Somewhere hears every word.' These are not the minimal requirements of a rational belief in immortality – the belief that I'll be *there* – as a participant in our 1993 conference put it. Rather, such words are the degraded remnants of a belief which has lost the soul in its words.

You describe my view as Immortality without Metaphysics. True. But what prevails at present is metaphysics without immortality.

L: People are talking as if a refutation of dualism, and of the notion of an immaterial substance, can be taken for granted. Could someone tell me, briefly, what that refutation is? I have no difficulty with the notion of an immaterial substance. What is the difficulty?

O: Let me try to answer that. One difficulty with the notion of an immaterial substance concerns its identity, or its reidentification. When you want to say that you are referring to the same substance that you were referring to before, what would count either for or against its identification?

A: I agree that you do not have to hold that a belief that God exists is prior to religious practice.

O: I am quite prepared to say, with Kierkegaard, that such a belief is incoherent. All I am saying is that there is even greater disagreement about how we proceed from that point. It seems to me that the ordinary believer does not believe in immortality in any figurative sense.

C: The believer puts his trust in the Resurrection, not in speculations about an empty grave.

F: Fear of the grave may contain confusion. Rush Rhees has said that it may seem like an everlasting solitary confinement. But he goes on to say that although human beings can be solitary in various circumstances, the grave is not one of them. The grave and what it contains is no more solitary than a river or a mountain. Here the grave is seen as part of the majesty of God's landscape.

B: But if we speak of belief in immortality as a religious experience, how is this different from what might be meant by an encounter with Christ?

F: The former would include a reference to my life as a completed whole. Wittgenstein said that he could make sense of a picture in which he stood before the Judgement Seat with an odd kind of body. Everything depends on the use we make of this kind of picture.

But talk of the Last Judgement involves a conception of my death, my completed life. By the way, conceptions of eternity are not confined to religion. Shortly after the exploding of the first atom bomb, a young couple walked out into the sea at Swansea with their young child. They did not want to live in such a world, and said, in a note, that now they would be together for eternity. What does that mean? They were not religious. But wouldn't it be absurd to react to the note by saying, 'That's false. The waves will separate the bodies soon enough?'

C: Bultmann was concerned with these issues in his *New Testament Theology* and *Commentary on St. John*. He speaks of 'walking in the spirit' and of being 'raised with Christ', and how we misunderstand what is involved if we try to objectify this in spatial relations.

D: Similarly, when 'existence' is denied of God, the point is not to censure saying 'God exists' or 'God does not exist', but to point out that by 'God' we do not mean an existent or an entity.

O: But I come back to the question of whether a person is really saying something in religious belief. Is he spouting or seriously referring? If he coherent or incoherent?

D: To answer such questions we need to pay attention to concept formation in religious belief.

G: No doubt this is so, but how does the formation take place? If religion is not cut off from other features of human life, how does one pass from one to the other? How are the bridges built? This is not only a conceptual question, but also a moral or religious question.

D: Well, consider from the Bible stories where that transition has happened; where people have moved from unbelief to belief. Saul on the road to Damascus, for example. The change happens to an intellectual man, but his intellect has nothing to do with it. The change is not unconnected with the rest of his life – that he was persecuting the Christians, for example. And the story tells us how he changed. But what we see there is not an explanation of how to get from unbelief to belief; it is not a case of getting from one to the other. We are not shown 'how to do it'.

Index